Manufacturing Strategy

Also by Terry Hill

Production/Operations Management

MANUFACTURING STRATEGY

The Strategic Management of the Manufacturing Function

Terry Hill

MACMILLAN

1746

First published 1985

Published by
MACMILLAN EDUCATION LTD
Houndmills, Basingstoke, Hampshire RG21 2XS
and London
Companies and representatives
throughout the world

Printed by Chanctonbury Press Ltd.

British Library Cataloguing in Publication Data
Hill, Terry
Manufacturing strategy.
1. Factory management
I. Title
658.5   TS155
ISBN 0-333-39477-1
ISBN 0-333-39478-X Pbk

To PM, AJ and JB

Contents

Preface   xiii

1   **International Comparisons**   1
  1.1   **Manufacturing Output**   2
  1.2   **Productivity: National Comparisons**   6
  1.3   **Productivity: Plant-level Comparisons**   9
  1.4   **Why has This Happened?**   15
        Failure to recognise the size of the competitive
        challenge   15
        Failure to appreciate the impact of increasing manu-
        facturing capacity   18
        Top management's lack of manufacturing
        experience   19
        The manufacturing manager's obsession with short-
        term performance issues   21
  1.5   **Manufacturing Strategy**   23
  1.6   **Conclusion**   25
  Notes and References   28
  Further Reading   30

2   **Manufacturing Implications of Corporate Mar-**
        keting Decisions   31
  2.1   **Strategic Dominance – Perspectives Over Time**   32

2.2 **Reasons for Manufacturing's Reactive Role in Corporate Strategy** **32**

The production manager's view of himself *33*

Production managers are too late in the corporate debate *34*

The 'can't say no' syndrome *35*

Lack of language *35*

Functional goals and measures *36*

Functional support for manufacturing is weak *37*

Tenure *38*

Top management's view of strategy *38*

2.3 **The Way forward** **39**

Linking manufacturing with corporate marketing decisions *39*

How it works *40*

2.4 **Establishing the Order-winning Criteria of Different Products** **45**

Order-winning criteria *45*

Price *45*

Product quality and reliability *47*

Delivery speed *47*

Delivery reliability *48*

Other criteria *48*

Order-winning versus qualifying criteria *49*

The procedure involved for understanding the criteria weightings chosen *50*

Identifying qualifying criteria with potential to become order-winning criteria *51*

Identifying qualifying criteria which are order-losing sensitive *51*

2.5 **The Outputs of Manufacturing Strategy** **52**

2.6 **Conclusion** **56**

Notes and References **57**

Further Reading **57**

3 **Choice of Process** **59**

3.1 **The Choice of Process** **60**

The manufacturing function *60*

The 'classic' type of process choice *61*

3.2 **The Business Implications of Process Choice** **67**

3.3 **Selected Business Implications of Process Choice** **69**

Project   72
Jobbing, latch and line   73
Jobbing   73
Line   75
Batch   76
Continuous process   78
3.4 **An Overview of Process Choice   79**
3.5 **Hybrid Processes   81**
Numerical control (NC) machines   82
Machining centres   83
Flexible manufacturing systems   83
Dedicated use of general purpose plant   86
Group technology   86
Mix mode assembly lines   88
Transfer lines   88
3.6 **Review of the Use of Numerical Control (NC) in Hybrid Processes   88**
3.7 **Profile Analysis   89**
3.8 **Conclusion   95**
Notes and References   97
Further Reading   98

4   **Focused Manufacturing   99**
4.1 **Focused Manufacturing   100**
Marketing   101
Increases in plant size   101
Manufacturing   102
Specialists as the basis for controlling a business   102
Looking for panaceas   103
Trade-offs in focused manufacturing   103
Plants-within-a-plant configurations   107
4.2 **Focus and the Product Life Cycle   108**
4.3 **Progression or Regression in Focused Manufacturing   112**
4.4 **Experience Curves   112**
Characteristic patterns   116
4.5 **Areas of Activity which will Affect the Rate of Cost Improvement   120**
Product redesign, substitution and standardisation   120
Labour efficiency   120
Economies of scale   122
Improved processes and methods   122

4.6   **Experience Curves and Manufacturing Strategy**   123
4.7   **Units of the Experience Curve**   126
4.8   **Experience Curves and Focus**   127
4.9   **Conclusion**   134
       Ways forward – halting the drift into unfocused manu-
       facturing   *137*
Notes and References   138

5   **Process Positioning**   141
5.1   **Reasons for Choosing Alternative Strategic Positions**   141
       Core elements of the business   *142*
       Strategic consideraitons   *142*
       Span of process and product technology   *142*
       Product volumes   *144*
       Yesterday's strategies   *145*
       Shedding difficult manufacturing tasks   *145*
5.2   **Issues Involved in Process Position Changes**   145
       Costs and investments   *147*
       Strategic considerations   *148*
       The managerial task   *149*
5.3   **Alternatives to Widening Internal Span of Process**   150
       Joint ventures and long-term contracts   *151*
       Customer/vendor relations   *152*
       Just-in-time production   *155*
5.4   **Conclusion**   155
Notes and References   156
Further Reading   157

6   **Manufacturing Infrastructure Development**   158
6.1   **Manufacturing Infrastructure Issues**   161
6.2   **Infrastructure Development**   163
6.3   **Important Infrastructure Issues**   165
6.4   **Some Organisational Issues**   166
6.5   **The Role of Specialists**   167
       Too many layers   *170*
6.6   **Operational Effects of Structural Decisions**   172
       The concept of an operator's job   *172*
6.7   **Strategy-based Alternatives**   174
       Functional teamwork concept   *174*
       The structure of work   *175*
       Cascading overheads   *176*

Quality circles or productivity improvement groups *176*
6.8 **Some Key Areas of Operational Control** **178**
6.9 **Control of Quality** **179**
6.10 **Control of Inventory** **182**
Function of inventory as a basis for control *183*
6.11 **Control of Manufacturing** **187**
Market related criteria *187*
Process requirement criteria *188*
Levels of control within an organisation *191*
Choosing between push or pull systems *192*
Some important issues when considering MRP and JIT *194*
6.12 **Conclusion** **196**
Notes and References **198**
Further Reading **200**

7 **Accounting and Financial Perspectives and Manufacturing Strategy** **201**
7.1 **Investment Decisions** **202**
7.2 **The Need for a Strategic View of Investments** **204**
Investment decisions must be based on order-winning criteria *205*
Excessive use of ROI distorts strategy building *206*
Government grants are not necessarily golden handshakes *208*
Linking investment to product life cycles reduces risk *210*
Manufacturing must test the process implications of product life cycle forecasts *212*
Investment decisions must quantify working capital and infrastructure requirements *213*
7.3 **Operating Controls and Information** **215**
7.4 **The Simplistic Nature of Accounting Information** **215**
7.5 **The Need for Accounting System Development** **218**
Allocate, not absorb overheads *219*
Create business related financial information *221*
Provide performance related financial information *222*
7.6 **Conclusion** **223**
Notes and References **225**

Index **227**

Preface

Currently in many industrial companies, strategic developments are predominantly based on corporate marketing decisions at the 'front end' with manufacturing being forced to react at the 'back end' of the debate. Due to the fact that manufacturing managers come later into these discussions, it becomes difficult for them successfully to influence corporate decisions. All too often, the result is the formulation and later development of strategies which manufacturing is unable to support successfully. That is not to say that this happens for want of trying: strong in the manufacturing culture is the work ethic. However, if the basic link between the manufacturing processes and infrastructure (i.e. manufacturing strategy) and the market is not strategically sound, then, by definition, the success of the business will suffer.

The many reasons why this exists are addressed in the book. Significant amongst them is that the life-style of typical manufacturing managers primarily concerns the day-to-day part of their task. It concerns operations detail and is output-orientated, while in strategic terms the role is seen as being reactive.

The purpose of the book is to attempt to lift manufacturing managers' thinking and to provide the necessary strategic perspective for the task in hand. It is intended to help them to analyse and discuss issues and to think strategically. Currently, the area of manufacturing strategy is short of concepts, ideas and language. This further hampers manufacturing managers in sustaining strategic argument. The book goes some way to redressing this state of affairs. It helps provide insights and to review manufacturing's corporate contribution through strategic perspectives rather than just through operational performance. It helps manufacturing managers not only to provide appropriate corporate-level inputs but also facilitates other executives to recognise and appreciate the strategic perspectives which eminate from manufacturing and need to be given due consideration within the corporate debate.

The manufacturing perspective forms the basis on which the book is written, but the approach taken places these issues within the rightful context of corporate strategy. Thus it recognises that in today's world the majority of companies will be unable to sustain success over a long period of time if it is based upon a single function's view of what makes strategic sense. Throughout, therefore, the book emphasises the essential requirement to link the marketing and manufacturing perspectives in order to determine what are the best strategies to adopt for the business as a whole.

In summary, the book is written as an attempt to

(1) Close the gap between manufacturing and marketing in terms of corporate strategy formulation.
(2) Provide a set of principles and concepts which are pragmatic in nature and designed to be applied to each different part of a business.
(3) Offer an analytical approach to the development of manufacturing strategy rather than advocate a set of prescriptive solutions. Each business and each part of each business is different. The resolution of strategy through prescription, therefore, is inappropriate. Furthermore, the complexity within manufacturing is such that it encourages companies to take strategic short cuts. As a consequence, prescriptive approaches seem attractive. The book argues strongly against this. In offering an approach to the development of manufacturing strategy and raising essential issues throughout, it provides a way of coping with this complexity. The principles and concepts outlined provide a basis for placing operational detail within an essential strategic framework.

Outlined in the book is a basic approach to developing a manufacturing strategy which has been successfully used in several companies. It does so by providing a logical, practical and successful way for manufacturing to interface with the marketing inputs into corporate strategy formulation. In so doing, it ensures that the 'front end' debate concerns not just the outward-looking stance of marketing but the outward-looking stance of the business as a whole. This reduces situations in which marketing-led strategies may be adopted which, in overall terms, will be harmful to the business. It does this by raising the level of awareness of what would be incurred for the total business by different decisions, a prerequisite for developing a sound strategic direction.

Many executives shy away from discussions on manufacturing because they see it as an area of intense detail. This is because, traditionally, manufacturing is presented in this form. The approach in the book is to group together relevant operational detail into key strategic issues, and to provide an understanding of how these can be applied in companies. The development of a strategic language also provides the opportunity of moving away from what often constitutes current practice – a discussion on operational problems. This is not only an inappropriate manufacturing contribution at the executive level, but it also has the effect of dulling the interest of other functions in taking on board the manufacturing issues involved. Strategic language, on the other hand, helps orientate and maintain the debate at the appropriate level. It stimulates executive interest and enables others to address the complexity by creating a manageable number of manufacturing variables.

The book comprises seven chapters. Chapter 1 sets the scene by drawing some important international comparisons at national, corporate and plant level. The figures embody a growing awareness of the fact that those countries which clearly emphasise the importance of manufacturing's contribution to business success have consistently outperformed other developed countries with a sound industrial tradition.

The core of the book is in the centre five chapters. The headings themselves highlight some of the key developments within manufacturing strategy. Together they form the substance of the language development besides the framework to be used in its formulation.

Chapter 2 explains the approach to be adopted and details what needs to be completed at each step. It includes some illustrations to help with this explanation. Chapter 3 deals exclusively with the choice of manufacturing process, the basis for that choice and the business implications which follow. Chapter 4 introduces the concept of focus and the need to align plants or each part of a plant to a defined set of tasks. Chapter 5 introduces the implications behind the decision which companies need to make at the strategic level where should they position themselves on the process spectrum. Although at first sight these latter two chapters appear solely to concern manufacturing process decisions, it is important to recognise that they are also a critical part of infrastructure formulation; for the size and shape of plants are significant factors in what constitutes an appropriate infrastructure, the subject of Chapter 6. This chapter introduces some important concepts as a way of providing the business with the insights necessary to formulate developments within their critical part of manufacturing. This approach therefore will enable these important, expensive and time-consuming tasks to be fashioned in support of the requirements of the business. It will enable them to be given strategic shape and direction rather than emanating from specialist perspectives.

The final chapter concerns the important area of accounting and finance, is important because it provides basic data used in the formulation of strategic decisions. As with Chapter 6, it is not intended to be a comprehensive statement of the art. It is intended to represent some production management views of serious shortcomings in this essential information provision. The professional accountant may find the approach used to be provocative. It is intended, however, to be more constructive than that. The issues raised are intended to be thought-provoking with the aim of challenging current practice and ideas as a way to stimulate improvement.

Finally, I trust that all who use the book find it helpful. It is vital that manufacturing takes its full part in strategic formulation, if industrial companies are to prosper in the face of world competition.

September 1985   TERRY HILL

International Comparisons

The year 1984, for so long the centre of attention created by Orwell's forecast of the future, symbolised a new stark reality – the impact of industrial competition. The cut and thrust and the struggle for giant companies to survive had, in most industrial nations, become, by then, an integral part of each industry's way of life. To close down a plant, once an anathema to business, had now become an acceptable course of action to follow based upon necessity or as an integral part of some comprehensive corporate strategic decision. The economic world of the 1980s is very different to that of the 1960s and 1970s.

For the most part, however, production decision-making in manufacturing industry has not changed to meet these new challenges. In most nations and most industries, manufacturing management still takes a subordinate role in strategic terms to the marketing and finance functions. It still concerns itself primarily with short-term issues. The argument of this book is that a strategic approach to manufacturing management is essential if companies are going to be able to survive, let alone hold their own or grow by competing effectively in domestic and world markets.

This chapter provides some national and corporate comparisons. It shows how some nations with strong industrial traditions have come to be outperformed, and attempts to set the scene by illustrating the extent of the changes which have taken place and comparing different approaches to the management of manufacturing. The final section turns its attention to the area of manufacturing strategy, not only to

1

link this chapter to the remainder of the book but also to start to high-light the increasing awareness of manufacturing as a strategic force at both national and corporate level.

1.1 Manufacturing Output

Comparative figures on manufacturing output over the period from 1970 to 1984 reveal that whereas some countries (notably Japan and

FIGURE 1.1
Comparative manufacturing output 1970–84 (1970=100)

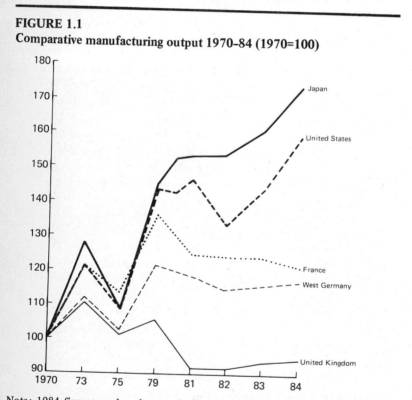

Note: 1984 figures are based upon the first three quarters and are not seasonally adjusted

Based upon Figure 7.1 in the *Economic Review* (1983) p.34 (UK), and updated from information supplied in OECD's *Indicators of Industrial Activity*.

the USA) have maintained sound growth during the 1970s and first half of the 1980s, others (in particular the UK) have declined – see Figure 1.1. To shed further light on these differences, Table 1.1 gives the percentage share for some of the 'main manufacturing' countries' exports of manufactured goods during the years 1969–1983.

TABLE 1.1
Main manufacturing countries' exports of manufactured goods – selected countries only

Year	Percentage share						
	France	Italy	Japan	Sweden	UK	USA	West Germany
1969	8.2	7.3	11.2	3.2	11.2	19.2	19.1
1970	8.8	7.2	11.7	3.4	10.6	18.6	19.9
1971	8.8	7.3	13.0	3.3	10.9	17.0	20.1
1972	9.3	7.6	13.2	3.3	10.1	16.2	20.2
1973	9.6	6.8	12.7	3.4	9.4	16.0	22.1
1974	9.2	6.8	14.4	3.3	8.8	17.0	21.6
1975	10.2	7.4	13.6	3.5	9.1	17.7	20.3
1976	9.8	7.1	14.7	3.4	8.4	17.3	20.6
1977	9.9	7.6	15.5	3.1	9.0	15.7	20.8
1978	9.8	7.9	15.6	3.0	8.9	15.3	20.8
1979	10.5	8.4	13.7	3.1	9.1	16.0	20.8
1980	10.0	7.9	14.9	2.9	9.7	17.0	19.9
1981	9.2	7.7	17.9	2.8	8.5	18.6	18.4
1982	9.2	8.0	17.4	2.8	8.5	17.7	19.5
1983[1]	9.9[3]	8.1	17.0	2.8	7.7	16.9	19.9
+(−)% change[2]	21	11	52	(12)	(31)	(12)	2

[1] The figures for 1983 reflect Quarter 1 only.
[2] +(−) % change is the difference between 1969 and Quarter 1, 1983 as a percentage of 1969.
[3] The 1983 figure for France is estimated.

Source: *Monthly Review of External Trade Statistics*, Department of Trade and Industry, Issue No. 96, Dec. 1983.

This, on the whole, reinforces the main message in Figure 1.1. Japan again demonstrated its improvement in the manufacturing sector showing by far the largest improvement in the period reviewed. It also illustrates West Germany's strong export position which has remained fairly constant throughout. Whereas the UK's decline in the same period is very marked.

To complete this initial review, the export–import trade ratios of manufacturing industries are given in Table 1.2 to provide an insight into the relative trading performance of main manufacturing nations. The figures reinforce the strong positions held by both Japan and West Germany and the decline in the UK performance. The USA, whilst still in a deficit position, showed improvement between 1972 and 1982.

TABLE 1.2
Export import ratios of trade for total manu-facturing industries, 1972 and 1982

Country	Export–import ratio, total manufacturing industries	
	1972	1982
Canada	0.9	1.1
France	1.1	1.0
Italy	1.3	1.3
Japan	2.8	3.0
United Kingdom	1.1	0.9
United States	0.8	0.9
West Germany	1.5	1.5

Source: OECD Science and Technology Indicators Unit, *Newsletter No. 8* (1984) pp. 6, 7.

The decline in the UK's competitive position in the world industrial markets is there for all to see. Loss of market share abroad, increased imports at home. UK industry has performed badly for a long time, whatever measure is used. A more in-depth review of her trading performance shows that from 1973, imports took an increasing market share for manufacturing goods overall whilst making significant and very worrying inroads into certain sectors – see Table 1.3.

TABLE 1.3
Ratio of UK imports to home demand for all manufacturing and selected sectors

Manufacturing sector	Imports/home demand ratio						1983
	1973	1979	1980	1981	1982	1983	(1973=100)
Motor vehicles and their parts	23	41	39	42	46	51	222
Paper, printing and publishing	19	19	19	20	20	20	105
Engineering							
mechanical	26	29	29	32	32	36	138
electrical and electronic	27	31	31	36	40	43	159
instruments	46	53	52	55	56	56	122
Chemicals and man-made fibres	22	30	29	31	34	33	150
Food, drink and tobacco	19	18	16	16	16	17	89
Textile industry	21	33	34	39	39	41	195
Clothing and footwear	18	29	29	33	33	34	189
Total manufacturing industry	21	27	26	28	29	31	148

Source: Central Statistical Office (CSO), *Annual Abstract of Statistics*, Table 12.1 'Import Penetration Ratio for Products of Manufacturing Industry', no. 121 (1985).

Against this background of decline it is interesting to note that successive UK Governments have tended to act on the sometimes painful premise that exposure to overseas competition is a necessary ingredient for the development of a strong, domestic manufacturing base. What is, however, of deep concern is that manufacturing industry's response to that exposure has been woefully slow. Many firms have tended to complain about 'unfair' external competition and have kept their corporate eyes on domestic rather than overseas competitors. The result is that they have adopted inadequate, reactive strategies because the consequences for manufacturing have not been appreciated. Typically, they have filled capacity by chasing orders, increasing variety and reducing batch sizes, leaving overseas competitors with substantial advantages in the higher-volume segments of their markets. Many businesses have failed to recognise, until too late in the day, that the sellers' markets of the 1950s and 1960s have long since passed and that the 1980s require new strategies which must aim to gain and maintain some specific and significant advantages against the most, not least powerful of their competitors.

Whereas the UK and US in particular were being buffeted by this new competitive surge, that was not so for some countries which seemed to have moved from strength to strength. Figure 1.1 has shown the continued rise in relative output in Japan. Similarly, certain Western European countries, notably West Germany, were also showing up well in the international league tables. Of deeper concern still for the UK, however, were the facts underlying these trends, especially that of competitive productivity.

1.2 Productivity: National Comparisons

The prosperity of nations is recognised as being dependent on their comparative productivity. In the past two decades of increasing competition, this has been brought sharply into focus. Although not a precise measure in the definctive sense of the world, it affords a way of assessing trends both for the performance of individual countries and their relative positions in appropriate world rankings.

Thus, there are two important dimensions of a productivity slowdown for any nation. The first is the rate of the slowdown itself, whilst the second is the cumulative effect of the slowdown on the comparative level of productivity between a country and its competitors.

Where the growth rate lags substantially behind that of other industrialised countries and does so for a protracted period, then a decline in living standards will follow and companies will find themselves at a serious competitive disadvantage. This in turn will lead, if it goes unchecked, to a position where recovery is the more difficult to achieve, and breaking free from the downward spiral, a major task.

Productivity measures the relationship between outputs (in the form of goods and services produced) and inputs (in the form of labour, capital, material and other resources). Although in practice productivity is not so simple to measure due to the global nature of the figures involved, it does provide an overall review of improvement and one which lends itself to trend analysis. Two types of productivity measurement are commonly used: labour productivity and total-factor or multi-factor productivity. Labour productivity measures output in terms of hours worked or paid for. Total-factor or multi-factor productivity not only includes the labour input but also all or some of the plant, equipment, energy and materials. However, when there is a change in a single-factor productivity ratio, it is important not to attribute the change solely to that one input. Owing to the interrelated nature of the total inputs involved, the change may well be influenced by any or all of the many variables which could contribute to the change. For example, production methods, capital investment, process technology, labour force, managerial performance, capacity utilisation, material input/usage rates, capacity scale and product mix are all potential contributors to productivity improvements. Furthermore, the relative importance of these will vary from nation to nation, industrial sector to industrial sector, company to company, plant to plant and one time period to the next.

Although it may be difficult to get a consensus on the quantitative dimensions of productivity measurement, the qualitative conclusions on the size and duration of the problem for the UK are clearly shown in Table 1.4.

Not only is the productivity slowdown itself disturbing, but the picture which emerges when comparisons are made with other leading industrial countries also adds to the justifiable level of concern. Besides the UK, Canada and the US have similar profiles with the latter coming bottom of the league table for the period 1960–81, as shown in Figure 1.2. Later figures confirm these differences. The rate of productivity

TABLE 1.4
Average annual rates of productivity growth in leading industrial countries in the periods 1960–73 and 1973–9 and the change which occurred in these two periods

Country	Rate of growth (%)		
	1960–73	1973–9	Change
Italy	7.8	1.6	(6.2)
Japan	9.9	3.8	(6.1)
Sweden	5.8	2.5	(3.3)
Canada	4.2	1.0	(3.2)
United States	3.1	1.1	(2.0)
United Kingdom	3.8	1.9	(1.9)
France	5.9	4.2	(1.7)
West Germany	5.8	4.3	(1.5)

Source: New York Stock Exchange, *US Economic Performance in a Global Perspective* (New York: NYSE, 1981), p. 19

increase in the fourth quarter of 1984 reinforced this gap. Japan achieved 10 per cent whilst France, West Germany, US and the UK achieved 7½, 6, 3½ and 2½ per cent respectively.

Whilst the change in the percentage growth rate was less in the UK and US than most of the other countries shown in Table 1.4, there is still a big gap between the UK and US rate of growth for 1973–9 and that for the countries at the top. Whilst West Germany and France are some 2½ times greater than the UK, they are almost four times greater than the US and more than four times greater than Canada.

The cumulative effect over the period 1960 to 1982 is clearly shown in Figures 1.2 and 1.3, and the enormity of the ever widening gap for the UK is a source of distinct, national concern.*

*More recent figures confirm this trend. In 1984, unit labour costs rose faster in the UK than in any of its major competitors. The figures were: UK, up 6 per cent; France, up 3 per cent; US up ½ per cent; West Germany, down 3 per cent, and Japan, down 6 per cent.

FIGURE 1.2

Trends of productivity growth rates (1960–81): indexed labour – productivity growth rates of manufacturing industries (1960=100)

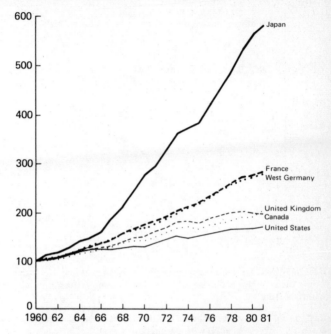

Note   In order to compare productivity growth rates, each country's growth rate for 1960 is assigned a value of 100. If this figure were to compare levels of productivity (instead of growth rates), it would show each country starting at a different level.

Source: Committee for Economic Development's Research and Policy Committee, *Productivity Policy: key to Nation's Economic Future*, April 1983, p.17. (With permission.)

1.3 Productivity: Plant-level Comparisons

Three examples are given to illustrate the company and plant level differences in productivity between countries and also to help reinforce the wide gap which exists. A report[2] on the toolmaking sector assessed the relative performance of 17 UK and West German companies in the

FIGURE 1.3
Loss of UK competitiveness

Unit labour costs: UK labour costs per unit of output in manufacturing, adjusted using the effective exchange rate, divided by competitors' unit labour costs in manufacturing.

Sources: London Business School, OECD and CBI staff estimates. Economic Directorate, CBI – Reprinted with permission[3]

product sectors of mould, large press tool and assembly equipment makers. It was essentially concerned with the overall achievement of comparable teams of management and workers. A performance ratio, based upon added value divided by total employment costs and adjusted for employee cost difference,[4] was used to compare the overall achievement of one company with each other company in the relevant product sector. Figure 1.4 shows the relative average performance of the UK and West German companies reviewed. The average performance of West German companies in each product sector was better than in their British counterparts by a factor of just under 20 per cent (mould makers), just over 30 per cent (large press toolmakers) and 25 per cent (assembly equipment makers).

FIGURE 1.4

Relative performance of British and West German companies by product sector

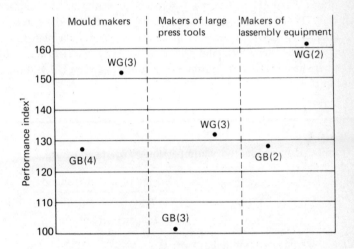

	Mould makers	Makers of large press tools	Makers of assembly equipment

Performance index[1]

	Number of companies concerned		
UK	4	3	2
West Germany	3	3	2

[1]Base of 100 for the lowest performing company in the total sample

Note: In each column the figure shown is the average for the companies in that sector in the country concerned, and the number in brackets is the firms involved.

Source: Gauge and Tool Sector Working Party's Report (1981), p.vii, Figure 1.

A more recent Anglo-German survey[5] revealed even higher productivity differences in a 1983–4 study of 25 UK and 20 West German firms in the metal-working trades. From within the larger survey, six pairs of firms, selected on the basis of matched, simple products, were analysed. In all six comparisons, the German firms showed higher labour productivity varying from 10 to 130 per cent with an average of some 63 per cent.

The third illustration provides the next three examples which were all taken from a Ford Motor Company series of presentations to suppliers in the early 1980s. The purpose was, in part, to highlight the extent of the productivity gap between European and Japanese car plants. The figures speak for themselves and illustrate not only the significant difference between Japan and Europe but also between the UK and other European plants.

TABLE 1.5
Engine plant productivity comparisons, Toyota and Ford

Aspect	Engine plant performance	
	Toyota (Japan)	Ford[1] (Europe)
Daily output per employee	9	2
Floor space (000 sq. ft)[2]	300	878

[1] The Ford engine plant was its 'latest'.
[2] The floor space comparisons were for similar output levels.

A comparison on assembly plant build (see Table 1.6) showed not only similar differences between Europe and Japan but also a significantly lower productivity achievement between the UK and continental European plants.

Similar figures quoted to represent 1979 productivity comparisons revealed that the number of units produced per head employed was as shown in Table 1.7.

Another comparison, this time between Volkswagen and Nissan, also supported this wide margin of difference with the annual number of cars produced per employee of 10.6 to 39.2 respectively, giving the almost identical ratio to that above, of 3.7 to 1.

The consequence of this is an erosion of markets owing to a significant price advantage. In an article on the US motor industry, the estimated employee costs per vehicle in 1979 for Ford (USA) and Toyo-

TABLE 1.6
Assembly plant productivity comparisons, Toyota and Ford

Aspect	Ford Transit		Toyota Hiace
	UK	Belgium	
Number per shift at similar build rate			
Directs	1024	643	350
Inspectors	83	68	15
Other indirects	929	287	45
Total	2036	998	410
Total manpower per unit build	12.5	7.2[1]	2.4

[1] This particular figure related to West Germany, not to Belgium.

TABLE 1.7
The number of units per employee category produced by Ford (Europe) and Toyota (Japan)

Labour category	Units per employee	
	Ford (Europe)	Toyota (Japan)
Direct labour	32	65
Indirect labour and staff	23	170
Total	13	47

Kogyo were $2464 and $491, respectively.[6] Based on the huge productivity and cost advantages described here, the surge in total output and the increase in export sales enjoyed by the Japanese vehicle manufacturers since the mid-1960s has been considerable (see Table 1.8).

TABLE 1.8
Japanese vehicle production, domestic sales and export sales 1966–83

Year	Japanese vehicles (millions)		
	Total production	Sales	
		Domestic	Export
1966	2.3	2.0	0.3
1970	5.2	4.1	1.1
1979	10.0	5.1	4.9
1980	11.0	5.0	6.0
1981	11.2	5.1	6.1
1982	10.7	5.2	5.5
1983	11.1	5.4	5.7
1984	11.5	5.5	6.0

Source: Motor Industry of Great Britain Society of Motor Manufacturing Traders and the Motor Industry Research Association.

The consequences of these productivity differences are reflected in the export–import ratio for 'motor vehicles' in some of the major manufacturing nations (see Table 1.9).

TABLE 1.9
Export-import ratio for motor vehicles in 1972 and 1982

Country	Export–import ratio for motor vehicles	
	1972	1982
Canada	0.9	1.2
France	2.0	1.3
Italy	1.5	0.8
Japan	25.2	48.2
UK	2.0	0.7
USA	0.6	0.5
West Germany	3.4	4.4

Source: OECD Science and Technology Indicators Unit. (1984)

1.4 Why Has This Happened?

The reasons why this has happened are many and varied. Some are unsubstantiated opinions, others are supported by fact. Some will be more relevant to some nations, sectors and companies, and others, less. However, learning from past failures is a step towards determining how to build a more successful competitive future.

Failure to recognise the size of the competitive challenge

There has been a failure, conscious or otherwise, of industry and society at large to recognise the size of the competitive challenge, the impact it was having and would have on our very way of life, and to recognise the need to change.

One illustration of UK industry's lack of awareness is provided in a selection from the corporate responses to the 1976 Select Committee of Science and Technology (Japan Subcommittee) seeking evidence on several aspects of Japanese industry. The subcommittee wrote in September 1977 to many leading British manufacturing companies and related associations seeking their views on a number of perspectives within Japanese industry. There follows a précis of some of the points raised in the replies received, with the name of the organisation, and particular aspect(s) to be addressed.

Ford Motor Company's comments on the success with which Japanese industry has handled its process and product development:[7]

> I am not sure that we have anything useful to contribute on this issue so far as the motor industry is concerned because all the processes and products used by the Japanese motor industry are known to us and their success depends on achieving economies of scale based on a large home market, on a different attitude adopted by labour in their industry and also on their apparent success in containing inflation more effectively than we have been able to do in this country.
>
> In short, as far as the motor industry is concerned the general superiority of the Japanese seems to me to be in the area of attitudes and economies rather than technology.

The reply also mentions that the Japanese 'are very competitive in their strategic thinking and their marketing plans, but . . . there is nothing they do in these areas either that is not known and practised by some of us at least in the motor industry in the West'.

Yet, less than three years later, the Ford Motor Company was holding seminars within all its major suppliers to detail the critical nature of the Japanese challenge and examining the stark comparisons of performance, amongst others, which were provided earlier in the chapter. Based on the improving percentage of the Japanese free world vehicle production (10 to 26 per cent from 1966 to 1979) and the decline in the European percentage (38 to 34 per cent) in the same period, Ford concentrated much of its discussion on the manufacturing perspective as the foundation for this challenge. As the Ford Report admitted, the extent and nature of the superiority was not appreciated until Ford went to see for themselves.

But Ford were not the only company which failed to appreciate the extent of the challenge.

Rank Organisation commented on the introduction of new products and improved production methods used by Japanese industry, as follows:

Whilst subscribing 'on the whole to the generalisation that Japanese industry has performed in the ways described, better than the UK' Rank considered that Japan 'would seem to have the following advantages compared with the UK, at least in the products/markets where they are conspicuously successful'.

The reply then lists seven advantages which were, in summary form:

(1) High prestige of industrial activity and careers management and technology.
(2) Ample supply of potential managers, engineers and technologists.
(3) Full support by operatives and trade unions to productivity increases and high quality attainment.
(4) Better personal motivation through taxes, rewards and strong work ethic.
(5) Unique relationship between government, banking and industry.
(6) Home market highly protected.
(7) Buoyant economy helps exploit new technologies and inventions.

Rank's reply then detailed three steps to be taken to help redress the situation. These related to points (1), (2), (4) and (6) above. Thus, like Ford, Rank in late 1977 was stressing not the key manufacturing and business issues (that is, aspects over which the company had substantial and significant control and direction) but aspects which were governmental or cultural in origin (that is, aspects over which they had little control and direction).

Yet in the early 1980s, the Rank/Toshiba television plant in Plymouth illustrated how the initial failure of the joint venture was turned into a successful manufacturing unit when Toshiba took full control. And, this is not the only example of initial failure being turned into success when Japanese management took over. Similar cases are provided from elsewhere including Motorola's TV assembly plant in Illinois taken over in the early 1970s by Matsushita, the Sony TV plant at San Diego, and the Sanyo Electric plants in Arkansas and California.

Further, apparent misunderstandings or lack of awareness of the nature and extent of competition were displayed in the content, tone and extent of other replies, for example, the Motor Industry Research Association.

These views, however, were not shared by all contributors. Many were aware of the differences in corporate attitude and priorities, thus providing a sharp contrast to the earlier examples:
Electrical Research Association replied:

> **Japanese industry is successful in those products it has chosen for world-wide marketing because there is a total commitment to manufacturing high quality, reliable goods on a very large scale, as much effort being committed to the production process and technology as the products themselves. In the United Kingdom we have very large resources and our best talent locked up in irrelevant basic research. Manufacturing industry attempts to survive with the minimum resources and too little skill and investment in the production and quality control process.**

EMI's response was similarly biased towards a recognition of the Japanese manufacturer's approach to markets and production. For instance,

- Japanese manufacturers study competitors' products, technologies and market needs in much greater depth than their European counterparts.

● Advanced developments are embodied in the products and in the manufacturing processes. This gives the commercial products a technological lead and a cost advantage – two significant factors in establishing a significant market position.

Some companies even recognised the gravity of the problem and the speed of response which must be made. For instance, BOC Ltd identified 'certain technical aspects of small batch manufacturing in which considerable practical experience has been obtained in Japan and for which no equivalent knowledge exists in the UK'. Linked machining centres which had been in operation for five years in Japan were not known to exist in the UK or even being contemplated by any British machine tool manufacturer. In summary, BOC's reply concludes that 'the action we in Britain take in the next two years can be critical in ensuring a continuing viable manufacturing industry in this field, and especially the machine tool aspect'.

Failure to appreciate the impact of increasing manufacturing capacity

World manufacturing capacity up to the mid-1960s was, by and large, less than demand and in this period companies could sell all they could make. The redressing of this capacity/demand imbalance heralded the growing prominence of marketing. In the 1970s, it then became the accounting/finance function which increased its influence. During this time, the manufacturing perspective within the corporate strategy resolution diminished. The result has been that many companies have become almost entirely marketing-orientated. New product introductions and product differentiation have, therefore, become the predominant corporate strategic approach. Market opportunities are explored leaving the aftermath for manufacturing to handle and solve. Couple this with the increasing pre-eminence of financial measures and the result has been a corporate policy in many UK companies where investment for product innovation and associated manufacturing requirements has been relatively plentiful, whilst that for process innovation has been relatively scarce. This is not so in Japan. A recent survey revealed that, whereas process engineering functions in North American and European companies were, respectively, 6 per cent and 8 per cent likely to get their project proposals approved, in Japan it was 27 per cent.[8] The consequences of this have been several.

(1) For many companies, it has resulted in a widening inability to meet changing patterns of demand. Classically, whilst manufacturing technology and the perceived manufacturing task were moving towards even more mass production and the economies associated with that direction, markets were responding to greater competitive pressures which, in turn, led to wider product ranges and resultant lower volumes.

(2) Strategic investment in manufacturing has, overall, been discouraged with the result that the process technology advantage enjoyed by our competitors continues to increase:

- Corporate performance is measured predominantly in terms of return on investment. In addition, the need to demonstrate twice yearly the expected progress to the business, its shareholders and the stock market puts unwise and unnecessary pressure on short-term performance. This, in turn, adds weight to the argument to keep investment low as a way of keeping returns relatively high.
- Top management's inexperience in manufacturing provides an unreceptive climate in which to consider strategic process investment. Risk aversion, so much a part of the corporate financial argument, also favours holding-off.

(3) The diminishing role of production in strategy has led to a corresponding lack of involvement in the corporate debate. One consequence has been that the engineering dimension has been the predominant basis on which process choices have been made. This has led to situations where processes have been installed which, though excellent in themselves, were not appropriate to the business needs. Tripping over white elephants from the past, has made managements wary of the future.

Top management's lack of manufacturing experience

Top management's lack of experience in manufacturing has further ramifications for a business. Considering the fact that manufacturing accounts for some 70–80 per cent of assets, expenditure and people, then it is imperative that senior executives fully appreciate the arguments and counter-arguments in manufacturing so as to ensure that the accompanying wide range of perspectives are taken into account when making important manufacturing decisions. Once large investments have been made then rarely does a company invest a second time to correct the mistake. This lack of experience is certainly not so in Japan and West Germany where a full and perceptive insight into manufacturing is seen as a prerequisite for top management.

However, the consequences of this knowledge gap do not stop here. As Wickham Skinner observes

> **to many executives, manufacturing and the production function is a necessary nuisance – it soaks up capital in facilities and inventories, it resists changes in products and schedules, its quality is never as good as it should be and its people are unsophisticated, tedious, detail-orientated and unexciting. This makes for an unreceptive climate for major innovations in factory technology and contributes to the blind spot syndrome.[9]**

And, this brings with it many important consequences. One is that senior executives do not perceive the strategic potential of manufacturing. Typically it is seen in its traditional productivity/efficiency mode with the added need to respond to the strategic overtures of marketing and finance. The result is that manufacturing concentrates its effort and attention on the short-term whilst adopting its classic, reactive posture towards the long-term strategic issues of the business.

A *Wall Street Journal* (Europe) and Booz-Allen Hamilton survey on 'The Management of Technology' based on over 200 chief executives in 16 European countries, listed amongst its 'significant findings' that there was 'a surprising emphasis by European executives on cost reduction as a primary objective of technology'. The European Panel Members 'rank cost reduction in the factory as by far their most important objectives for technology'. That attitude clashes significantly with the findings of comparable studies among US and Japanese executives. Those business leaders display a far more aggressive attitude, ranking innovation in the form of new products, improved product performance or improved customer service higher. It goes on to quote one view, which was supported by a number of Europe's leading executives, that there is 'a desire to extend the life of the smoke stack industry. Many view technology as a way to extend the current product line past the point where it could go otherwise'.[10]

The survey also reveals that compared with the US, chief executives in European companies do not see their role as comprising an important co-ordinating function between R & D and marketing (see Table 1.10) – 'chief executives should be working hard to link the marketing and research and development departments. The most aggressive US and Japanese firms are doing this. But many European firms aren't.'

TABLE 1.10
Chief executives' role in R & D – US and Europe

Aspects of chief executive's role	Per cent of chief executives performing this role	
	Europe	US
Singles out and follows strategically important projects	36	58
Reviews major development projects above a financial threshold	19	58
Reviews all R & D programmes early and periodically	16	34

Source: *Wall Street Journal* (Europe) and Booz-Allen Hamilton Inc., *The Management of Technology*, The European Panel of Chief Executives No. 1, Feb. 1984, p. 8.

The production manager's obsession with short-term performance issues

The emphasis within the production manager's role has, in turn, been directed towards short-term issues and tasks. The overriding pressures to meet day-to-day targets and the highly quantifiable nature of the role have reinforced the tendency of manufacturing executives to concern themselves with this feature to the exclusion of the important long-term. The skills of production managers are high on short-term tasks such as scheduling, maintaining efficiency levels, controls, delivery, quality and resolving labour problems.

Skinner rightly believes that

most factories were not managed very differently in the 1970s than in the 1940s and 1950s. Manufacturing management was dominated by engineering and a technical point of view. This may have been adequate when *production* management issues centred largely on

efficiency and productivity and the answers came from industrial engineering and process engineering. But, the problems of operations managers in the 70s had moved far beyond mere physical efficiency.[11]

However, this predomonance of the short-term is reinforced by the view which companies have of the production management role. An analysis of job advertisements in the period 1970–9 revealed that of all the aspects mentioned concerning job content, 50 per cent for managers and 52 per cent for directors concerned the need for day-to-day management and a knowledge of support functions. Similarly, the appropriate work experience mix which a suitable applicant would need revealed that for managers, 54 per cent of all mentions referred to their experience record as production managers and use of management controls and techniques. For directors it accounted for 51 per cent of all mentions. In contrast, the same ten-year analysis revealed a correspondingly low emphasis on, or requirement for, the long-term, corporate contribution. The job content mentions were 8 per cent and 13 per cent for managers and directors with typical work experience of applicants at 3 per cent and 4 per cent respectively.[12]

But, the production job has changed from one which concerns maintaining steady state manufacturing by sound day-to-day husbandry to one which is multidimensional. It is now increasingly concerned with managing greater complexity in product range, product mix, volume changes, process flexibility, inventory, cost and financial controls and employee awareness due to the more intensive level of domestic and international competition.

This is the nature of the new task. No longer are the key issues solely confined to operational control and fine-tuning the system. The need is for broad, business-orientated manufacturing managers but companies have produced too few of them. The use of specialists as the way to control our businesses has increasingly led to a reduction in the breadth of a line manager's responsibilities which has narrowed the experience base. Furthermore, many manufacturing managers have been outgunned by specialist argument and found themselves unable to cope with the variety of demands placed upon them. The response by many has been to revert increasingly to their strengths. This has, therefore, reinforced their short-term role and their inherently reactive stance to corporate strategic resolution.

Manufacturing executives do not, on the whole, explain the important, conceptual aspects of manufacturing to others in the organisation.

Seldom do they evaluate and expose the implications for manufacturing of corporate decisions, so that alternatives can be considered and more soundly based, corporate decisions agreed. Part of the reason for this is that there is a lack of developed language to help provide a way of explaining the corporate production issues involved. Lacking, therefore, in strategic dimension, manufacturing has often been forced into piece-meal change achieving what it can as and when it has been able. The result has been a series of intermittent responses lacking corporate co-ordination.

1.5 Manufacturing Strategy

What has happened in the last decade and a half is that countries such as Japan and West Germany have gained the competitive upper hand, and this advantage has been achieved through manufacturing. The Japanese, in particular, have gone for existing markets and provided better goods with few, if any, inherent benefits derived from material and energy resources.

One of the keys to this achievement through manufacturing has been the integration of these functional perspectives at the level of corporate strategy debate, and it is appropriate now to explain what this embodies and how it differs from the conventional approaches to the management of production. In broad terms, there are two important roles which manufacturing can offer as part of the strategic strengths of a company.

The first is to provide manufacturing processes which will give the business a distinct advantage in the market-place. In this way, manufacturing will offer to provide a marketing edge through distinct, unique technology developments in its process and manufacturing operations which competitors are unable to match. This role is quite rare, but examples include Pilkington's float glass process.

The second way is to provide co-ordinated manufacturing support for the essential ways in which products win orders in the market-place at a level which is better than its competitors are able to do. In this way, manufacturing develops a set of policies in both its process choice and infrastructure design (for example, controls, procedures, systems and structures) which are consistent with the existing way(s) that products win orders whilst being able to reflect future developments in line with changing business needs. Most companies share access to the same processes and thus technology is not inherently different. Similarly, the systems, structures and other elements of infrastructure are equally universal. What is different is the degree to which manufacturing matches process and infrastructure to those criteria which win orders. In this way, manufacturing constitutes a co-ordinated response consistent with the business needs and which will embrace all those aspects of a company for which manufacturing is responsible.

To do this effectively manufacturing needs to be involved throughout the whole of the corporate strategy debate to explain, in business terms, the implications of corporate marketing proposals and, as a result, be able to influence strategy decisions for the good of the business as a whole. Too often in the past, manufacturing has been too late in this procedure. Corporate executives have tended to assume that competitive strategies are more to do with, and often in fact are one and the same as, marketing initiatives. Implicit, if not explicit, in this view are two important assumptions. The first is that manufacturing's role is to respond to these changes rather than to make inputs into them. The second is that manufacturing has the capability to respond flexibly and positively to these changing demands. The result has been an inability to influence decisions which has led to a posture which appears to be forever complaining about the unrealistic demands placed upon production.

The need for a manufacturing strategy to be developed and shared by the business is not only to do with the critical nature of manufacturing within corporate strategy but also a realisation that many of the decisions are structural in nature. This means that they are hard to change. Unless the issues and consequences are fully appreciated by the business, then it can be locked into a number of manufacturing decisions which will take years to change. These can range from process investments on the one hand, through to human resource management practices and controls on the other. Decisions not in line with the needs of the business can contribute significantly to a lack of corporate success. To change them is costly and time consuming. But even more significantly, they will come too late. The development of a corporate policy comprising a co-ordinated set of main function inputs will mean that the business would be able to go in one consistent, coherent direction based on a well argued, well understood and well formed strategy. This is achieved, in part, by moving away from argument, disagreement, misunderstanding and short-term, parochial moves based on interfunctional perspectives, to the resolution of these differences at the corporate level. Currently, marketing led strategies leave the aftermath to be resolved by manufacturing, who without adequate, appropriate guidance or discussion and agreement at the corporate level, resolve the issues as best they can largely from their unilateral view of what is best for the business as a whole.

In the majority of cases, manufacturing is simply not geared to the business's corporate objectives. The result is a manufacturing system, good in itself, but not designed to meet company needs. Manufacturing left in the wake of corporate decisions is often at best a neutral force, and even sometimes inadvertently pulls in the opposite direction. Seen as being concerned solely with efficiency, the question of production's strategic contribution is seldom part of the corporate consciousness.

What does all this mean for production managers? One clear consequence is the need to change from a reactive to a proactive stance. The long-term inflexible nature of manufacturing means that the key issues, and there are many of them, involved in process choice and infrastructure development need to be reflected in business decisions with the business being made aware of the implications for manufacturing of proposed corporate changes. When this is achieved, the strategy decisions which are then taken reflect what is best for the business as a whole. So, manufacturing management's attention must increasingly be towards strategy. This does not mean that operations are unimportant. But the balance and direction of management activity needs to reflect the relative impact on business performance of strategy and operations whilst recognising that both need to be done well. Top management have, by and large, perceived corporate improvements as coming mainly through broad decisions concerning new markets, takeovers and the like. However, the building blocks of corporate success are to be found in creating effective, successful businesses where manufacturing supports the marketing requirement within a well chosen, well argued and well understood corporate strategy.

1.6 Conclusion

The emphasis in successfully managed manufacturing functions is increasingly towards issues of strategy. And, there is evidence of a growing awareness of this fact. For example, the Advisory Council for

Applied Research and Development's booklet, *New Opportunities in Manufacturing: the Management of Technology* specifically recommended for industry that 'companies in manufacturing should review the balance of their senior management and ensure that the role of a suitably qualified board member includes responsibility for manufacturing strategy'.[13] When surveys on manufacturing in Europe, Japan and North America posed questions under the heading on which 'activities or programmes the business unit is planning to focus on during the next two years to improve operations' the percentage responses shown in Table 1.11 were recorded against the item 'defining a manufacturing strategy'.[14]

TABLE 1.11
The percentage responses in 1983 and 1984 confirming plans to define a manufacturing strategy in the next two years as a way of improving operations

Year	% responses		
	Europe	Japan	North America
1983	34	30	42
1984	41	not available	51

It is important to stress that top management needs to pay a great deal more than lip service to the task of ensuring that manufacturing's input into the strategic debate is comprehensive and that the agreed corporate decisions fully reflect the complex issues involved. Much determination will need to be exercised to ensure that the more superficial approaches to incorporating the wide ranging aspects of manufacturing into corporate decisions are avoided. The rewards for this are substantial. An analysis of the US automobile industry concluded that

> **most explanations of this Japanese advantage in production costs and product quality emphasize the impact of automation, the strong support of central government, and the pervasive influence of national culture. No doubt these factors have played an important role, but the primary sources of this advantage are found instead in the Japanese ... execution of a well-designed strategy based on the**

shrewd use of manufacturing excellence ... The Japanese cost and quality advantage ... originates in painstaking strategic management of people, materials and equipment – that is, in superior manufacturing performance.[15]

The implications for manufacturing executives are that they must begin to think and act in a more strategic manner. In an environment traditionally geared to meeting output targets, the pressure on manufacturing has been to manage reactively, and to be operationally efficient rather than strategically effective. It has been more concerned with doing things right (efficiency), than doing the right things (effectiveness). This has over the years created the view that this comprises the appropriate manufacturing task and contribution. Furthermore, it has given rise to the related assumption that any other posture would imply negative attitudes, with manufacturing appearing to be putting obstacles in the way of achieving key corporate objectives. At times this puts manufacturing in the vicious circle of corporate demands on manufacturing, manufacturing's best response, a recriminating corporate appraisal of that response, new corporate demands for improved manufacturing performance and so on. The purpose of this book is to help avoid the all too common corporate approach to manufacturing by providing a set of concepts and approaches which together create a platform from which manufacturing can make a positive, strategic contribution to developing powerful competitive strategies. But, manufacturing executives must first accept that they need to manage their own activities strategically, and this is almost as much a change in management attitude as it is an analytical process.

The purpose of thinking and managing strategically is not to just improve operational performance or to defend market share. It is to gain competitive advantage and it implies an attempt to mobilise manufacturing capability to help gain this competitive edge. Kenichi Ohmae,[16] a leading Japanese consultant with McKinsey, suggests that when managers are striving to achieve or maintain a position of relative superiority over competitors the management mind works very differently than the way it does when the objective is to make operational improvements against often arbitrarily set, internal objectives.

This chapter has highlighted the tendency for manufacturing to place more emphasis on operational efficiency than on competitive advantage. The danger for the business is that manufacturing gets so used to absorbing and responding to demands that reacting becomes the norm. Each crisis is viewed as a 'temporary situation' which often militates against recognising the need to fundamentally review strategies. By the time that this need becomes obvious the business is often at a serious competitive disadvantage.

The aims of this book are to reverse the reactive response and short-term perspectives held by manufacturing of its contribution to the business, to turn the role into one which seeks to manage manufacturing strategically and to set out the managerial and corporate issues which need to be addressed to establish competitive advantage. All, however, is not lost. There is much evidence that in many of the traditional manufacturing nations the capability exists to turn domestic manufacturing around and to challenge and beat overseas competition in both home and world markets. There are already examples of that turnaround in competitive performance, but the key ingredients include tough, professional management, combining strategic analysis of key issues with that intuitive, creative flair, for so long directed at primarily solving operational problems.

It is imperative that manufacturing managers take the initiative. For some organisations or functions within a business, the *status quo* even suits them. In those same organisations, manufacturing is played off against a forever changing set of objectives and targets, and it hurts. If manufacturing waits for other corporate initiatives they will not come soon enough. The lack of empathy and understanding by top management towards manufacturing often means that when difficulties arise, the preferred course of action is to get rid of the problem by selling-off the business or buying-in from outside. The causes of the problem are seldom addressed. Companies should realise that there are no long-term profits to be made in easy manufacturing tasks – anyone can provide these. It is in the difficult areas where profits are to be made. Furthermore, selling off inherent infrastructure can lead to an inability to effectively compete in future markets. The critical task facing manufacturing managers is to explain the essential nature of manufacturing in business terms and this must embrace both process technology and infrastructure development.

Notes and References

1. Confederation of British Industry, *News Release,* pp. 50, 85, 15 March 1985.

2. Gauge and Tool Sector Working Party, 'Toolmaking: a Comparison of UK and West German Companies' (National Economic Development Office, 1981).
3. CBI Economic Directorate *Pay, Profits and Jobs* (1980).
4. Gauge and Tool Sector Working Party's Report, 1981, p. 1a and Appendix A on pp. 20–21.
5. A. Daly, D.M.W.N. Hitchens, and K. Wagner, 'Productivity, Machinery and Skills in a Sample of British and German Manufacturing Plants', National Institute of Economic and Social Research *National Institute Review* No 111, Feb. 1985, pp. 48–61.
6. W. J. Abernathy *et al.*, 'The New Industrial Competition', *Harvard Business Review*, Sept/Oct. 1981, p. 80.
7. Second Report from the Select Committee on Science and Technology, 1977/78. 'Innovation, Research and Development in Japanese Science-based Industry', vols 1 and 2 (HMSO Aug. 1978). These corporate responses provided as appendixes to the Minutes of Evidence taken before the Select Committee on Science and Technology (Japan Subcommittee) are as follows:

Page(s)	*Appendix*	*Company*	*Date*
109	1	Ford Motor Company	Oct. 1977
111–112	3	Rank Organisation	Oct. 1977
179	31	Motor Industry Research Association	Oct. 1977
180	32	Electrical Research Association	Nov. 1977
131	17	EMI Group	Nov. 1977
110	2	BOC	Sept. 1977

8. Boston University Research Report Series, 'The 1983 Global Manufacturing Futures Series', Apr. 1983, p. 18.
9. W. Skinner, 'Operations Technology: Blind Spot in Strategic Management', Harvard Business School Working Paper 83–85 (1983) p. 11.
10. *Wall Street Journal* (Europe) and Booz-Allen Hamilton Inc., European Panel of Chief Executives, No. 1, 'The Management of Technology', Feb. 1984, p. 3.
11. W. Skinner, 'Operations Technology', p. 6. These views are also confirmed by the author in his book entitled *Production/Operations Management* (Prentice-Hall, 1983) pp. 23 and 24.
12. T.J. Hill *et al.*, 'The Production Manager's Task and Contribution', CRIBA Working Paper No. 94 (University of Warwick, UK) July 1981, pp. 27 and 32.
13. Advisory Council for Applied Research and Development', *New Opportunities in Manufacturing: the Management of Technology* Cabinet Office: London, HMSO, Oct. 1983) p.48.

14. J. G. Miller and T. E. Vollman, 'The 1984 Manufacturing Futures Project: Summary of North American Survey Responses', School of Management, Boston University, May 1984; K. Ferdows and A. de Meyer, *The State of Large Manufacturers in Europe: Results of the 1984 European Manufacturing Futures Survey* (The European Institute of Business Administration (INSEAD)) Apr. 1974, and J. G. Miller, J. Nakane (Waseda University, Systems Science Institute, Tokyo) and T. E. Vollman, *The 1983 Global Manufacturing Futures Survey* (School of Management, Boston University, Apr. 1983).
15. W.J. Abernathy, 'The New Industrial Competition', pp, 73–74.
16. Kenichi Ohmae, *The Mind of the Strategist* (McGraw-Hill, 1982) pp. 36–7.

Further Reading

Confederation of British Industry's Report, 'Pay and Productivity', Sept. 1983.
Foreign Press Centre, Japan. Science and Technology Agency's, 'Summary of White Paper on Science and Technology for 1981', Aug. 1983.
US Sub-committee on Employment and Productivity of the Committee on Labor and Human Resources, United States Senate 'Productivity and the American Economy: Report and findings', Sept. 1982.

Manufacturing Implications of Corporate Marketing Decisions

Companies invest in processes and infrastructure in order to make products and sell them at a profit. Consequently, the degree to which manufacturing is aligned to the product needs in the market-place will make a significant contribution to the overall success of a business. The size and fundamental nature of the manufacturing contribution is such, however, that the wrong fit will lead to the business being well wide of the mark. Many executives are still unaware 'that what appear to be routine manufacturing decisions frequently come to limit the corporation's strategic options, binding it with facilities, equipment, personnel and basic controls and policies to a non-competitive posture which may take years to turn round'.[1]

The reason for this is that companies having invested inappropriately in process and infrastructure, cannot afford to re-invest to put things right. The financial implications, systems development, training requirements and the time it would take to make the changes would leave it, at best, seriously disadvantaged. To avoid this companies need to be aware of how well manufacturing can support the market-place and be conscious of the investments and time dimensions to change current positions into future proposals.

2.1   Strategic Dominance – Perspectives Over Time

In broad terms, the changing world demand/capacity balance has brought with it a change in the fortunes of different functions. Up to the mid-1960s, many industries had enjoyed a capacity/demand relationship which favoured manufacturing. This, together with post-war growth, helped create the dominance of the manufacturing function in many corporations. As the demand/capacity balance began to even out, and selling into existing and new markets became more difficult, the power base of corporate influence began to swing away from manufacturing and heralded the rise of marketing. By the mid-1970s the impact of recessions and energy crises had, in turn, opened the door to the influence of accounting and finance. These varying fortunes, however, rarely seemed to be based upon what was best for the total good of the business, but more on which functional perspective appeared to provide the key which opened the door to corporate success or salvation. The consequence was that, those functions which were out in the cold were themselves left without due corporate influence.

However, in times of increasing world competition, an over-capacity in many sectors of manufacturing industry, an increasing scarcity of key resources and decreasing product life cycles there is an overriding logic for businesses to incorporate all the key functional perspectives when determining policy decisions. Why then does this not happen? In many organisations, manufacturing adopts or is required to take a reactive stance in corporate deliberations. Yet how can the function which controls such a large slice of the assets, expenditure and people, thus underpinning the very welfare of a company, be left out?

2.2   Reasons for Manufacturing's Reactive Role in Corporate Strategy

The fact that manufacturing executives have an exacting and critical corporate role to play is undisputed. Why then do they adopt their current role and why does this situation exist and not appear to be improving?

The production manager's view of himself

One of the major contributions to this situation appears to be that production managers also see themselves holding a reactive corporate brief. They too define their role as being one which requires them to react as well as possible to all that is asked of the production system. They see their role as:

● The exercise of skill and experience in effectively coping with the exacting and varying demands placed on manufacturing.
● To reconcile the trade-offs inherent in these demands as best they can.

Thus, rarely do they adequately contribute to the making of corporate decisions which result in a demand on manufacturing.

They do not explain the different sets of manufacturing implications created by alternative policy decisions and changes in direction. They fail, by default, to contribute at the corporate level and hence to help the company arrive at decisions which embrace all the important business perspectives.

The company's view of the production manager's role

Production managements' perceived role of reacting to the demands placed upon it and a prime concern for the short term which this implies, is reinforced by the corporate view of manufacturing's contribution and hence the qualities which incumbents should possess. Many companies typically promote operators to foremen, foremen to managers and managers to directors with scant regard for the change in emphasis which needs to take place and with little help to make this transition a success. One major UK company, recognising the important corporate contribution to be made by its manufacturing executives undertook a series of tailor-made courses in manufacturing strategy. The first of these comprised sixteen factory managers who, during the course, reflected that as a group their aggregate company service exceeded 300 years, yet the collective training they had received to help them prepare for their manufacturing executive roles was less than 30 days.

On a broader front, a survey of UK recruitment advertisements in the *Sunday Times* from 1970 to 1979[2] revealed that, in terms of the appropriate work experience of suitable applicants or the content of the job being advertised, whereas the number of mentions concerning the corporate or long-term contribution to be made by production managers and executives was very low, the number concerning the day-to-day management task was relatively high (see Table 2.1). In terms of both previous experience and job content the contrast was a stark illustration of where the emphasis lay.

TABLE 2.1
The corporate long-term compared to the day-to-day short-term perception of production executives' jobs and relevant experience of suitable applicants

Job category	Mentions as a percentage of the total in UK recruitment advertisements 1970–79	
	Corporate policy long-term/ corporate contribution	Day-to-day management/ record of production management
Production managers		
Work experience	3	34
Job content	8	23
Production directors		
Work experience	4	32
Job content	13	27

Production managers are too late in the corporate debate

Production managers are often not involved in corporate policy decisions until these decisions have started to take shape. This position having been partly created by the last two points will, once established, tend to become standard practice. The result is that production executives have less opportunity to contribute to decisions on strategy alternatives and, as a consequence, always appear to be complaining about the unrealistic demands made of them and the problems which invariably ensue.

The 'can't say no' syndrome

The 'can't say no' syndrome is still the hallmark of the production culture. But this helps no one. Manufacturing executives tend to respond
to corporate needs and difficulties without evaluating the consequences
or alternatives which need to be considered and then explaining these
to others. Rarely is it a yes or no decision. The need to be able to say
'no' from a total business perspective and with sound corporate related
arguments is an important part of any senior executive's role, and
manufacturing is no exception. At this time, the production manager
accepts the current and future demands placed upon the systems and
capacities he controls and then goes away to resolve them. In this way
he decides between corporate alternatives but only from a narrow
functional perspective of what appears best for the business. It is
essential that this changes. Resolving corporate related issues in a unilateral way is not the most effective method to resolve the complex
alternatives on hand. This resolution needs corporate debate to ensure
that the relevant factors and options are taken into account so an
appropriate corporate decision can be concluded.

For strategic decisions need to encompass the sets of important
trade-offs which are embodied in alternatives which have their roots in
the process and infrastructure investments associated with manufacturing and which are reflected in the high proportion of assets and
expenditure under their control.

Lack of language

On the whole, production managers do not have a history of explaining
their function clearly and effectively to others in the organisation. This
is particularly the case in terms of the manufacturing strategy issues
which need to be considered and the production consequences which
will arise from the corporate decisions under discussion. On the other
hand, marketing and financial executives have explained their function
well. They can talk about policy alternatives in a straightforward and
intelligible manner.[3]

The reason for this difference cannot, however, be wholly placed at
the production manager's door. The knowledge base, concepts and
language have not been developed in the same way. Consequently,
shared perspectives within manufacturing, let alone between functions,

are not held, which adds fuel to the lack of inter-functional understanding.

To illustrate this last point, just review the number of books and
articles written and postgraduate and post-experience courses provided
in the area of manufacturing strategy compared with the other major
functions of marketing and accounting/finance and to those disciplines
which purport to relate to business such as operational research and
organisational behaviour. Similarly, a check on the faculty mix within
major business schools clearly reveals the disproportionate allocation
of resources between these various areas and an understanding of why
these critical developments in manufacturing have not been forthcoming.

Functional goals and measures

In many organisations, the managers of different functions are measured
in terms of their departmental efficiency (an operational perspective)
and not in terms of overall effectiveness (a business perspective).
Furthermore, their career prospects are governed by their performance
within the functional value system. As a consequence, this leads to
managers making trade-offs which are sub-optimal for the business as
a whole.

Figure 2.1 illustrates this dichotomy. A typical accountant or sales-
man when receiving a customer order will look at one figure as being
significant – the total value of the order placed. For them, sales value is
the important measure of business relevance.

In the same situation, manufacturing managers will look at the order
make-up. For them, the business relevance of an order is not its value
but its volume and product mix. It is this aspect which determines the
ease with which an order can be made in terms of the process configurations already laid down. It is this which will reflect manufacturing's
ability to meet the cost base of the product(s) involved and hence the
profit margin which will result.

Where marketing is measured by the level of sales turnover achieved,
each £1 of sales in their value system will carry the same weight as any
other £1 of sales. Hence, all sales are deemed equal. In reality, however,
this is not the case. Orders are not of the same value to a business. The
higher the degree of fit between the anticipated volumes and product
mix and the actual sales, then the more the target levels will normally

FIGURE 2.1
**The dichotomy of business views illustrated by the different figures
included on typical customer order paperwork**

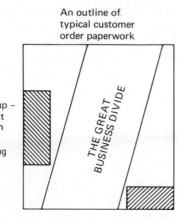

be met. Product costs based upon one level of volumes and process configurations based upon a given product mix are rarely, if ever, realigned with incremental volume and mix changes. Even the costing base which underpins initial forecasts is rarely, if ever, adjusted each time the market picture changes. A *great business divide*, therefore, separates the two realities of the market-place and manufacturing. The simplistic measure of total sales value disguises those product characteristics so essential to manufacturing's ability to sustain cost and profit margin structures in a business.

Functional support for manufacturing is weak

Building on the last point, many companies exercise control of their business through establishing specialist functions with, originally, the prime role and *raison d'être* of supporting the needs of the line and, in particular, manufacturing. However, in most firms the clarity of this perspective is now at best blurred, and at worst distorted. Typically, the performance of these specialist departments is measured in terms of their own functionally derived goals and perspectives rather than line management and hence business requirements. Getting adequate and timely resources committed to the manufacturing needs of a business is difficult.

Competing in different value systems, being measured against different performance criteria and gaining prominence and promotion through different departmental opinions of what constitutes importance within their contribution has gradually fragmented the business. It has created a situation where shared perspectives and overlapping views are left to individual accomplishment and endeavour rather than in response to clear corporate direction (these issues are covered in more detail in Chapter 6).

Tenure

Over the last two decades there has been a growing tendency to reduce the length of tenure for job incumbents, which militates against a manager's responsibility to provide for the necessary level of continuity. The short-term perspectives which result not only affect functional continuity but also discourage longer-term corporate perspectives from being pursued and implemented. The result is an inclination to maintain the *status quo* and to meet functional goals above all else. In times of change, neither of these promotes the corporate goodwill. Instead it leads a manager into taking decisions which are unduly weighted towards the standpoint of how they will affect him politically in the future rather than how they will affect the business's competitive position.

Top management's view of strategy

The authors of business plans and corporate marketing reviews look outward from the business. Top executives associate themselves with these activities, seeing them as legitimate corporate strategy issues. They concentrate their attention on the external environment in which the business operates.

Manufacturing plans are built in line with the stated business needs and are based upon the internal dimensions of the processes involved, and top executives are less likely to associate themselves with these activities. Typically they request a manufacturing strategy statement from the production executive without becoming involved in its structure and development. They assume that it is not an inherent part of their role, which increases the difficulties in establishing a corporate strategy through dialogue and understanding.

A key task in corporate strategy, however, is matching these two perspectives, the resolution of which has been abdicated by top management or at best has occurred outside the boundaries of their business awareness.

2.3 The Way Forward

What then is required is an orientation based neither on products/market/production interface, so that the degree of fit between the proposed marketing strategy and manufacturing's ability to support it proposed marketing strategy and manufacturing's ability to support it, is known at the business level and objectively resolved within corporate perspectives.

For this to take place, relevant internal information which explains the company's manufacturing capabilities needs to be available within a business as well as the traditional marketing information which is primarily concerned with the customer and the market opportunities associated with the company's products. It is not sufficient that such information should be available – and often it is not. To be effective, the ownership of its use must be vested in top management. As with other functions, manufacturing strategy is not owned by manufacturing. It requires corporate ownership. Senior executives need to understand all the strategic inputs in the corporate debate, for without this understanding the resolution between conflicting or non-matching functional perspectives cannot be fully investigated. What results is that individual functions are left with handling the trade-offs involved.

In this way, the business inappropriately delegates this key task and finds itself only able to exercise control over the decisions taken in a global, after-the-event way.

Linking manufacturing with corporate marketing decisions

There is no short-cut to moving forward. There are, however, five basic steps to be taken. These provide an analytical and objective structure in which the corporate debate and consequent actions can be taken.

Step 1   Define corporate objectives.
Step 2   Determine marketing strategies to meet these objectives.
Step 3   Assess how different products win orders against competitors.
Step 4   Establish the most appropriate mode to manufacture these sets of products – process choice.
Step 5   Provide the manufacturing infrastructure required to support production.

These are, in one sense, classical steps in corporate planning. The problem is that most corporate planners treat the first three steps as interactive with 'feedback loops' and the next two as linear and deterministic. While each step has substance in its own right, the really critical issue is that each has an impact on the others – hence the involved nature of strategy formulation. This is further exacerbated by the inherent complexity of manufacturing and the general failure to take account of the essential interaction between marketing and manufacturing strategies. What is required, therefore, is an approach which recognises these features and yet provides an ordered and analytical way forward.

The approach which is suggested to link manufacturing with corporate marketing decisions is schematically outlined in Table 2.2. It has been presented in the form of a framework to help express the stages involved in outline form. The approach to be followed provides the key to stimulating corporate debate about the business in such a way as to enable manufacturing to assess the degree to which it can support products in the market-place. It is an approach which has been researched and tested successfully in several industries and different sizes of business.

How it works

The objective of using this framework is to produce a manufacturing strategy for a business (Steps 4 and 5). In all cases this will include a review of existing products plus a review of proposed product introductions. Furthermore, the review will be based upon current and future market expectations. This is for the simple reason that manufacturing needs to support a product over the whole and not just a part of its life cycle and hence it is this total decision which the business needs to address. As product requirements change, so will manufacturing's task. The range of support requirements, therefore, will invariably affect the choice of process (Step 4) and infrastructure (Step 5) con-

TABLE 2.2
Framework for reflecting manufacturing policy issues in corporate decisions (steps involved)

1	2	3	4	5
Corporate objectives	Marketing strategy	How do products win orders in the market place	Manufacturing strategy	
			process choice	infrastructure
• growth • profit • return on investment • other financial measures	• product markets and segments • range • mix • volumes • standardisation versus customisation • level of innovation • leader versus follower alternatives	• price • quality • delivery speed reliability • colour range • product range • design leadership	• choice of alternative processes • trade-offs embodied in the process choice • role of inventory in the process configuration	• function support • manufacturing systems • controls and procedures • work structuring • organisational structure

Note: Although the steps to be followed are given as finite points in a stated procedure, in reality the process will involve statement and restatement, for several of these aspects will impinge on each other.

sidered appropriate for the business over the whole life cycle of each product or product family. Levels of investment will also need to reflect this total support, and the varying degrees of mismatch over the life cycle between the product requirements and manufacturing process and infrastructure capability will need to be understood and agreed. In this way, the business will make conscious decisions at the corporate level. It will exercise its due responsibility for resolving trade-offs between the investment required to reduce the degree of mismatch and the ramifications for the business by allowing the mismatch to go unaltered.

However, to get to Steps 4 and 5 the earlier three steps need to be taken. With some understanding of what is to be achieved in a manufacturing strategy statement, it is now opportune to go through each step in turn and then to explain how the necessary interrelations between these parts come together as a whole to form a corporate strategy for a business.

Step 1   Corporate objectives

Inputs into corporate strategy need to be linked to the objectives of the business. The essential nature of this tie-up is twofold. In itself it provides the basis for establishing clear, strategic direction for the business and demonstrates both the strategic awareness and strategic willingness essential to corporate success. Secondly, it will define the boundaries and mark the parameters against which the various inputs can be measured and consistency established thus providing the hallmarks of a coherent corporate plan.

For each company, the objectives will be different in nature and emphasis. They will reflect the nature of the economy, markets, opportunity and preferences of those involved. The important issues here, however, are that they need to be well thought through, hold logically together and provide the necessary direction for the business.

Typical measures concern profit in relation to sales and investment, together with targets for growth in absolute terms or with regard to market share. Additionally, businesses may wish to include employee policies and environmental issues as part of their overall sets of objectives.

Step 2   Marketing strategy

Linking closely to the provision of the agreed corporate objectives, a marketing strategy needs to be developed and will often include the following stages:

1. Market planning and control units need to be selected with the aim of bringing together a number of products which have closely related market targets and often sharing a common marketing programme. In this way, it will help to identify a number of manageable units with similar marketing characteristics.
2. The second stage involves a situational analysis of product markets which comprises:
   (a) current and future volumes.
   (b) end-user characteristics.
   (c) industry practices and trends.
   (d) identifying key competitors and a review of the business's relative position.
3. The final stage concerns identifying the target markets and agreeing objectives for each. This will include both a broad review of how to achieve these, together with the short-term action plans necessary to achieve the more global objectives involved.

In addition, it will be necessary for the company to agree the level of service support necessary in each market and an assessment of the investments and resources necessary to support these throughout the business.

The outcome of this will be a declaration to the business of the product markets and segments the strategy proposes whilst identifying the range, mix and volumes involved. Other issues pertinent to the business will include the degree of standardisation/customerisation involved within each product range, the level of innovation and product development it proposes to the business and whether it should be a leader or follower in each of its markets and the extent and timing of these strategic initiatives.

Step 3   How do products win orders in the market place?

Manufacturing's task is to provide better than the company's competitors those criteria which enable the products involved to win orders in the market-place. This step, therefore, is the essential link between corporate marketing proposals and commitments and the manufacturing processes and infrastructure necessary to support them (see Figure 2.2).

FIGURE 2.2
How order-winning criteria link corporate marketing decisions with manufacturing strategy

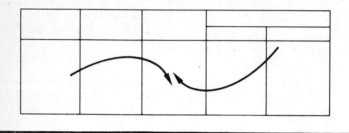

Typical order-winning criteria include price, quality, delivery speed and delivery reliability. However, not only will these be of more or less importance one to another but they will also change over time. The procedure to be followed and the important issues to be addressed are covered in some detail later in this chapter.

Step 4   Process choice

Manufacturing can choose from a number of alternative processes in order to make the products involved. The key to this choice is volume and the order-winning criteria involved. Each choice, therefore, needs to reflect the set of trade-offs involved for the various products in both current and future terms. The issues embodied in these trade-offs are both extensive and important. Chapter 3, therefore, has been devoted to the aspect of process choice where the implications embodied in this fundamental decision will be dealt with in much detail.

Step 5   Manufacturing infrastructure

Manufacturing infrastructure comprises the non-process features within production. It encompasses the procedures, systems, controls, payment schemes, work structuring alternatives, organisational issues and so on which are involved in the non-process aspects of manufacturing. Chapter 6 discusses and illustrates some of the major areas involved.

Whilst the five steps discussed above comprise the elements of manufacturing strategy development, it is not intended here to treat the first two steps in other than a somewhat superficial way – they are dealt with rigorously in other textbooks.[4] The purpose of including them, therefore, is to both demonstrate the integral nature of strategy formulation and reinforce the interaction nature of the procedure involved. However, of the remaining three steps mentioned above, process choice and manufacturing infrastructure are dealt with extensively in later chapters. Step 3, which concerns the order-winning criteria of different products is now discussed in some detail.

2.4 Establishing the Order-winning Criteria of Different Products

The procedure involved for establishing the order-winning criteria of different products requires marketing to review all current and proposed products and to divide them into types having similar order-winning characteristics. Note, however, that this will often be different to the market planning and control units identified in the marketing strategy section and hence will need to be signalled at this earlier stage. The next phase is to provide actual and forecast sales volumes for current and relevant future time periods. The selection of the future time periods will be chosen as those appropriate to the business itself. When this information has been gathered marketing have to award percentages to each relevant order-winning factor for each family of products. An illustration is given in a later example, Table 2.3. Weighted percentages have to be assessed for both current and relevant future time periods.

Order-winning criteria

Typical order-winning criteria are discussed in the following section. To help distinguish between the issues involved, it is important to recognise from the outset that some order-winning criteria do not fall within the jurisdiction of manufacturing. For example, after-sales service, being the existing supplier to a customer, technical liaison capability and design leadership are features provided by functions other than manufacturing. It is a corporate decision whether or not to allocate resources to provide this particular feature or by dint of past endeavours. However, within the mix of order-winning criteria over a product's life cycle, manufacturing will normally be at the forefront of this essential provision.

Price

In many markets, and particularly in the growth and maturity phases of the product life cycle (see Figure 2.3), price becomes an increasingly important order-winning criterion. When this is so, manufacturing's task

---

FIGURE 2.3
Product life cycles

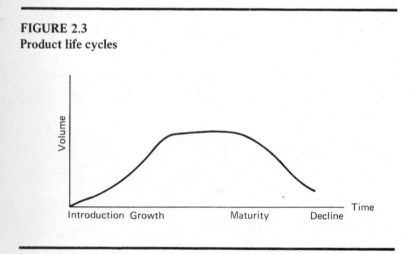

---

is to provide the low costs necessary to support the price sensitivity of the market-place, thus creating the level of profit margin necessary to support the business investment involved and create opportunity for the future. As in many of the pertinent analyses in manufacturing, highlighting the pockets of significant cost will give direction to the areas where resource allocation should be made and management attention given.

In most UK manufacturing companies, direct and indirect labour is only a small part of the total cost. Materials followed by overheads are often the two main areas of cost, a factor which should be reflected in the information provision, allocation of resources and frequency of review. The likelihood is, however, that they are not.

Product quality and reliability

As mentioned earlier, order-winning criteria can be provided by any number of functions within the business. For instance, leadership in product design will often be the reason for winning orders especially in the early stages of a product's life cycle. However, this is not based upon manufacturing's performance but upon engineering design capability, and corporate support and funding for this activity. Whereas product quality and reliability, while in part based upon design, are primarily provided through the manufacturing processes of the business. Hence, where a business wins orders at least in part through manufacturing's ability to maintain the necessary levels of product quality and reliability then this becomes a function of the production task.

Delivery speed

In some markets orders may be won, at least in part, through a company's ability to deliver more quickly than its competitors, or when it is able to meet the delivery date required when only some or even none of the competition can do so. Products which compete in this way, therefore, need a manufacturing process which can respond to this requirement. There are two perspectives to the issue of delivery speed. The one is where the process lead time, whilst being shorter than the delivery time required by the customer, is difficult to achieve because the current order loading on manufacturing capacity plus the process lead time to complete the order is greater than the delivery time required (see situation 1, Figure 2.4). The resolution of this is through either a short-term increase in capacity (e.g. overtime working), by rescheduling existing jobs or using a combination of both.

The other is where the process lead time is greater than the customer delivery requirement (see situation 2, Figure 2.4). In these situations, manufacturing (for a given process technology), can only meet the customer's delivery requirement by either increasing short-term capacity or holding inventory and thus reducing the process lead time by completing part of manufacturing before the order point and hence in anticipation of winning these types of orders. In addition, scheduling changing may be used to facilitate the accomplishment of the task but will not in themselves resolve this type of situation.

Where process lead time and existing order backlog do not exceed

FIGURE 2.4
Situations where delivery speed is an order-winning criterion to be provided by manufacturing

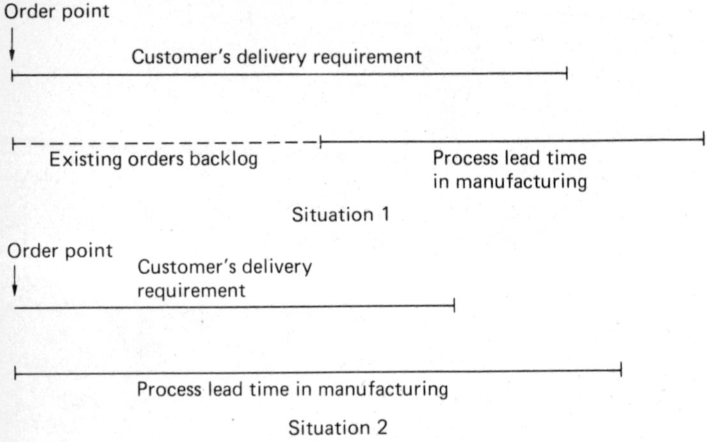

Order point

Customer's delivery requirement

Existing orders backlog   Process lead time
in manufacturing

Situation 1

Order point
Customer's delivery
requirement

Process lead time in manufacturing

Situation 2

the customer's delivery requirement, then the criterion of delivery speed is not an issue (see Figure 2.5).

Delivery reliability

The aspect of delivery reliability concerns the manufacturing task of supplying the products on or before the delivery due date. For manufacturing, this would involve considerations of capacity, scheduling and inventory holdings principally in terms of work-in-progress and finished goods.

Other criteria

The four criteria described above tend for most products to be the most common, certainly in terms of manufacturing provision. However, there will be other criteria which appertain to particular products and these need to be ascertained by marketing and explained in the procedure.

FIGURE 2.5
A situation where delivery speed is not an order-winning criterion

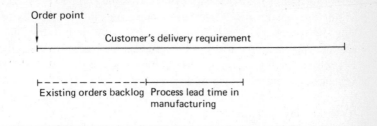

You will notice from the examples given below that most of these criteria are primarily non-manufacturing in origin or provision, and this distinction needs to be made clear during the discussion, an aspect which is dealt with later in the chapter. Similarly, the manufacturing task has to be clearly defined.

- *Technical liaison* – the provision by the supplier of the technical in-house capability to support product development particularly towards its introduction in the early stages of its manufacture.
- *Meeting a launch date* – where companies are linked to either a customer's or their own launch dates, the essential nature of meeting these schedules is obvious. The task requires effective co-ordination of the other departments involved, customer/marketing liaison and the ability to control current product requirements so that efficient manufacturing takes place whilst development work is completed on time.
- *Product and colour range* – in some instance, products win orders due, in part, to the range of products offered to the consumer. In other or the same instances, product sales may be enhanced due to the width of colours offered. In both instances, manufacturing's task is to provide the product support for these.

Order-winning versus qualifying criteria

It is important when discussing the order-winning criteria to distinguish between those which win orders in the market-place and those which qualify the product to be there. For example, when Japanese companies entered the UK colour television market in the 1970s, they changed the way in which products won orders from predominantly price to product quality and reliability. The relatively low product quality and reliability of existing television sets meant that in the changed competitive forces of this market, existing producers were losing orders through quality to the Japanese companies, i.e. existing manufacturers were not providing the criteria which qualified them to be in the market-place. By the early 1980s, product quality was raised by those concerned so that they are now qualified to be in the market. As a result, the most important order-winning criterion in this market has reverted back to price.

For manufacturing, therefore, it means that it must provide the qualifying criteria in order to get into or stay in the market-place. But those will not win orders. They merely prevent a company losing orders to its competitors. Once the qualifying criteria have been achieved, manufacturing then has to turn its attention to the ways in which orders are won and to ideally provide these better than anyone else.

Also, in the case of price, if this is not the predominant order-winning criterion, then it does not mean that a company can charge what it wishes. Whilst it needs to recognise that it does not compete on price and therefore should exploit this opportunity, it has to keep its exploitation within sensible bounds. Failure to do so will, in turn, start to increasingly lose orders to those who are more competitively priced. Hence, in this situation a company will have turned a qualifying criterion (i.e. a product highly priced within some limits) into an order-losing criterion where the price has become too high.

The procedure involved for understanding the criteria weightings chosen

When the criteria have been designated for each 'family' of products, the next step is for marketing to determine the weightings for each relevant criterion. This involves designating percentage points to each criterion for both current and future volumes. In this part of the procedure, the discussion centres around not only the individual weights but also the reasons why any changes in emphasis are anticipated in the future. Where changes do occur, it is essential for the business to understand that the task is to support the full range of criteria together with the changes in emphasis involved. As explained earlier whereas some of these will be non-production features, the major thrust will in fact be from manufacturing. Certainly the provision of any significant changes in emphasis anticipated in the future will be manufacturing based and the need to reconcile the process and infrastructure investments appropriate to meet the changing requirements will need to be fully discussed, understood and eventually agreed by all concerned.

A final word concerns the order-winning criteria put forward by marketing and the percentage weightings proposed. There is a danger, certainly when this procedure is first adopted, that marketing will include a host of criteria and often, partly as a result of not distinguishing between their relative importance, spread the percentage points, thus failing to help identify the critical order-winning feature(s). The discussions explained earlier which involve the questioning and understanding of the criteria and weightings selected need to ensure that this situation does not arise. The need for marketing to clearly identify how orders are won is an essential prerequisite to develop an appropriate corporate manufacturing strategy.

Identifying qualifying criteria with potential to become order-winning criteria

Part of Step 3 requires marketing to indicate any qualifying criteria associated with the different sets of products with the potential to become order-winning criteria (for instance, the earlier examples of the changed role of quality in the UK colour television market). In this way, a corporate decision on whether to invest in manufacturing so as to initiate this change can be considered. The impact it would have on market share, the time it would take for competitors to catch up and the investments involved in bringing about this change would be some of the issues to be addressed in this corporate strategy decision.

Identifying qualifying criteria which are order-losing sensitive

The final phase of Step 3 is for marketing to identify any qualifying criteria which are order-losing sensitive. It is important here for manufacturing to be fully aware of any qualifying criterion which is distinctly sensitive in order-losing terms. Where these are identified, the discussion which follows is aimed at appreciating the degree of order-losing sensitivity and the degree of risk the business is prepared to accept. Trade-offs between the costs, investment and sales can then be understood and decisions based on these be taken.

2.5   The Outputs of Manufacturing Strategy

There are two outputs which accrue from the use of this framework. The first concerns a manufacturing review of the implications for manufacturing processes and infrastructure support for current and future products and volumes. As depicted in Figure 2.6 this involves assessing the implications for manufacturing processes and infrastructure of selling products in terms of current and future volumes. This will result in an assessment of the degree of match between what exists in manufacturing and those processes and infrastructure features needed to provide the order-winning criteria involved.

FIGURE 2.6
Assessing the implications for manufacturing processes and infrastructure of order-winning criteria

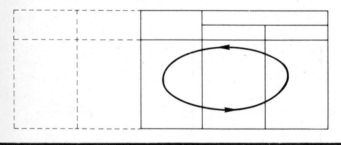

Similarly, this will be completed for all future product proposals as well as the essential biannual review designed to pick up any volume or order-winning criteria changes which may make a significant difference to the incremental change which has taken place over time as measured against the relevant base year. In this way, the changes in match and mismatch are monitored, thus detecting incremental marketing changes which have occurred over time and which often otherwise go unnoticed. Only by reviewing current and future requirements against the original decisions can the full change be assessed.

*   *   *

To illustrate the way in which this initial part of a manufacturing strategy is developed, a short summary of the work completed with a

UK manufacturing company is provided. The company supplied electrical and electronic parts to original equipment (OE) suppliers whose products had life cycles varying between seven and twelve years with an agreement to manufacture spares for a further five years following the last OE orders. Table 2.3 outlines the order-winning criteria weightings for three of the products involved each supplied to a different customer but considered to be representative of the product range as a whole.

The three examples illustrate products at different stages in their product life cycles. Product A is one which by 1988 will have moved into spares volumes and reflects the change from a price sensitive product to one where price is significantly less important. Product B is an example of a product scheduled to be introduced by 1986 and illustrative of the move from non-manufacturing to manufacturing order-winning criteria and the increasing price sensitivity of the market. Product C, on the other hand, illustrates a product which will by 1986 have entered its mature phase, with orders being won mainly on price with an important element of delivery speed.

The preparation of this information enabled manufacturing to establish the appropriate way to meet the low volume spares requirements of Product A and to clearly recognise the price insensitivity associated with these volumes. With Product B it highlighted the emphasis which would eventually be placed on price whilst with Product C it signalled the need to provide a high degree of delivery speed and the process and inventory alternatives which needed to be considered. As a whole, it also drew attention to the different mix of order-winning criteria which existed throughout the product range and the different manufacturing tasks involved. In this way, manufacturing was able to establish appropriate responses to each market rather than attempting to meet these wide-ranging differences by a single strategy.

*   *   *

The second output is, that having determined the manufacturing strategy position and the necessary investments and the time period for change involved, these now form part of the corporate strategy debate as illustrated in Figure 2.7.

The consequences of this are that the company as a whole is now required to review the business in both marketing and manufacturing terms. It changes the style and substance of corporate decisions from functionally-based arguments and perspectives to ones which address functional differences by resolving the trade-offs involved at the busi-

TABLE 2.3
The weekly volumes and order-winning criteria weightings for three product families considered representative of the whole product range

| Order-winning criteria | Product, time-scale and weightings | | | | | | | | |
| | Product A | | | Product B | | | Product C | | |
	1985	1986	1988	1985	1986	1988	1985	1986	1988
Design capability	–	–	–	40	–	–	–	–	–
Handling design modifications	–	–	–	–	20	–	20	–	–
Technical liaison support	–	–	–	20	20	–	20	–	–
UK-based supplier	10	–	–	10	10	10	20	–	–
Existing supplier	10	60	90	10	20	30	–	30	30
Price	60	40	10	20	30	60	30	40	40
Delivery speed	20	–	–	–	–	–	10	30	30
Weekly volumes	2500	1500	50	–	300	700	3000	4000	4000

FIGURE 2.7
Manufacturing's input into the corporate strategy debate

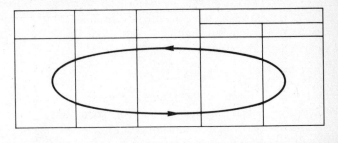

ness level. This corporate resolution therefore leads to an agreed understanding of what are the

- business objectives
- marketing strategy adopted,
- manufacturing strategy required.

In reality, it will lead to one of four positions based upon the degree of fit between the marketing and manufacturing strategic interface.

(1) Where the interface is sufficiently close and requires little, if any, adjustment.
(2) Where the interface is not sufficiently close but the corporate decision is not to invest the required time and money to bring it closer to (1) above.
(3) Where the interface is not sufficiently close and it is decided to change the marketing strategy so that the mismatch is reduced and moves towards (1) above.
(4) Where the interface is not sufficiently close and the time and investment is allocated to enable manufacturing to bring its processes and infrastructure to that required to support the marketing strategy and so move towards (1) above.

In situations (3) and (4) the company decides to reposition marketing and manufacturing respectively in order to bring about the position described in (1). In the case of (2), it is most essential that the reality of the mismatch is translated into manufacturing targets and budgets in order to present a manageable, achievable and hence controllable task. In this way, the inadequacies of manufacturing's performance against budget are separated from the consequences of the corporate strategy decision to accept the mismatch involved. The business is, therefore, able to learn the extent of the consequences resulting from the manufacturing/marketing interface mismatch and use this vital information in its future strategic decisions.

*   *   *

An example to illustrate the interactive nature of manufacturing strategy developments is provided by a medium-sized company involved in electronics and particularly with applications in telecommunications. On reviewing its product range in one segment of the market in a way similar to that illustrated in Table 2.3, it became clear that by the late 1980s and early 1990s the market would be very price sensitive. The analysis revealed that typically the weighting could be 70 points on price and the remainder on delivery speed. This pattern was the case except in one segment of the market where the company enjoyed a distinct technological advantage over its European competitors. An analysis of the process investment necessary to remain competitive over the next years forced the company to select those markets in which it wished to remain. This enabled it to direct its investment thus concentrating its limited resources in segments where it would be more able to compete or where it had a technology advantage. The consequence was that it reduced its product range and began the series of process investments necessary to enable the company to compete effectively in its chosen market segments.

2.6 Conclusion

In the past, manufacturing's role in terms of its corporate contribution has been perceived by the company as a whole as being the provider of requests. Corporate strategy debate has stopped short at discussing the implications of decisions in terms of manufacturing. And this has been based on two incorrect assumptions, that:

(1) Within a given technology, manufacturing is able to do everything.

(2) Manufacturing's contribution concerns the achievement of efficiency rather than the effective support of the business needs.

The result for many companies is that not only have the profit margins they once enjoyed been eroded, but also the base on which to build a sound and prosperous business in the future is no longer available. Without the frequent manufacturing strategy checks necessary to evaluate the fit between the business and manufacturing's ability to provide the necessary order-winning criteria of its various products, then the absence of these essential insights leaves a business vulnerable and exposed. In times of increased world competition, being left behind can be sudden and fatal. In many cases, averting the end is the only option left. Turning the business around, however, will only be achieved by switching from an operational to a strategic mode, and one which will require a corporate review of the marketing and manufacturing perspectives involved in the alternatives to be considered and the financial implications of the proposals involved.

Notes and References

1. W. Skinner, 'Manufacturing – Missing Link in Corporate Strategy', *Harvard Business Review*, May–June 1969, p. 136.
2. T. J. Hill *et al.* 'The Production Manager's Task and Contribution', CRIBA Working Paper No. 94, July 1981 (University of Warwick).
3. This argument was put forward in T. J. Hill's article, 'Manufacturing Implications in Determining Corporate Policy', *International Journal of Operations and Production Management*, vol. 1, no. 1, p.4.
4. These include K. R. Andrews, *The Concepts of Corporate Strategy* (Irwin, 1980); M. E. Porter, *Competitive Strategy* (New York: Free Press, 1980); C. W. Hofer and D. Schendel, *Strategy Formulation: Analytical Concepts* (St Paul: West Publishing Co., 1978).

Further Reading

Buffa, E. S., *Meeting the Competitive Challenge: Manufacturing Strategy for US Companies* (Irwin, 1984).
Christensen, C. R., Andrews, K. R., Bowers, J. L., Hamermesh, R. G. and Porter, M. E., *Business Policy*, 5th ed (Irwin, 1982).
Grant, J. H. and King, W. R., *The Logic of Strategic Planning* (Boston: Little, Brown, 1982).

Gudnason, C. H. and Riis, Jo, 'Manufacturing Strategy', *OMEGA Int. Jnl of Mgmt Sci.*, vol. 12, No. 6, pp. 547–55 (1984).

Porter, M. E., *Competitive Advantage: Techniques for Creating and Sustaining Superior Performance* (Collier-Macmillan, 1984).

Skinner, W., *Manufacturing in the Corporate Strategy* (New York: John Wiley, 1978).

Skinner, W., 'The Decline, Fall, and Renewal of Manufacturing Plants', *Industrial Engineering*, Oct. 1974, pp. 33–8.

Choice of Process

The way in which a business decides to make its products is a choice which many executives believe to be based upon the single dimension of technology. As a consequence, they leave this decision to engineering/ process specialists on the assumption that they, being the custodians of technological understanding, are best able to draw the fine distinctions which need to be made. By designating those specialists as the appropriate people with whom this decision should rest, a situation is created in which the important manufacturing and business perspectives are at best given inadequate weight and in many instances are omitted altogether.

This chapter describes the manufacturing and business implications of process choice and in so doing highlights the importance of these issues when making investment decisions. In this way, it helps to broaden the view of manufacturing currently held by senior executives and provides a way of reviewing the manufacturing implications of marketing decisions, hence facilitating the manufacturing input into corporate strategy. This ensures that the necessary marketing/manufacturing interface is made and that the strategies adopted are business rather than functionally led.

3.1   The Choice of Process

When choosing the appropriate way in which to manufacture its products, a business will take the following steps:

1. A decision on how much to buy out, which in turn determines the
   make-in task.
2. To identify the appropriate engineering/technology alternatives to
   complete the tasks embodied in each product. This will concern
   both the make-in components and the bringing together of them
   with the bought-out items in order to produce the final product
   specification at agreed levels of quality.
3. To choose between alternative manufacturing approaches to completing the tasks embodied in providing the products involved. This
   will need to reflect the market in which a product competes and the
   volumes associated with those sales. Existing factories will often find
   that their existing processes are not ideal. This issue is dealt with
   later in the chapter when the important insights into process choice
   have been covered.

The choice of process concerns step 3 in this procedure. It will
need to embody the decisions made in the other two steps and to recognise any constraints imposed by them. However, whilst these constraints
alter the dimensions within the decision (e.g. what is involved) they do
not alter its nature. The essence of the choice is linked to the appropriate way to manufacture given the market and associated volumes
involved.

However, having stressed the optimal nature of process choice, there
are certain constraints which have an overriding impact on this decision.
What these are and how they limit business options will be explained
as part of the next section.

The manufacturing function

The principal manufacturing function is to take inputs (materials and
labour) and convert them into products. To complete this, a business
usually has a range of choices to make between different modes of
manufacturing. They usually choose one or, as is often the case, several
ways. The fundamental rationale for arriving at this decision, however,
must be to ensure that the choice of process is the one best able to

support the company competitively in the market-place. To understand what is involved in this decision there are several important perspectives which have to be taken into account. Each choice of process will bring with it certain implications for a business in terms of response to its markets, manufacturing capabilities and characteristics, the level of investment required, the unit costs involved and the type of control and style of management which is appropriate. To help understand these, it is necessary to review the process choices available. There are five classic types of manufacturing process – project, jobbing, batch, line and continuous process. However, in many situations, hybrids have been developed which blur the edges between one process and the next. These hybrids will also be discussed in terms of what they are, how they relate to the classic types and what they mean for a business.

Before going on to describe the choices of process involved, it is worth noting here that of the process choice types, the two extremes (namely, project and continuous process) are associated with a particular product type (e.g. civil engineering and foods/liquids, respectively), a point which will be addressed later in the chapter. However, even though a firm may find that in reality it has little option but to choose the one, appropriate process (e.g. oil-refining and continuous processes are for all intents and purposes inextricably linked), in manufacturing strategy terms, it is still of paramount important that a company is clearly aware of the precise nature of the business implications involved in the choice it is 'forced' to go along with, and that the trade-offs associated with these dimensions are fixed.

The 'classic' types of process choice

Project

Companies which produce large scale, one-off, complex products will normally provide these on a project basis. Examples include civil engineering contracts and aerospace programmes. It concerns the provison of a unique product requiring large scale inputs to be co-ordinated so as to achieve a customer's requirement. The resource inputs will normally be taken to the point where the product is to be built since it is not feasible to move it, once completed. All the activities, including the necessary support functions will usually be controlled in the form of a total system for the duration of the project. Resources will be allocated to the project and reallocated once their part of the task is complete or at the end of the project.

The selection of project as the appropriate process is based upon two features. The product is a one-off, customer specified requirement and, secondly, it is often too large to be moved or simply cannot be moved once completed. The latter criterion is such an overwhelming facet of this decision that products of this nature will always be made using the project choice of process. However, businesses will also be concerned with determining how much of the product to make away from site and how best to provide the parts or sections which go into the structures made on site. These will, in turn, often be produced using a different choice of process than project. These decisions need to be based upon other criteria which will become clear in the descriptions of these other choices which now follow.

Jobbing, unit or one-off

Job shops meet the one-off (i.e. unique) order requirements of customers, for example purpose-built tooling. The product involved will be of an individual nature and requires that the supplier interprets the customer's design and specification whilst applying relatively high level skills in the conversion process. A large degree of this interpretation will normally be in the hands of the skilled employee whose experience in this type of work will be an essential facet of the process. The design having been specified, what happens in jobbing is that one, or possibly a small number of skilled employees if the task is very time consuming, will be largely responsible for deciding how best to complete the task on hand and for carrying out the work. It may also include a level of responsibility over scheduling, liaison with other functions and some involvement with the arrangements for outside subcontracted phases where necessary.

This one-off provision means that the product will not again be required in its exact form or, if it is, the demand will tend to be irregular with long time periods between one order and the next. For this reason, therefore, investment in the manufacturing process (e.g. in jigs, fixtures and specialist plant) will not normally be warranted.

Batch

When a company decides to manufacture using batch processes it does so because it is providing similar items on a repeat basis usually in larger

volumes (quantity × work content) than associated with jobbing, *
This type of process, however, is chosen to cover a wide range of
volumes as represented in Figure 3.1 by the elongated shape of batch
compared to the other processes. At the low volume end, the repeat
orders will be small and infrequent. In fact, some companies producing
very large, one-off items will adopt a batch rather than a jobbing process
approach to their manufacturing. When this happens, the work content
involved will be high in jobbing terms and often the order quantity is
for a small number of the same but unique items. At the high volume
end, the order quantities may involve many hours, shifts or even weeks
of work involving the same product at one or more stages in its designated manufacturing route.

The procedure followed in batch is to divide the manufacturing task
into a series of appropriate operations which together will make the
products involved. The reason is simply to determine the most effective
manufacturing route so that the low cost requirements of repeat, higher
volume markets can be best achieved. At this stage, suitable jigs and
fixtures will be identified in order to help reduce the processing times
involved, the investment in which is justified by the total product
throughput over time.

Each order quantity is manufactured by setting up that step of the
process necessary to complete the first operation for a particular
product. The whole order quantity is now completed at this stage.
Then, the next operation in the process is made ready, the total order
quantity is completed and so on until all the stages required to make a
product are completed. Meanwhile, the process used to complete the
first operation for the product is then reset to complete an operation
for another product and so on. Thus, capacity at each stage in the
process is used and reused to meet the different requirements of different orders.

Examples include moulding processes where one mould to produce
an item is put into a machine. The order for that component or product
is then produced, the mould is taken off, the raw materials may have to
be changed and a mould for another product is put into the machine
and so on. Similarly, in metal machining processes, a machine is set to
complete the necessary metal cutting operation for a product and the
whole order quantity is processed. When finished, the machine in

*Note that companies do manufacture order quantities of one on a batch basis.
In this instance, what underpins their decision on which process to adopt is the
repeat nature of a product, not the size of an order quantity.

question is reset to do the required metal cutting work on another item while the order quantity of the first product goes on to its next stage which is completed in another part of the process. At times, an order quantity may have more than one stage completed on the same machine. Here the same principle applies with the process reset to perform the next operation through which the whole order quantity will be passed.

Line

With further increases in volumes (quantity × work content), investment is made to provide a process that is dedicated to the needs of a single or normally small range of products. The width of the product range will be determined at the time of the investment. In a line process, products are passed through the same sequence of operations. The standard nature of the products allows for this and hence changes outside the prescribed range of options (which can be very wide, for example with motor vehicles) cannot be accommodated on the line itself. It is the cumulative volume of the product range which underpins the investment. Hence, the wider the product range then normally the higher is the investment required in the process in order to provide the degree of flexibility necessary to make these products. Where the options provided are very wide and the products involved of high cost or of a bulky nature then the more likely is the company to make these on an order basis only. Thus, for example, there will normally be a longer delay when purchasing a motor vehicle (especially if several options are specified) than say a domestic appliance. The underlying reason for this is the different degree of product standardisation involved. The motor vehicle, therefore will be made against a specific customer order and the domestic appliance to stock.

Continuous process

With continuous process, a basic material(s) is passed through successive stages or operations and refined or processed into one or more products; for example, petrochemicals. This choice of process is based upon two features. The first is very high volume demand, and the second is that the materials involved lend themselves to be moved easily from one part of the process to another; for example, fluids, gases and foods.

The high volume nature of the demand justifies the very high investment involved. The processes are designed to run all day and every day with minimum shutdowns due to the high costs of starting up and closing down. Normally, the product range is quite narrow and often the products offered are purposefully restricted in order to enhance volumes within the other products in the range. For example, UK oil refining companies do not offer either one or five star petrol, with three star petrol no longer available on all petrol station forecourts. In this way, companies have restricted the range of octanes and hence increased the volumes associated with the grades that are provided.

In continuous process, the other feature is the nature of the materials being processed. Whereas in line there were manual inputs into the manufacture of the products as they passed along, in continuous process the materials will be transferred automatically from one part of the process to the next, with the process monitoring and self-adjusting flow and quality. The labour tasks in these situations are predominantly involved in checking the system.

Choices of processes within a business

The five classic processes have been described separately because they are discrete choices. However, most businesses will select two or more processes as being appropriate for the products they manufacture. A typical illustration of this is the use of batch processes to make components for products and the choice of line to assemble components into final products. The reason why this occurs is that the work content associated with most components is insufficient to create the level of volume which would justify a more dedicated process, such as line.

Markets and product volumes

The explanation of the five classic processes stressed throughout that the underlying factor when choosing the process most appropriate to manufacturing the products is *volume (i.e. quantity × work content)*. The link between the demand for a product and the investment in processes to complete this task is fundamental to this decision. As volumes increase, the justification for investing in processes dedicated to make that product(s), increases. High utilisation of plant underpins the investment. Similarly, if processes will not be high utilised by one product they need to be chosen so that they are sufficiently flexible to meet the manufacturing needs of other products. Businesses when choosing processes, therefore, need to distinguish between the technology required to make a product and the way in which the product is then manufactured. On the one hand, the process technology choice concerns the engineering dimension of providing a process which will form, shape, cut etc. a product to the size and tolerances required. On the other hand, the manufacturing dimension concerns determining the best way to make a product. This decision rests on the basis of volumes. As volumes rise, the appropriate choice will change as illustrated in Figure 3.1.

FIGURE 3.1
Choice of process related to volumes

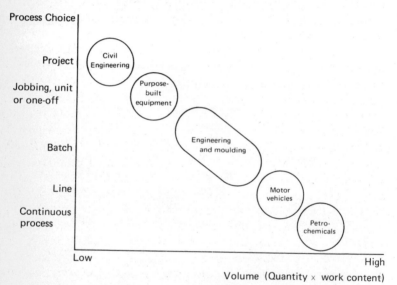

Source: Developed from the initial work by R. H. Hayes and S. C. Wheelwright in their article 'Link Manufacturing Process and Product Life Cycles', *Harvard Business Review*, Jan–Feb. 1979, pp. 133–40 and also in Chapter 2 of Hill, *Production/Operations Management* (Prentice-Hall International, 1983).

The choice of process, therefore, needs to be understood not in engineering terms but in terms of manufacturing constraints and other business dimensions. Understanding how well a process can support the order-winning criteria of a product, the implications for a company in terms of its infrastructure and so on are fundamental to this strategic decision and are dealt with in the following section.

3.2   The Business Implications of Process Choice

It has already been explained that market characteristics and product volumes are the underlying factors in choosing the appropriate process. In addition, the nature of the product is also a factor in this decision in terms of the two extremes in Figure 3.1, namely, project and continuous process.

Hence, the procedure used is to first assess the market/volume dimension. This then forms the basis for choosing which process is appropriate to best meet these critical business needs. The engineering dimension provides the initial set of alternatives concerning the ways to meet the requirements of the product. However, it is at this juncture that the engineering dimension finishes and the manufacturing and business dimensions start. Phase 1 links the market/volumes to the process choice (the manufacturing dimension which also takes into account the engineering dimension described earlier, - A1 and B1 in Figure 3.2. Phase 2 automatically picks up the corresponding point on each of the various manufacturing and business implications given in Table 3.1; A2 and B2 respectively in Figure 3.2. However, what tends to happen in many companies is that whilst the engineering dimension is recognised the manufacturing and business dimensions are unforeseen. In companies the engineering proposal currently underpins the major part of a process investment decision and this in turn, is based upon the forecast market/volumes which form part of the corporate marketing strategy. However, the manufacturing and business implications embodied in a proposal are given scant recognition. But, it is these issues which bind manufacturing and hence regulate its ability to respond to the business needs. Once the investment is made not only are the processes fixed, but also the whole of the manufacturing infrastructure is fixed. The result is that this decision dictates the extent to which manufacturing can support the needs of the market-place, the essence of business success.

When Phase 1 in Figure 3.2 is completed, the choice of process is designated. However, at the same time it stipulates the position on the vertical dimensions which will accrue as a result. Hence, Phase 2 is inextricably tied to Phase 1. Therefore, the decisions in Phase 1 cannot be taken in isolation. The choice has to embrace both Phase 1 and Phase 2. Only in this way will an organisation avoid falling into the Cyclopean trap from which it will take years to extricate itself. Only in this way will a business take into account the short and long term

FIGURE 3.2
The engineering dimensions and the manufacturing and business dimension phases involved in process choice

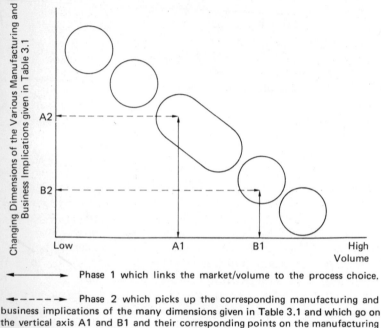

Phase 1 which links the market/volume to the process choice.

Phase 2 which picks up the corresponding manufacturing and business implications of the many dimensions given in Table 3.1 and which go on the vertical axis A1 and B1 and their corresponding points on the manufacturing and business implications dimensions, A2 and B2.

implications which emanate from the decision to manufacture using one choice of process as opposed to another.

To help explain the business implications of process choice, the perspectives involved have been placed into four categories – products and markets, manufacturing, investment and cost, and infrastructure. Furthermore, the issues for illustration and discussion have been chosen on the basis of their overall business importance. However, there are many other issues which are equally important to understand but which have distinct operational rather than strategic overtones.[1]

The critical issue embodied in Table 3.1 is to illustrate how each perspective reviewed changes between one choice of process and another. Thus, when a company decides to invest in a process, it will also have determined at the same time, the corresponding point on each dimension within these four categories. It is necessary, therefore, for companies to understand this and to be aware of the trade-offs embodied in that choice.

Table 3.1 contains many generalised statements which are intended to relate the usual requirements of one type of process to the other four. It can be seen that in almost all cases there is an arrow drawn between jobbing and line. This is intended to indicate that as a process moves from jobbing/low volume batch through to high volume batch/ line then progressively the particular characteristic will change from one form to the other. The reason for this approach is to help explain the implications of these choices and to examine the consequences which will normally follow.

It is important to bear in mind that companies selling products typically made using the project process will also need to make decisions on how much is made away from the site and then transported in. Today, many parts of a civil engineering structure, for instance, are made off-site by jobbing, batch or line processes and then brought in as required. Similarly, products with the fluid, semi-fluid or gaseous characteristics necessary to avail themselves of a continuous process choice may also be made on a batch process basis. Thus, the changing business characteristics displayed in Table 3.1 illustrate the sets of alternatives embodied in these choices as well.

Finally, Table 3.1 has been so arranged as to illustrate the linked relationship between jobbing, batch and line choices as opposed to the more distinct process/product relationship existing in project and continuous process which was described earlier. As a consequence the section which follows adopts this division.

3.3   Selected Business Implications of Process Choice

This section of the chapter takes the dimensions provided in Table 3.1 and further explains the implications involved. In order to help to link the four categories of products and markets, manufacturing, investment and cost, and infrastructure, these are explained under each of the process choice headings. Furthermore, in order to emphasise the separate nature of project and continuous process, and the linked

TABLE 3.1
Selected business implications of process choice

Aspects		Typical characteristics of process choice			
	Project	Jobbing, unit or one off	Batch	Line	Continuous process
PRODUCTS AND MARKETS					
Type of product	Special/small range of standards	Special	↑	Standard	Standard
Product range	Wide	Wide	↑	Narrow: standard products	Very narrow: standard products
Customer order size	Small	Small	↑	Large	Very large
Level of product change required	High	High	↑	Low and within agreed options	None
Rate of new product introductions	High	High	↑	Low	Very low
What does the company sell?	Capability	Capability	↑	Products	Products
How are orders won?					
Order-winning criteria	Delivery/quality/ design capability Price	Delivery/quality/ design capability Price	↑	Price	Price
Qualifying criteria	Price	Price		Quality/design	Quality/design
MANUFACTURING					
Nature of the process technology	Orientated towards general purpose	Universal	↑	Dedicated	Highly dedicated
Process flexibility	High	High	↑	Low	Inflexible
Production volumes	Low	Low	↑	High	Very high

	Mixed	Labour		Plant	Plant
Dominant utilisation	Mixed	Labour	→	Plant	Plant
Changes in capacity	Incremental	Incremental	→	Stepped change	New facility
Key manufacturing task	To meet specification/delivery schedules	To meet specification/delivery dates	→	Low cost production	Low cost production
INVESTMENT AND COST					
Level of capital investment	Low/high	Low	→	High	Very high
Level of inventory					
Components/raw material	As required	As required	Very high →	Planned with buffer stocks	Planned with buffer stocks
Work-in-progress	High[1]	High[1]	→	Low	Low
Finished goods	Low	Low	→	High[2]	High[3]
Percent of total costs					
Direct labour	Low	High	→	Low	Very low
Direct materials	High	Low	→	High	Very high
Site/plant overheads	Low	Low	→	High	High
INFRASTRUCTURE					
Appropriate organisational control	Decentralised/centralised	Decentralised	→	Centralised	Centralised
Style	Entrepreneurial	Entrepreneurial	→	Bureaucratic	Bureaucratic
Most important production management perspective	Technology	Technology	→	Business/people	Technology
Level of specialist support to manufacturing	High	Low	→	High	Very high

[1] This would depend upon stage payment arrangements.
[2] However, many businesses here only make against customer schedules, or on receipt of a customer order.
[3] The finished goods inventory in, for instance, oil refining is stored in the post-processing stages of distribution and at the point of sale.

nature of jobbing, batch and line the order in which these are discussed is project, followed by jobbing, batch and line coming under one general section with continuous process at the end.

Project

Products and markets

Companies choosing project processes sell capability. They sell their experience, know-how and skills to provide for a customer's individual needs. Hence, they are in a market which will require a high level of product change and new product introductions. Its product range will be wide, with low unit sales volumes. It will win orders on aspects such as design capability, quality or delivery speed/reliability, with price normally acting as a qualifying rather than an order-winning criterion.

Manufacturing

Orientated towards general purpose equipment with some specialist plant to meet particular product, design or structural features, project processes are highly flexible coping with the low product volumes of the market and the design changes which will occur during production. Changes in capacity mix or in total can be made incrementally with the key tasks being on-time completion and meeting the specification as laid down by the customer.

Investment and cost

The capital investment in plant and other processes will tend to be low but with some high cost items which may be purchased or hired depending upon their potential usage, availability, costs and similar factors. Due to the opportunity to schedule materials, the inventory at this stage will be on an as-required basis. Work-in-progress levels will be high but normally much of this will be passed on to the customers by stage payment agreements. In a make-to-order situation, finished goods are small with immediate delivery on completion. The key cost will normally be materials, and sound purchasing arrangements and work-in-progress usage and control are essential.

Infrastructure

Due to the uncertainties in the process and the need to respond quickly to any customer derived changes, the organisational control should be decentralised supported by an entrepreneurial rather than a bureaucratic style. In addition, however, once the business grows there will also be a need to centrally control key items of plant, internal specialist/engineering skills and other purchased commodities/skills to ensure they are effectively scheduled by project and between projects. It is essential for the production manager to have a relevant technology grounding in order to appreciate and respond to unforeseen difficulties and problems of a technical as well as a non-technical nature and to effectively use the local and centrally based specialist support.

Jobbing, batch and line

In order to explain how these three choices are linked and yet how they each differ, jobbing, batch and line are discussed under the same section, with each being dealt with under a separate subsection. Furthermore, as batch often links the change in dimensions between jobbing and line, the latter two are dealt with first in order to help describe batch within this overall perspective.

Jobbing

Products and markets

In essence, a jobbing business sells its capability to manufacture to a customer's requirements. The only restrictions it has concern the range of skills provided by its workforce or limited by its processes. Thus, it handles a wide product range competing on aspects other than price. This does not mean that the business can charge any price it decides. But, providing the price is within what is reasonable for the market (and that includes provisions for additional delivery speed or post-start modifications) then price is a qualifying rather than an order-winning criterion.

Manufacturing

As a consequence of the products it provides and markets it serves, the manufacturing process is flexible and needs to be geared to this flexibility with its major concern surrounding the utilisation of its labour skills, with processes being purchased to facilitate the skilled operator to complete the task. Changes in capacity can be achieved incrementally. The order backlog position which exists in make-to-order markets will allow manufacturing the opportunity to look forward and make any foreseen adjustments in capacity ahead of time. The key manufacturing task is to complete the item to specification and on time, as normally this one-off item forms an integral part of some greater business whole as far as the customer is concerned.

Investment and cost

Although many items of equipment in jobbing can be very expensive, as a general rule this investment is low compared to batch and line. In addition, material will tend to be purchased only when an order has been received, with material delivery forming part of the total lead time. Work-in-progress will be high with all jobs, on average, being half-finished, while the make-to-order nature of its business means that products are despatched once completed. There will tend to be few specialist and other support functions which leads to a relatively lower plant/site overhead cost. These functions will be largely part of the skilled worker's task which together with the high labour content normally makes this the highest portion of total costs. Materials will tend to be low; where there are expensive materials involved, invariably these will be on a customer-supplied basis.

Infrastructure

On the organisational side, it is important to recognise that the control and style needs to be decentralised in structure and entrepreneurial in nature so as to respond quickly and effectively to meet the inherent flexibility requirements of this market. For this reason, the production executive has to understand the technology involved as this forms an important part of his contribution to business decisions (e.g. in accepting an order, confirming a delivery quotation or providing part of the specialist inputs into a business).

Line

Products and markets

When a line process is chosen, it reflects the other end of the spectrum to jobbing. The business sells standard products which to be successful are sold on price and are associated with large customer orders. The level of product change is usually prescribed within a list of options and outside this, the product is not normally available. Product design and quality are determined at the outset to meet the perceived needs of the customer.

Manufacturing

In order to provide low manufacturing costs the process is dedicated to a predetermined range of products and is not geared to be flexible outside this range due to the high costs of change. In addition, this provides the opportunity to maintain the necessary quality levels throughout the process. Production volumes are high and need to be so in order to achieve the high level of plant utilisation necessary to justify the investment and to underpin the cost structures involved. Output changes are more difficult to arrange due to the stepped-change nature of capacity alterations.

Investment and cost

The key to low manufacturing costs is the high process investment which goes hand-in-hand with line. The volumes involved allow schedules of raw materials and components to be planned with associated buffer stocks to cover the uncertainty of supply. Work-in-progress inventory will be low. Although finished goods will tend to be high, many businesses will only make standard products against customer schedules or on receipt of an order. Also, products offering many optional extras (e.g. motor vehicles) will tend to have a policy of only making to a specific order. Hence, even in times of relatively low sales, you have to wait for your new car. Finally, the high areas of cost tend to be in materials/bought-out components and site/plant overheads, with direct labour a relatively small part of the total.

Infrastructure

As the choice of a line process represents a high volume business then a more centralised organisation, controlled by systems, is more appropriate. On the manufacturing side, the key production executive task concerns the business/people aspects of the job with specialist support providing the technical know-how involved in terms of both products and processes.

Batch

Products and markets

In between jobbing and line comes batch. This is chosen to cover a very wide range of volumes (as illustrated by the elongated shape depicted in Figures 3.1 and 3.2) and links the low/high volume and make-to-order/ standard product businesses. In most cases the choice of batch rather than jobbing as the appropriate way to manufacture the products involved, signals the fact that the production volumes (i.e. quantity x work content) have increased, are of a repeat nature but are insufficient to dedicate processes solely to them as would be the case in line. Some unique orders with a high volume content may also be done on a batch basis.

At the low volume end of batch, the processes are able to cope with a high degree of product change and a high level of new production introduction. Here, the business is orientated towards selling capability with, however, price starting to become a more important order-winning criterion due to the volume and repeat nature of the products. At the high volume end of batch, products have become increasingly standard, order sizes are becoming larger, product change is lower, all of which illustrate the shift in product/market characteristic towards line.

Manufacturing

It can be deduced from the product/market features that batch processes usually have to cope with a wide range of both products and production volumes. In order to be able to handle this task, these processes will be of a general purpose nature offering a high degree of flexibility. With some plant, the utilisation will be low; with other, plant will have been purchased to meet the needs of a product or to offer distinct process advantages (e.g. numerical control (NC) machines, machining centres and flexible manufacturing systems), each of which will be described in a later section. In these cases, high investment will normally be justified on a usage basis and the aim will be to utilise the capacity to the full.

In order to help underpin the total process investment, many UK companies adopt a deliberate policy of increasing the utilisation of plant in three ways:

1. Putting a wide range of products through the same set of processes.
2. Usually manufacturing many of the same products in a single order or batch quantity (hence the name). In this way, the number of set-ups are reduced which both decreases the setting costs and increases effective capacity.
3. Making products wait for processes to become available. This policy, together with the order quantity decisions above, leads to a work-in-progress inventory investment which, in relation to the size of the business, tends to be very high compared to jobbing and particularly line.

Investment and cost

As the products/markets move towards the high volume end of the spectrum then a business, in order to be competitive, will increasingly invest in its batch processes in order to achieve the low manufacturing cost requirement of these markets. As explained earlier, many UK companies exploit this still further by putting more products through the same processes and hence increasing overall utilisation. However, the major trade-off associated with this policy is the very high investment in work-in-progress inventory. The raw materials/components and finished goods inventory levels will in turn be associated with the make-to-order or make-to-stock nature of the business. As with all companies in these mid-volume markets, the nearer it is to a make-to-order situation the more the characteristics of that market will prevail, and vice versa. The make-up of total costs is no exception.

Infrastructure

As the business moves away from the low volume end of the continuum then centralised controls and a bureaucratic style become more appropriate. The increasing complexity of this growth will change the nature of the specialist functions where design and production engineering will be an increasingly important support to manufacturing. The production manager's role will be bound up with appreciating and recognising the critical business issues involved, providing co-ordination throughout and spearheading the development of manufacturing systems.

At the low-volume end of batch, the characteristics though not the same will be, in many situations, more akin to those in jobbing. It is important, therefore, to recognise the extent and trends in these changes and ensure that the necessary adjustments take place.

Continuous process

Markets and products

At the other end of the volume spectrum, companies choosing continuous process will be selling a narrow range of standard products in markets where product change and the rate of product introductions are low. The company will be selling products rather than capability and the large customer orders will be won principally on price.

Manufacturing

In a price sensitive market, the key manufacturing task will be low cost production. To help keep costs low, the process will be highly dedicated where the cost structure is based upon high production volumes leading to a need to achieve high plant utilisation. The fixed nature of capacity also creates restrictions when increases or decreases in output are required, with the decision based upon whether or not to build a new facility on the one hand or how often to run the plant (known as 'campaigning') on the other.

Investment and cost

The high plant investment and high volume throughput associated with continuous process offers the opportunity to keep raw material inventory on a planned usage basis with built-in buffer stocks to cover uncertainties. Work-in-progress will be relatively low in total throughput terms with inventory in finished goods high. This is because of the need to maintain throughput levels at all times against fluctuating sales patterns. In many cases, however, finished goods are held in the extensive distribution system of a business and sometimes at its own retail outlets (e.g. on garage forecourts).

Owing to the high process investment, direct labour costs are small with the highest cost usually in materials. Site/plant overheads in this process will be high owing to the need to support the process and handle the high throughput levels involved.

Infrastructure

The high volume nature of these businesses lends itself to a centralised, bureaucratic organisation control and style. Manufacturing performance is measured against budgets, variance analysis is the order of the day and investment proposals are centrally monitored. An understanding of the process and product technology is important when running a production unit together with the ability to co-ordinate the high level of specialist support provided for manufacturing.

3.4   An Overview of Process Choice

In order to help clarify the issues involved in process choice, an overview of how these alternatives link to one another is now described. The first important fact to stress is that each of the choices embodies a totally different approach to manufacturing a product. Although described in some detail in the chapter, a short explanation of these differences will serve to reinforce this important point.

Project – used for one-off products which have to be built on site because it is difficult or impossible to move them once they have been made. Consequently, the resources involved need to be brought to the site and released for reuse elsewhere when they are no longer needed.
Jobbing – used for one-off products which can be moved once completed. The responsibility for making the product is normally given to a skilled man who decides how best to make it and then completes all or most of the operations involved including checking the quality at each stage.
Batch – with an increase in volumes and the repeat nature of products, companied select batch as the effective way to meet the requirements involved. Because the products are repeated, companies can consider investment at each of the manufacturing steps necessary to make them. This includes engineering time to decide how best to make a product, through to jigs and fixtures to facilitate the completion of certain operations and equipment purchased with an eye to making these and

other products with similar characteristics. However, the volumes involved do not warrant the purchase of dedicated equipment. The operations necessary to complete a product are, therefore, not linked and are said to be decoupled.

Line – when demand is sufficient to justify dedicating equipment solely to making a specified range of products, then a line process is normally chosen. The operations necessary to complete a product are linked together so that each product goes from one operation directly to the next and so on. The operations necessary to complete a product in this instance are said to be coupled.

Continuous process – when the demand for a product is such that the volume required necessitate a process being used all day and every day then further investment is justified. The equipment in this instance is designed to automatically transfer the product from one stage to the next, check the quality within the process and make adjustments where necessary. The investment associated with this is warranted by the volumes involved.

Therefore, as also illustrated in earlier diagrams, Figure 3.3 shows a gap between the five choices outlined in order to emphasise the distinctions made above. Furthermore, it also makes the point that whereas there will sometimes be a transition from jobbing to low volume batch, from low volume to high volume batch, from high volume batch to line or from high volume batch to continuous process, the same will not apply between project and jobbing or from line to continuous process. Similarly, when volumes reduce towards the end of a product's life cycle the reverse movement will take place, but again it will only go as illustrated in Figure 3.3.

Transition in these instances refers to the possibility that a business may, as volumes increase or decrease, change its choice of manufacturing accordingly. Project and continuous process, however, are prescribed by the nature of the product itself and the volumes involved. In this way, businesses with these characteristics are precluded from considering any other choice of process in terms of a transitional movement as described here and shown in Figure 3.3. However, those products which lend themselves to being produced using continuous process (e.g. fluids, gases and foods) can and often are produced on a batch basis where the production volumes involved are not adequate to justify the high investment associated with continuous process.

When product volumes increase or decrease, then companies should ideally realign their choice of process in keeping with that which is

FIGURE 3.3
Potential transitions between the different choices of process

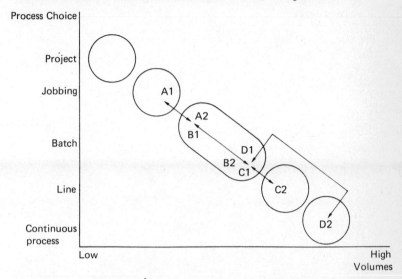

◄————————► This shows four potential volume transitions which typically may face a business. The first example shows a move from one-off, *low-volume (A1) to repeat order, low-volume demand (A2) for a product of vice versa and the change in manufacturing process which should ideally accompany this movement. Examples B1 to B2, C1 to C2 and D1 to D2 show similar demand changes at different points on the volume scale and requiring similar decisions concerning the realignment of the process choice.

*One-off is a description of uniqueness, not order quantity.

more appropriate to the new level of volumes. Many companies, however, find themselves unable or unwilling to commit the fresh investment necessary to complete this realignment especially where the volume movement experienced is downward.

3.5 Hybrid Processes

Earlier in this chapter it was stated that some hybrid processes had been developed which were a mix of two of the five classic processes. Some of the more important hybrid developments are now explained, and to help position these in relation to the classic processes, they are included together in Figure 3.4.

FIGURE 3.4

The position of some hybrid processes in relation to the five classic choices of process

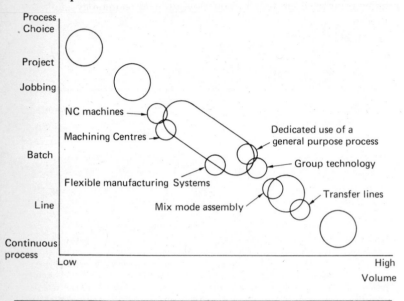

Numerical control (NC) machines

An NC system[2] describes a process which automatically performs the required operations according to a detailed set of coded instructions. As mathematical information is the base used, then the system is called numerical control. The operation of machine tools (the first applications were applied to metal cutting processes such as milling, boring, turning, grinding and sawing but in recent years the range of NC applications includes tube bending, shearing and different forms of cutting) is from numerical data stored on paper or magnetic tapes, tabulating cards, computer storage or direct information. Compared with conventional equipment, NC machines offer increased accuracy, consistency and flexibility even with the need to meet very complex manufacturing requirements. Thus, design changes and modifications require only a change in instruction, nothing more.

However, the trade-off against conventional plant is the increased investment associated with NC processes. In addition, it brings with it variations for the operators, setter and supervisor in terms of their role, the level of specialist support and skill requirements together with the problems involved in the introduction of new technology and associated changes.

Machining centres

Machining centres, which first appeared in the late 1950s, combine NC operations previously provided by different machines into one machining centre. With tool changing automatically controlled by instructions on the tape, and carousels holding up to 120 tools and more, the underlying rationale for this development is to maximise the combination of operations completed at a single location. In this way, a machining centre changes the pattern of work-in-progress inventory associated with the classic process which could be adopted as an alternative, namely batch. Just as in line, a part now goes through a number of operations in sequence and thus changes the process design from functional to product layout. However, if the pre- and post-machining operations are performed on another process choice (e.g. batch) the relevant point on the dimensions in Table 3.1 would then change accordingly. Machining centres as with all NC-based processes pick up an increased level of flexibility in relation to an alternative non-NC process due to the nature and level of the capital investment involved. These and other issues are discussed in the section 'Review of the use of numerical control (NC) in hybrid processes' on page 88.

Flexible manufacturing systems

Flexible manufacturing systems (FMS) are a combination of standard and special numerical control (NC) machines, automated materials handling and computer control in the form of direct numerical control (DNC)[3] for the purposes of extending the benefits of NC to mid-volume manufacturing situations.[4] Whereas NC equipment and particularly machining centres cater for relatively low volume demand, much less attention has been given to improving manufacturing's approach to mid-volume, mid-variety products, although this accounts for a large part of the products which would fall into the batch range of volumes.

FMS are designed around families of parts. It is the increased volumes associated with the range of products which justifies the investment on the one hand and the inherent flexibility of the NC equipment on the other which combine to create the rationale of FMS in this mid-volume segment of demand. Classical families of products are:

1. By assembly: grouping parts together that would be required to make a single assembly (e.g. an engine assembly). The system would be designed to allow the user to order against an assembly requirement, rather than scheduling order quantities for each part through an appropriate series of functionally laid out processes.
2. By type: categorising parts by type in terms of a range of similar products. This would then relieve higher volume production processes of the low to mid-volume part numbers and thus reduce the number of change-overs involved. This aggregate family demand justifies the capital investment with the inherent flexibility within the FMS allowing a relatively wide range of products to be considered and facilitating the balancing and rebalancing of the workload as product mix and volumes change.
3. By size and similar operations: the specification of the FMS in this situation reflects the physical size of the parts and the particular operations which need to be completed. Again, the flexibility within the system extends the range of work with which it can cope and allows high utilisation owing to its ability to handle product mix and volume changes.

A typical series of events in processing a part in FMS (see Figure 3.5) is as follows:

- A DNC system directs a cart carrying an empty fixture to a load station and also advises the loader which part is to be loaded.
- On completion the loader signals that it is now ready and the computer directs the part to the first operation selecting, if available, the lowest backlog potential.
- The part is automatically unloaded, the appropriate NC program selected and the work completed.
- This procedure will be followed until the part is finished whence it goes to the unloading area and out of the system.

The philosophy of FMS is the same as that of machining centres, i.e. maximising the combination of operations completed at a single location. The additional capital investment, as with other forms of process

FIGURE 3.5
An example of a 15-station random FMS provided as a 3-stage installation

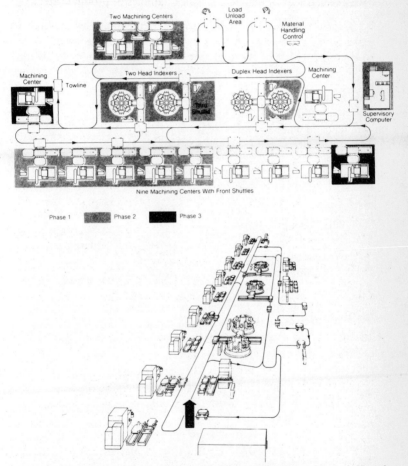

Source: Kearney & Trecker Corporation, *KT's World of Advanced Manufacturing Technologies* (2nd edn, 1983) (with permission).

choice such as group technology and transfer lines (see over) and also line will bring with it both lower cost and lower work-in-progress inventory advantages. These trade-offs will be discussed more fully at the end of this section on hybrid processes.

Dedicated use of general purpose plant

The first three hybrid processes concerned the use of NC equipment as the basis for the process change. However, there are alternative hybrid processes which can be adopted using non-NC equipment. Two are described here. The first concerns the dedicated use of general purpose plant.

Where the volume of a specific part is such that it can justify the allocation of a process to its sole use, then manufacturing does so. In this instance the dedication is not in the plant itself but in the use of a general purpose process. Thus, the potential flexibility and other characteristics illustrated in Table 3.1 of a general purpose process are still retained and when volumes reduce will be reclaimed.

Group technology

The underlying difference between batch and line processes is one of volume. What group technology does is to gain for batch processes some of the advantages inherent in high volume, line situations. It does this by changing the process or functional layout associated with batch manufacturing, into the product layout associated with line (see Figure 3.6).

The approach adopted is to separate out those processes which do not lend themselves to the application of group technology due to factors such as the level of investment involved and health considerations (e.g. noise or process waste/fumes). The next step is to group together families of like products. The criteria for this selection are similar to those outlined under the section on FMS. However, note that the process flexibility inherent in group technology applications is not of the same order as in FMS.

The third step is to determine the process configuration necessary to manufacture each product family involved and to layout the cell or line to reflect the manufacturing routings involved. The final stage is to complete a tooling analysis within each family, with a twofold aim. The first is to group together those parts within the family which can use the same tooling. This then forms the basis for scheduling in order to reduce setting time. The second is to include this feature as part of the design prerequisites for future products.[5]

The implications of group technology for a business are that the enhanced volumes have moved the point on the horizontal axis in

FIGURE 3.6
Group layout, its relationship to functional (batch) and line (product) layouts to illustrate the transition from the former to the latter

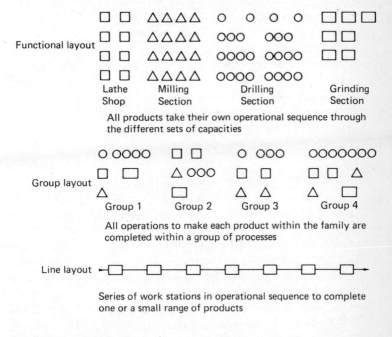

Source: Terry Hill, *Production/Operations Management*, p. 101 (with permission).

Figure 3.4 towards the higher volume end. In so doing, the process choice of group technology substitutes the point on many of the Table 3.1 dimensions associated with a batch process, to that of line. Most importantly, it creates an inherently less flexible process in that to reuse any spare capacity brought about by a decrease in product family volumes will not be easy or even possible without moving the location of the plant, itself a form of process investment. The key advantages to be gained from group technology include reduced lead times and lower work-in-progress inventory together with a series of advantages associated with any form of small scale manufacturing unit. A detailed review of these issues is provided elsewhere (see reference 5 at the end of the chapter).

Mix mode assembly lines

Mix mode assembly lines, as the name suggests, are assembly lines which are designed to cope with a range of products in any scheduled combination. This is achieved by the use of computer controlled flow lines which schedule work in terms of the overall production requirement and the short-term workloads at the various stations. The increased range of products which can be catered for and which, in turn, justify the investment, is achieved by the increased expenditure necessary to achieve the higher flexibility. In this way, mix mode assembly lines are designed to cope with high volume batch products by transferring the basis of the production from batch to line and thereby altering all the trade-offs examined earlier in Table 3.1.

Transfer lines

The last hybrid process to be discussed is transfer lines. Where the volume demand for products is very high, further investment is justified. As shown in Figure 3.4, transfer lines are a hybrid between line and continuous process. This illustrates the features involving this process where the high demand justifies investment designed to reduce the manual inputs associated with a line process and move more towards a process which not only automatically moves a part from one station to the next but also automatically positions, completes the task and checks the quality as an in-built part of the process. Furthermore, deviations from the specified tolerances will be registered and automatic tooling adjustments and replacements will often be part of the procedure involved. In order to achieve this, the process is numerically controlled in part or in full which provides the systems control afforded, in part at least, by the operator in the line process.

3.6   Review of the Use of Numerical Control (NC) in Hybrid Processes

Whereas the *dedicated use of a general-purpose process and group technology* are derived from alternative uses of non-NC processes, the other four hybrid processes are based upon the concept of numerical control in one form or another.[6]

The last section explained and Figure 3.4 illustrates that the basis for the choice between one NC hybrid process and the other is volume. As with the choices between the five classical processes which were outlined in Table 3.1, the implications for these choices have to be understood and taken into account at the time of their selection (see Figure 3.7). It is important here to recognise that the NC base of these processes brings with it a level of flexibility which is far greater than that inherent with non-NC alternatives. This means, therefore, that the process is more able to cope with a wider range of products and to handle product mix changes over time. However, dedication in these alternatives starts to be introduced when processes are brought together to meet the needs of a given range/family of products. In order thereafter to reuse these, further and often substantial investment will have to be made to relocate, adapt or change existing processes and their configuration to meet the needs of other products. This change is illustrated by the gap between machining centres and FMS. As the choice moves to the other end of the spectrum, the implications of dedication will begin to take hold.

Figure 3.7 illustrates the rationalised use of NC-based processes as they relate to volume. Thus, in the same way as with the classic processes described earlier, whilst volume is the basis for choice, two other equally important dimensions must be a part of this decision. The first is the changes in volume expected over time. The second is the host of implications to the business which need to be understood and be taken into account when arriving at this decision. Some of these are shown in Figure 3.7 but Table 3.1 provides a more complete list.[7]

3.7 Profile Analysis

A company needs to have a comprehensive understanding of the changing implications to its business as alternative processes are chosen, and then to use this concept as an important input into the corporate strategy debate. In fact, it forms the blocks on which to build the strategic, manufacturing dimension. Assessing how well existing process choices fit an organisation's current product requirements and making appropriate choices of process to meet future products are critical manufacturing responsibilities, owing to the high investment associated with the outcomes of these decisions.

FIGURE 3.7
Hybrid NC process choice related to volume

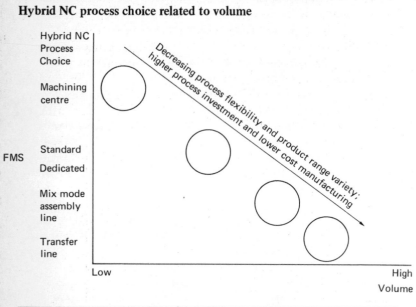

The purpose of this assessment is to evaluate and where necessary improve the degree of fit between manufacturing's ability to support the different order-winning criteria of the company's products in terms of the current and future ways in which they will win orders, i.e. manufacturing's strategic response within the business. In many instances though, companies will be unable or unwilling to improve the degree of fit, due to the investment, executive energy or time scales involved. Instead they will be prepared to live with the trade-offs involved. In such circumstances, however, this decision will enable *profile analysis* to be based on an increased awareness of the corporate position and to be taken as a conscious choice between alternatives. It is this level of strategic alertness to which many companies have not aspired.

Profile analysis is a way to ascertain the degree of fit between the choices of process which have been made or are proposed to be made and the order-winning criteria of the product(s) under review. The procedure to complete a *product profile* involves, first, selecting from the implications listed in Table 3.1* and setting these down for each analysis. A business will need to complete this procedure for the different families of products based upon the marketing perspective referred to earlier in the chapter. The basis for the selection will be to reflect the critical dimensions of the market-place, manufacturing, investment, cost and infrastructure as they appertain to a business and the product family under review.

The next step is to profile a product by positioning it on each of the implications selected. In this way, it tests the level of correlation between the market needs and manufacturing's current or proposed response to their provision. The more consistency that exists between the products/markets and the manufacturing, investment/cost and infrastructure elements of the business then the straighter will be the profile line. Inconsistencies between the market and manufacturing's inherent ability to meet the product performance criteria (both order-winning and qualifying criteria) will show in the dog-leg shape of the profile which will result.

Where the marketing needs have changed over time then the effect on the degree of fit between manufacturing's support for, and the market itself can be assessed and described. One such illustration is provided by Table 3.2 which shows the 1978 and 1983 profile for a company and its products. The incremental marketing changes in this six-year period had had the cumulative effect of moving, in a leftward direction, this company's position on several of the relevant product/market dimensions. However, the order-winning criteria had remained the same and without the required process and infrastructure investment and change, manufacturing had increasingly been less able to cope effectively. The result was that profits tumbled and ROI dropped from almost 30 per cent to less than 5 per cent. Furthermore, given the 1983 product profile which existed, then manufacturing would be unable to improve its performance, and hence redress this situation without the necessary re-investment involved. As Table 3.2 illustrates, the level of inconsistency between the actual 1983 position on the vertical axis and where it should have been (see Figure 3.2, which explains the Phase 1 and Phase 2 steps in manufacturing strategy development) has resulted in a profile mismatch. This, therefore, explains and illustrates the level

---

*The dimensions actually used in the example given in Table 3.2 are drawn from a wider range than those provided in Table 3.1. They include several operational perspectives[9] which were an essential part of the particular corporate picture being drawn.

TABLE 3.2

A profile analysis for a company in which the mainstream products have been profiled. The 1983 profile illustrates the dog-leg shape which reflects the inconsistencies between the high-volume batch process and infrastructure and the 1983 market position

	Typical characteristics of process choice[1] and the company's 1978 and 1983 product profile		
Some relevant product/market, manufacturing and infrastructure aspects for this company	Jobbing, unit, one-off	Batch	Line

Products and markets			
Product range	Wide		Narrow
Customer order size	Small		Large
Frequency of product changes required by the market	Many		Few
Frequency of schedule changes required by customers	High		Low
Order-winning criteria	Delivery/design capability		Price

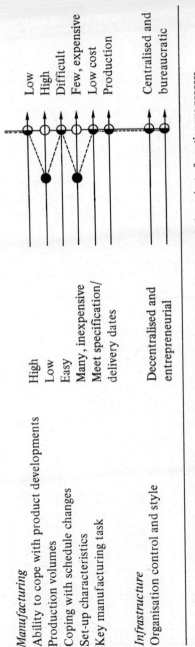

Manufacturing		
Ability to cope with product developments	High	Low
Production volumes	Low	High
Coping with schedule changes	Easy	Difficult
Set-up characteristics	Many, inexpensive	Few, expensive
Key manufacturing task	Meet specification/ delivery dates	Low cost
		Production

Infrastructure		
Organisation control and style	Decentralised and entrepreneurial	Centralised and bureaucratic

[1] The process choices open to the company whose profile is represented here did not include project of continuous process.

O 1978 company position on each of the chosen dimensions and the resulting profile ——— .

● 1983 company position on each of the chosen dimensions and the resulting profile ------- .

of inconsistency involved. In such situations, companies face a number of alternative choices:

(1) Live with the mismatch.
(2) Go some way to redressing the profile mismatch by altering the marketing strategy.
(3) Go some way to redressing the profile mismatch by investing in and changing manufacturing and its infrastructure.

Alternative (1) affords companies the opportunity to consciously make a decision on the trade-offs involved. It does not in any way imply this to be an incorrect strategic choice. What it does do is to bring a company's expectations more in line with reality, makes it aware of the real costs of being in different markets, changes the measures of performance by distinguishing between those which are based upon business related decisions and those which are based upon functional achievement, and raises the level of corporate consciousness about the overall conse-

FIGURE 3.8
The level of inconsistency on all points of the dimensions on the vertical axis – Phase 2 of the procedure (see Figure 3.2)

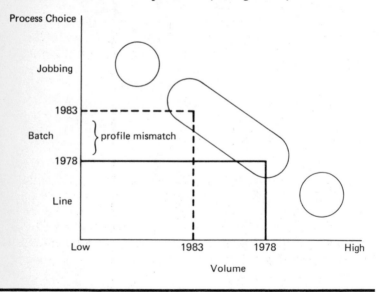

quences of maintaining product profile *status quo* or the decision to improve or widen any *mismatch* which may exist. Furthermore, future decisions concerning new products are now more able to incorporate these essential perspectives and hence arrive at decisions which reconcile the diverse functional perspectives under the mantle of what is best for the business.

Alternatives (2) and (3) concern ways of straightening existing or consciously avoiding the creation of new mismatches which may be taken independently or in unison. *Alternative (2)* represents the influencing of corporate policy through changes or modifications to existing or proposed marketing strategies. In this way, the implications for manufacturing of marketing decisions are addressed and included as an integral part of the corporate strategy debate. Thus, manufacturing is able to move from the reactive stance it currently takes to a proactive mode, so essential to sound policy decisions.

Alternative (3) on the other hand, involves a company in the decision to invest in the processes and infrastructure of its business to either enable manufacturing to become more effective in its provision of the order-winning criteria and support in the market-place for existing products, or to establish the required level of support for future products. As in *Alternative (2)* therefore, it enables manufacturing to switch from making a reactive to making a proactive response to corporate marketing decisions. Thus, by receiving pertinent inputs at the strategic level, the business now becomes more fully aware of the sets of implications involved and is thereby able to arrive at strategic options based upon the relevant and comprehensive inputs necessary to make sound judgements at the strategic level.

3.8 Conclusion

Establishing the level of mismatch between its current processes and current business and the adjustment it must or is able to achieve, or making the appropriate choice of process for future products are difficult and critical production management tasks. Difficult, in that the decision is complex. Critical, in that the process investment will be substantial and changes will be expensive and time-consuming to implement.

The danger is that companies will lean solely on the engineering/

technology dimension for the choice of process answer. *But, it is not an engineering solution*. The engineering input concerns providing alternative, technological options which will enable the product to be manufactured. However, the choice of process concerns how manufacturing is then completed. This will involve the product/market, investment/ cost and infrastructure besides the manufacturing dimensions all of which have been examined in this chapter.

Engineering prescriptions, technology solutions seeking problems or the belief that panaceas are on hand, have been instrumental, in part, for UK manufacturing's current uncompetitive position. Couple this with a marketing led strategy in some businesses which has over-reached itself or the more universal impact of incremental marketing changes which, over time, have altered the business without a strategic recognition of the consequences involved, and the result has been to facilitate the erosion of large, traditional markets by our competitors. Other companies, persuaded by the apparent desirability of new markets or the short-term solution to get out of tough manufacturing industries have also left the way clear in these high-volume, established markets. However, there is no long-term future in easy manufacturing tasks. The short-term may appear attractive but tomorrow matters.

Successful manufacturing nations have been systematically picking off many existing UK and other industrial nations' markets by a combined marketing/manufacturing strategy so creating, at the expense of its competitors, a sound industrial base essential to a nation's long-term prosperity and growth.

Corporate decisions on process choice entail going through the initial conceptualisation, justification and finally implementation of the procedures described here. There are no short cuts. Understanding the complexity of a business and determining the strategic direction so necessary for its success are by-products of hard work and basing decisions on informed insights. The manufacturing inputs into the corporate strategy debate and its outcomes have invariably been too little and too late, but to compete effectively in the future this will have to be redressed. Only when an informed corporate resolution of the interfunctional differences within a business is achieved will a company be in charge of its own destiny.

Notes and References

1. Many of these additional issues are illustrated and discussed in Hill, *Production/Operation Management* Prentice-Hall, 1983), pp. 28–36.
2. More advanced NC systems were introduced in the late 1960s in the form of computer numerical control (CNC) which replaced the hard-wired control unit of the NC system with a stored program using a dedicated mini-computer. Hence, the memory storage rather than paper-tape input makes the process more reliable and more flexible in terms of program changes. Direct numerical control (DNC) systems consist of a number of NC and/or CNC equipment connected to a centralised computer. The centralised source of information provided by DNC helps in the control of manufacturing. Flexible manufacturing systems (FMS) combines the DNC principle together with the other features described in the relevant section on p. 83.
3. Ibid.
4. P. R. Haas, 'Flexible Manufacturing Systems – a Solution for the Mid-volume, Mid-variety Parts Manufacturer' SME Technical Conference, Detroit, Apr. 1973 and J. J. Hughes *et al.*, 'Flexible Manufacturing Systems for Improved Mid-volume Productivity', *Proceedings of the Third Annual AIEE Systems Engineering Conference*, Nov. 1975.
5. A fuller explanation is given in Hill, *Production/Operations Management*, pp. 100–4; also refer to G. A. B. Edwards, *Readings in Group Technology* (Machinery Publishing Company Ltd, 1971), and J. L. Burbidge, *The Introduction of Group Technology* (Heinemann, 1975).
6. NC refers to the operation of machine tools from numerical data stored on paper or magnetic tape, punched cards, computer storage or direct information. The development of machining centres result from the concepts of NC. In a machining centre, a range of operations are provided. A carousel with up to 120–150 tools (i.e. embodied in the centre) from which the program will select as required and with some taking place simultaneously as required. Consequently, a machining centre is able to cope not only with a wide range of product requirements but it can also be scheduled to complete one-offs in any sequence desired. More advanced NC systems include computer numerical control (CNC) systems using a dedicated mini-computer to perform NC functions and direct numerical control (DNC) which refers to a system having a computer controlling more than one machine tool. A DNC system includes both the hardware and software required to drive more than one NC machine simultaneously. To do this, DNC uses a computer which may be a mini-computer, several microcomputers linked together, a mini-computer linked to a large computer or a large computer on its own.
7. A fuller range including operational issues is provided in Hill, *Production/Operations Management*, pp. 28–36.

Further Reading

Blois, K. J. 'Market Concentration – Challenge to Corporate Planning', *Long Range Planning*, vol. 13, Aug. 1980, pp. 56–62.

Burbridge, J. L. 'The Simplification of Material Flow Systems', *International Journal of Production Research*, vol. 20, no. 3, pp. 339–47 (1982).

Dale, R. G., Burbidge, J. L. and Cottam, M. J. 'Planning the Introduction of Group Technology', *International Journal of Operations and Production Management*, vol. 4, no. 1, pp. 34–7.

Financial Times Survey, 'Manufacturing Automation', 5 Feb. 1985, pp. 17–22.

Goldhar, J. D. 'Some Summary Thoughts – Manufacturing, Technology and Corporate Strategy', presented at the Society of Manufacturing Engineers, Manufacturing Productivity Solutions 1982 Conference, Detroit, 14–17 Nov. 1982.

Goldhar, J. D. and Jelinck, M. 'Plan for Economies of Scope', *Harvard Business Review*, Nov./Dec. 1983, pp. 143–8.

Harvard Business School, 'Types of Production Process and Their Characteristics' 8–678–071 (revised 1978).

Hayes, R. W. and Wheelwright, S. C. *Restoring our Competitive Edge – Competing through Manufacturing*, Ch. 6, 'The Technology of Manufacturing Processes' (John Wiley, 1984).

Hyer, N. L. and Wemmerlov, U. 'Group Technology and Productivity', *Harvard Business Review*, July-Aug. 1984, pp. 140–9.

Leonard, R. and Rathmill, K. 'The Group Technology Myths', *Management Today*, Jan. 1977, pp. 66–9.

Linder, J. O. 'Flexible Production Organisation – a Discussion of Efficiency', Paper, Department of Industrial Management, Chalmers University of Technology, Göteborg, Sweden.

Malpas, R. 'The Plant after Next', *Harvard Business Review*, July-Aug. 1983, pp. 122–30.

Miller, S. S. 'Making Your Plant Manager's Job Manageable', *Harvard Business Review*, Jan–Feb. 1983, pp. 69–74.

Schmenner, R. W. *Production/Operations Management – Concepts and Situations* (Science Research Associates (USA), 1981).

Zelenovie, D. M. 'Flexibility – a Condition for Effective Production Systems', *International Journal of Production Research*, vol. 20, no. 3, pp. 319–37 (1980).

Focused Manufacturing 4

Manufacturing is inherently a complex task and managing this complexity is one of the key corporate roles. The complexity involved, however, does not emanate from the intrinsic nature of the individual tasks which comprise the job. In all but highly technical, customised market segments, it is not difficult to cope with the technology of either the product or the process. In most situations, the process technology and wherewithal to make the product involved have been brought in from outside, with appropriate engineering and technical know-how provided inside to support the manufacturing requirement and underpin any necessary development. In a similar way, product design and the associated technology falls under the auspices of the customer and/or the design function. Hence, neither the process nor product technologies are generally either difficult to understand or manage from the viewpoint of the manufacturing function.

What creates the complexity then is not the technology dimension but the size of the task in terms of the number of aspects and issues involved, the interrelated nature of these and the level of fit between the manufacturing strategy task and the internal process capability and infrastructure.

In all instances, the level of complexity involved is derived largely from or can be controlled by the corporate strategy decisions made within the business itself. However, whereas the number and inter-related nature of the tasks and issues involved are more readily identified as a fundamental characteristic of complexity (the small-is-beautiful

99

syndrome[1]), the fit between the manufacturing strategy task and the internal process capability and infrastructure has only recently received close attention. And it is these latter issues which come under the heading of 'focused manufacturing'.

4.1   Focused Manufacturing

Focused manufacturing deals with the issue of linking an organisation's manufacturing facilities to the appropriate competitive factors of its business(es) with the aim of enabling that company to gain a greater control of its competitive position. However, one of the most difficult tasks in managing manufacturing is responding to the different demands made on the facilities in terms of the market-place. This is not only due to the wide and often diverse nature of these demands but also the level of complexity generated in the corresponding parts of the manufacturing function, including suppliers. Many companies are now finding that focusing the demands to which individual facilities must respond can achieve a marked reduction on the level of complexity involved in managing those operations. This, in turn, results in an improved overall performance.

When explaining focus the word narrow or narrowing is often used as part of this description. For example, Skinner who was the first to expound the benefits of focused plants argues that 'a factory that focuses on a narrow product mix for a particular market niche will outperform the conventional plant, which attempts a broader mission',[2] However, taken at face value this argument can be misleading. Many companies do not have the 'narrow product mix' alternative alluded to here. The issue of focus, therefore, is more accurately explained in Skinner's fuller definitions which formed part of his fourfold view for effecting basic changes in the management of manufacturing. Two of these were:

> **Learning to focus each plant on a limited, concise, manageable set of product, technologies, volumes and markets**
> **Learning to structure basic manufacturing policies and supporting services so that they focus on one explicit manufacturing task instead of on many inconsistent, conflicting, implicit tasks.**[3]

The emphasis here is on a limited and consistent set of tasks, which will often be far from the layman's definition of narrow. So, to avoid confusion and the implication of a simplistic resolution of the infinitely complex reality of business, the dimension of narrow should be omitted. It is the homogeneity of tasks and the repetition and experience within manufacturing of completing these which is the basis of focused manufacturing. Thus, focusing the demands placed on manufacturing will enable resources, efforts and attention to be concentrated on a defined and homogeneous set of activities, so allowing management to identify the key tasks and priorities necessary to achieve a better performance. However, in most plants the recognition, let alone the achievement of a meaningful level of plant focus, is rarely understood. There are several factors which have contributed to this position over the last fifteen to twenty years.

Marketing

Marketing-led strategies are usually based on the principle of growth through extending the product range. Invariably what happens is that new products (even those requiring new technologies) are manufactured, partly at least, on existing processes and almost always within the same infrastructure. The logic for this is based on the principle of the economies derived from using existing plant capacity where possible and being supported by the existing overhead structure. Over time, the incremental nature of these marketing changes will invariably alter the manufacturing task. 'The result is complexity, confusion, and worst of all a production organisation which, because it is spun out in all directions by a kind of centrifugal force, lacks focus and a doable manufacturing task.'[4] The factory is increasingly asked to provide the different order-winning criteria for a range of products with the result that it makes a series of compromises.

Increases in plant size

Faced with a shortage of capacity, the attractions of on-site expansion prove irresistible. The tangible arguments of cost and overhead advantages plus the provision of a better hedge against future uncertainty provide the basis against which the alternatives are measured. Rarely argued or taken into account are the costs of the associated uplift in complexity, and the resulting bureaucracy that develops as factories try to cope. The piecemeal or incremental nature of these changes further hides or disguises the changes which are taking place. Schmenner[5] concludes that

> **big plants usually have formidable bureaucratic structures. Relationships inevitably become formal, and the worker is separated from the top executives by many layers of management. All too often managers are shuffling the paperwork that formal systems have spawned ... Although there has to be some formality in plant operations, too much can wipe out the many informal procedures that keep plants nimble and able to adapt to change.**

Manufacturing

To aggravate the situation of compromise described in the last section, manufacturing in these circumstances will almost always not have a definition of its task. It will be required to perform on every yardstick with these often changing from one day to the next depending on the pressures from both within and outside the business. The result is that manufacturing, without an agreed strategy, will respond as best it can, independently deciding on the best corporate compromises or trade-offs involved. The result invariably is reduced plant performance.

Specialists as the basis for controlling a business

The use of specialists is the hallmark of the way in which management perceives the appropriate basis for controlling a business. 'These professionals, quite naturally, seek to maximize their contributions and justify their positions. They have conventional views of success in each of their particular fields. Of course, these objectives are generally in conflict.'[6] Furthermore, the essential link between the activities of specialists and the major functions of a business requires close co-operation and understanding. Too often that is not present. The failure of companies to clearly define the focus of their business exacerbates this problem. Without this direction there is insufficiently shared understanding of what is required. Thus, support systems, controls, information provision and other features of infrastructure are not developed in line with the appropriate and agreed corporate needs. Trade-offs are not made, therefore, against the shared understanding of the business. They are assessed on the fragmented and unco-ordinated views and advice of specialists and based on what seems best at the time, rather than an agreed strategic appreciation of competitive performance.

Looking for panaceas

Emanating somewhat from the last point is the underlying approach by many businesses to seek the resolution to problems through the application of panaceas. Most companies will be able to point to examples of this syndrome by recalling their own versions of redundant solutions. The latest example of a long line in manufacturing is exalting businesses to adopt the 'best' of the Japanese system as a matter of course rather than one effective way of meeting a defined need. Although in themselves such developments are not without their potential, often substantial, contribution to business success, they need to be derived from strategic discussion and in line with the appropriate focus. After all, it took those Japanese companies who have developed these approaches some thirty years to 'perfect' their ideas and to fit these approaches carefully to the business need. The panacea approach will at best only distract management from the essential resolution of its strategic direction, and at worst will imply that there is no longer any need to be concerned – all is in hand.

Trade-offs in focused manufacturing

Choice of focused manufacturing implies trade-offs. In arriving at this decision, however, it is important to distinguish between the gains associated with size reduction and manageable units and those which accrue from the approach adopted towards achieving focused manufacturing. Whilst a reduction in size may well go hand-in-hand with the decision to focus, it is important to separate those advantages which will be shared by any decision to reduce size and those which will be unique to each choice. Hayes and Wheelwright[7] suggest three different approaches to focusing facilities and provide a summary of the advantages and disadvantages for each alternative (see Table 4.1).

A volume split recognises the different process and infrastructure requirements of high and low production and focuses parts of the plant based upon this critical manufacturing difference. A product/market

TABLE 4.1
Advantages and disadvantages of alternative approaches to focusing facilities

Advantages	Disadvantages
Volume split (high volume versus low volume)	
Exploits economies of scale, where appropriate	Duplication of production processes, overhead, and inventories
Permits focusing on either cost effectiveness or production flexibility	Low volume plants can become orphans if not monitored carefully
Encourages customised development of production and management systems for products at different stages of their life style.	
Product/Market split	
Very responsive to market/customer needs and priorities	Duplication of resources across several facilities
Facilitates new product introduction introduction	Product transfers become awkward
Permits specialisation by market segment	Tendency to become unfocused as market shifts (high and low volume products produced in same plant)
Simplifies product cost estimation	Load imbalances develop as different markets grow at different rates
	Less emphasis on, and concentration of, technical skills in market-dominated environments
Process split	
Concentrates technological expertise	Impedes radical changes in products or processes
Less duplication of equipment for producing common parts	Slows organisation's response to totally new product/

Easier to balance loads among plants and keep utilisation high

Can develop customised process control systems

Encourages standardisation

market requirements

Longer cycle times and large pipeline inventories

High cost of co-ordination

Source: R. H. Hayes and S. C. Wheelwright, *Restoring Our Competitive Edge.*[7] With permission.

---

split orientates the parts of the plant towards a particular customer or set of product requirements with this aspect providing the basis for focus. A process split groups similar processes together in order to gain advantages such as concentrating expertise, improved utilisation and reducing total investment.

The approach to be followed when establishing the basis for choice, however, is the need to reflect the order-winning criteria of the products concerned which require to be carefully evaluated and then matched to the relevant plant focus. Not doing this will often lead to an inappropriate choice being made on the one hand, and resulting in a failure on the other to understand the rationale on which to base future decisions as businesses consider change or are forced to change.

*   *   *

A major UK supplier of components and products to the private, commercial and off-highway home and export vehicle markets reviewed one of its principal manufacturing facilities in the early 1980s. The accumulated complexity derived from its attempts to cope with product range increases, volume changes and the growing original equipment (OE)/spares mix had created a factory which was difficult to manage, had high work-in-progress investment and yet was increasingly unable to meet either the delivery needs of its customers or a satisfactory level of return on its investment.

In order to reduce the manufacturing task to a manageable size, it decided to create several 'units' based on a product/market split. In this way, it argued that it would best be able to reflect the needs of its customers whilst reducing its work-in-progress investment requirements. In order to test the validity of the approach it initially took the smallest manufacturing unit within the product/market split and, as it was convenient, relocated the processes and infrastructure for this within an unused part of the existing site. The first review highlighted a series of gains which were, when analysed, predominantly to do with the small-is-manageable philosophy. A more testing analysis, however, showed that the order-winning criteria for different parts of this and the other product/market units were not being addressed any more specifically than before the reorganisation. What had happened was that the company had merely created smaller versions of the larger whole which, in fact, mirror-imaged the problems of the bigger manufacturing units except those associated with plant size. The high and low volumes linked to OE and spares demand respectively called for different order-winning criteria. The appropriate split here would have been to separate out units based on volume in order to create the necessary link between the manufacturing task and the market. The gains owing to small size would automatically follow.

*   *   *

A large company involved in the manufacture of electronics in the late 1970s was facing the decision on where to site its thick film facility. At the time it had a manufacturing unit in two geographically separate sites and needed to double its overall capacity in the near future in order to meet the anticipated growth in thick film application. The alternatives were either to spread the increase over both sites or to re-examine its process needs and reflect these in the plant selection. On reviewing this problem two issues were recognised as being funda-mental to the choice. The first concerned the widening quality demands of products, and the second the extent to which each location could attract an adequate level of infrastructure support in terms of engineer-ing and development. Discussions on the effects of these implications provided the company with the opportunity to recognise that in its case the process requirements associated with more exacting product specifi-cations, low volumes, development activities and the necessary high calibre of engineering and specialist support came together to form a coherent set of process and infrastructure requirements. Whereas, the demands on the process and support staff for the low product specifi-cation and high volumes required a different set of processes and infrastructure. With this now clearly established and the availability and likelihood of attracting sufficient engineering and specialist staff at each location identified, the choices fell into place. In addition, by keeping the process capabilities separate for the two groups of products the problems of establishing, identifying and maintaining the quality requirements for items with very different levels of product specifica-tion were considerably reduced. In this way, therefore, the plant focus choice based upon process split enabled the company to recognise, appreciate and take account of the key practical constraints involved, to reflect these within the focused manufacturing decision, thus aligning the plant to the different market segments.

Plant-within-a-plant configurations

One of the important trade-offs implicit, if not explicit, in focused manufacturing is that of plant size versus the economies of organisational scale. Although the ideal would be plants individually focused to the needs of the markets and arranged on the basis of the alternatives given in Table 4.1, this is often not practical on two counts. First, many companies own existing sites together with the sizeable investment in the bricks and mortar, utilities, plant, offices and other facilities they have provided over the years in line with the needs of the business. Secondly, as businesses change, there is a real danger that the type of manufacturing complexity associated with lack of focus could gradually permeate some of the plants. Where rearrangement is constrained due to the size of initial plants, their geographical location and the distribution difficulties involved, process and infrastructure support considerations and the like then the flexibility of overall size (i.e. the larger the factory then the greater the permutations available) can often be to a company's advantage. However, although this second aspect may not be a major issue for many companies, the first constraint is.

The way to proceed (as inferred in the earlier example of the supplier to the vehicles markets) in these situations is to adopt the plant-within-a-plant (PWP) resolution to providing focus. In this way, sites are physically divided (i.e. with walls, different entrances and other facilities) thus providing a 'separate' plant within which manufacturing is focused to the needs of different parts of its total business. This reduces units to a more manageable task, attracting the advantages of both focus and smaller size.

Whilst the trade-off for these distinct and often critical gains is the apparent loss of economies of organisation size, what happens in addition is that PWP provides the opportunity to review overheads in line with each focused manufacturing plant. In this way, these judgements are found to be much easier to make owing to the improved clarity between business needs/direction and overhead requirement. The amorphous mass takes on shape which in turn allows each part of the business to reflect its needs with its overhead provision whilst the total business now has the opportunity to assess the relative contribution of each part to its overall success.

Focused manufacturing creates a structure in which each plant or PWP has its own facilities in which it can concentrate on every element of work that constitutes the manufacturing task. Each part of the facility comprises its own processes and infrastructure which are developed in line with each task. This not only provides significant gains in terms of sustaining the qualifying and meeting the order-winning criteria but also decreases the likelihood of the agreed focus being undermined, known as *focus regression.*

4.2 Focus and the Product Life Cycle

In the last section the three principal ways on which to base a focus split were discussed. However, of these the most important is usually volume. The link between volume and order-winning criteria as presented in Table 3.1 (pp. 70-1) was clearly established and explained. An important illustration of this concerns the nature of the product life cycle and the changes in volumes and order-winning criteria which take place over time.

* * *

A European-based company had moved, over a number of years, from Product A to Products B and C with Product D to be introduced in the near future. All four products basically performed the same task for the customer – more sophisticated, but the same task. As is often the case, there was a considerable overlap between the life of one product and that of another. As a result, there was a need to manufacture more than one range at a time, plus spares for each range. The spares service was part of the company's commitment to the past, as well as demonstrating to its current customers that they would be provided for in the future. In order, therefore, to establish the *whole* of the manufacturing task it was necessary to review the *whole* of the corporate marketing requirements as this would provide a true picture of the issues involved. A review of these products is summarised in Table 4.2.

Product A was based upon a mechanical technology and was no longer sold as part of a new contract. Sales were restricted to spares or replacement equipment in existing installations. The processes required to make this product were specific to this range as the other three

TABLE 4.2
Changes over time in production volumes and the main manufacturing task for current and future products

Aspect	Product			
	A	B	C	D
Production volumes				
Current	Low spares volumes	Large	Low	–
In two to three years	Low – little change	Decreasing	Increasing	Low
Manufacturing task based upon agreed order-winning criteria				
Current	Delivery speed	Cost reduction	Quality/ delivery reliability	
In two to three years	Delivery speed	Cost reduction	Cost reduction	Quality/ delivery reliability

products were based upon electronic product technology and required different processes. Products C and D emphasise the trend in product development reflecting the rapid advance in microtechnology.

The company whilst maintaining the process capability unique to meeting the spare parts and replacement equipment sales of Product A, currently produced both Products B and C on the same processes. With Product D already being earmarked as the next stage in the product development, the question facing manufacturing was, which processes were appropriate to meet both the technical and market requirements of the three products based on similar technology. The decision concerned the principle of *product and process focus*.[8] This concept helps a company to look at its present and future product decisions in terms of manufacturing, by considering what type of focus would best suit the corporate marketing needs. Being *product focused* means that the manufacturing facility is designed on a general purpose basis and is thus able to meet the needs of a range of products, including product development and low volumes. When a plant is *process focused*, it is designed to meet the needs of a relatively narrow range of products, normally with high volumes and/or similar process requirements. Such a plant is therefore specialised in order to meet the low-cost requirements of a price sensitive market.

The manufacturing strategy adopted by this company for its electronic products had been based on the provision of a general purpose production process and it was manufacturing Product B and C and intended to manufacture Product D in this way. This decision had been taken to meet three main objectives:

1. To cope with known product development with an existing facility and so avoid the need to plan for new facilities at each stage.
2. To minimise total product costs for all items, accepting that this may not be possible for individual products.
3. To be better able to handle fluctuating volumes owing to variable demand patterns from major customers.

However, by the very nature of general purpose processes, each product will be assumed to have similar order-winning criteria and hence, a similar manufacturing task will be appropriate. In this situation, these processes would be suboptimal in meeting the cost-reduction requirements of Product B and later those of Product C.

A facility to provide the existing and future market requirements would need to encompass the characteristics of both a product and process-focused plant as described earlier. To provide these in one process will always lead to a compromise through a series of trade-offs. However, where this trade-off is between the key order-winning criteria of different products, it is necessary to make alternative focused manufacturing provision.

This distinction is shown in Figure 4.1 by a product focus/process

---

FIGURE 4.1
Orientation of a particular manufacturing facility[9]

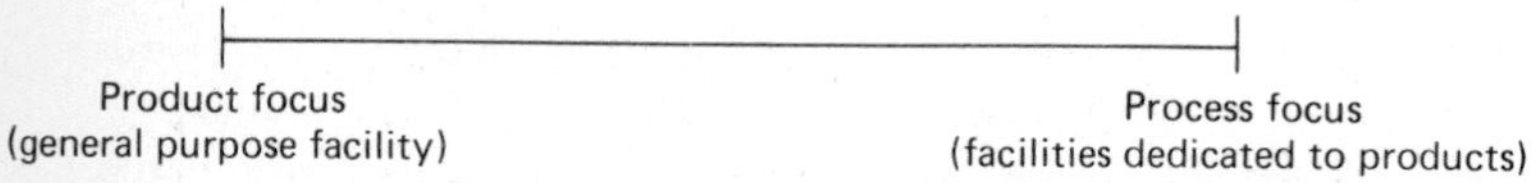

| Product focus | Process focus |
| (general purpose facility) | (facilities dedicated to products) |

focus continuum. Establishing where a production facility stands on this spectrum and in which direction it is evolving will provide a firm with the opportunity to review where it is and where it should be in terms of manufacturing's support of marketing. In this way it provides one of the essential inputs into the corporate strategy development by highlighting the degree of match between the marketing and manufacturing strategies bringing the company's attention to any current levels of difficulty and the possible ways forward to provide what is best for the business as a whole.

In the example described earlier the company in developing its manufacturing strategy became aware of the type of focused manufacturing appropriate to its products as they went through their life cycles and as illustrated in Figure 4.2.

In the early stages of growth, the implications for manufacturing will be towards handling less predictable sales volumes, product and process modifications and customer orientation. The provision of these will usually best be met by the capability and flexibility characteristics which are inherent in product focus. In the period of maturity, the high volume sales and the product technology having been fixed, attention is totally directed towards processes, with low cost manufacturing becom-

---

FIGURE 4.2
A typical product life cycle and its relationship to focus

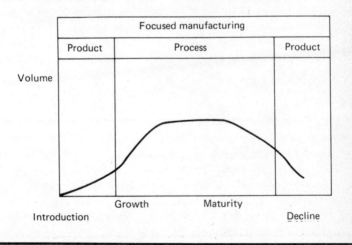

ing predominant (i.e. process focus). Finally, in the period of product decline, the manufacturing requirements revert back to a product focused facility due to the change in volumes and order-winning criteria.

4.3   Progression or Regression in Focused Manufacturing[10]

By definition, a single manufacturing process cannot provide the aspects of product and process focus at the same time. The recognition of the critical trade-offs to support the corporate marketing requirements is an essential component of a sound manufacturing strategy. In practice, however, every facility faces some variety in terms of corporate marketing requirements for its products. It is essential to be aware of these fluctuations in variety and to evaluate the consequences of these changes. The increase in product variety within the company described earlier and the associated differences required by these products over time, led to an increased diffusion between products and processes. This, in turn, led to movement away from its preferred focus, known as *focus regression*. On the other hand, for a facility to become increasingly competitive it needs to take appropriate steps to achieve greater movement towards its preferred focus, known as *focus progression*. For this to take place it would be necessary for the company described earlier to align Products B and C and later Product D to their appropriate focus. For, only in this way could the key task be addressed by manufacturing for the different products at the respective stages in their product life cycles.

4.4   Experience Curves

Evidence clearly shows that as experience accumulates, performance improves, and the experience curve is the quantification of this improvement. The basic phenomenon of the experience curve is that the cost to manufacture a given item falls in a regular and predictable way as the total quantity produced increases. The purpose of this section is to draw attention to this relationship and its role in the formulation of manufacturing strategy. It is helpful to note that whilst the cost/volume relationship is the pertinent corporate issue, some of the examples will in fact relate price to volume because the information, not being company derived, uses average industry price as a convenient substitute.

It is in almost everyone's experience that the price of a new product declines after its initial introduction and as it becomes more widely accepted and available. However, it is not so commonly recognised that, over a wide range of products, the cost follows a remarkably consistent decline. The characteristic pattern is that the cost declines (in constant £s) by a consistent percentage each time cumulative production is doubled. The effects of learning curves on labour costs have been recognised and reported over the last forty years beginning with studies on airframe production in the USA prior to the Second World War. However, experience curves are distinctly different to this. The real source of the experience effect is derived from organisational improvement. Although learning by individuals is important, it is only one of many improvements which accrue from experience. Investment in manufacturing processes, changes in production methods, product redesign and improvements in all functions in the business account for some part of the significant experience related improvements.

The experience curve is normally drawn by taking each doubling of cumulative unit production and expressing the unit cost or price as a percentage of the cost or price before doubling. So an 80 per cent experience curve would mean that the cost or price of the one hundredth unit of a product is 80 per cent that of the fiftieth, of the two hundredth, 80 per cent that of the one hundredth and so on. Figure 4.3 shows the experience curve for integrated circuits in the period from 1964 to 1972, and also illustrates the basic features of these curves, which are now explained.[11]

1. The horizontal axis measures the cumulative quantity produced on a logarithmic scale. Figure 4.4(a) and (b) shows the same information plotted on a linear and logarithmic scale, respectively. The information on Figure 4.4(a) reveals a smooth curve and the implied regularity of the relationship between unit cost and total volume. However, Figure 4.4(b) shows the same information plotted on double logarithmic scales. This presentation shows percentage changes as a constant distance, along either axis. The straight line on the log–log scale in Figure 4.4(b) means that a given percentage change in one factor has resulted in a corresponding percentage change in the other. The nature of that relationship determines the slope of the line which can be read off a log–log grid.

FIGURE 4.3

Experience curve for integrated circuits

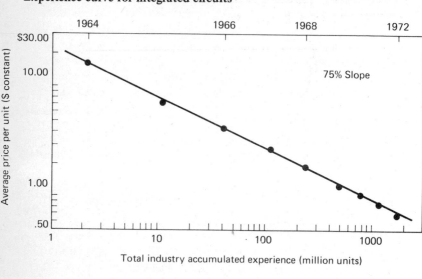

Source: Boston Consulting Group. With permission[12]

2. Returning to Figure 4.3, the logarithmic scale shows that many doublings of production can be achieved early on but later, vastly larger quantities are needed to double the cumulative unit volumes then involved. This implies, as one would expect, that movement down the experience curve slows with time. Initially, additional growth in annual volumes can offset this but the levelling in demand associated with the mature stage in the product life cycle and the eventual saturation and later decline through technical obsolescence will slow the rate of progress down the curve.

3. The vertical axis of the experience curve is usually cost or price per unit and is also expressed logarithmically. However, the cost or price per unit must be adjusted for inflation to allow comparisons to be drawn over time. Figure 4.3 shows that improvements further down the curve become, in absolute terms, quite small. Thus, as progress is made down the curve, each incremental movement will both take longer and yield less.

FIGURE 4.4
Cost/volume or price/volume relationship expressed on (a) a linear and (b) a log–log scale

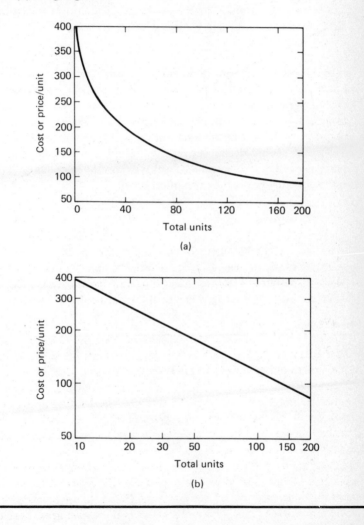

The characteristic decline in cost or price per unit established by the Boston Consulting Group's (BCG) work in the 1960s and early 1970s, was between 20 and 30 per cent for each doubling of cumulative production. Although the BCG claim that this can go on (in constant £s) without limit and despite the rate of experience growth, in reality this tends not to happen for the reasons expressed earlier.

Furthermore, it is important to stress that the experience curve characteristics are phenomenological in nature. They portray a relationship between cost or price and volume which can, but does not necessarily, exist. Consequently, the BCG concludes that

> **these observed or inferred reductions in costs as volume increases are not necessarily automatic. They depend crucially on a competent management that seeks ways to force costs down as volume expands. Production costs are most likely to decline under this internal pressure. Yet in the long run the average combined costs of all elements should decline under the pressure for the company to remain as profitable as possible. To this extent the relationship is of normal potential rather than one of certainty.[13]**

Characteristic patterns

Data on price and total industry volumes are readily available for many products and show, in general, that the price/volume relationship has characteristic patterns.[14] Where prices are underpinned by paralleled costs then the slope is a straight line as shown in Figure 4.5. Products

---

FIGURE 4.5

A stable pattern between price and cost reduction

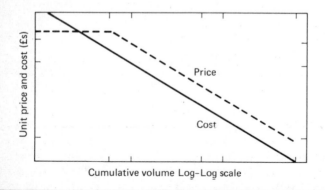

Cumulative volume Log-Log scale

which follow this trend tend to be those associated with high growth, highly competitive, technological industries such as the integrated circuits example given earlier in Figure 4.3. Often, as shown in Figure 4.5, prices may in the earlier years be set to establish market acceptance or to gain entry into a market. Depending upon each firm's lateness of market entry then the point at which experience will provide the opportunity for costs to decline to a level which creates margin, will differ.

Three further examples serve to illustrate this pattern. Figures 4.6, 4.7 and 4.8 show the constant price per ton reduction of crushed and broken limestone, the price of a Model T Ford during the period from 1909 to 1923 and the price for random access memory (RAM) components respectively.

FIGURE 4.6
Experience curve for the crushed and broken limestone industry between 1925-1971

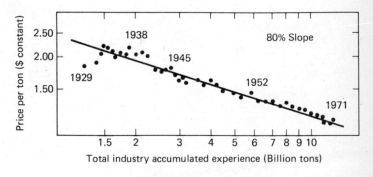

Total industry accumulated experience (Billion tons)

log–log scale

Source: Boston Consulting Group. With permission[15]

Sometimes prices do not decline as fast as costs in the early years, see Figure 4.9. In this example, whilst the cost/volume experience curve remains constant, the price/volume slope is in different phases as illustrated. In Phase A (Figure 4.9) prices are set to create an initial market. However, by maintaining a relatively high price during Phase B,

FIGURE 4.7
Experience curve for the model T Ford

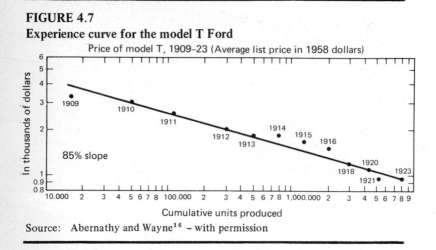

Price of model T, 1909–23 (Average list price in 1958 dollars)

Source: Abernathy and Wayne[16] – with permission

FIGURE 4.8
70 per cent experience curve for random access memory (RAM) components in the period 1976–84

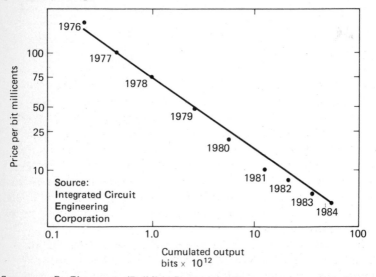

Source: P. Ghemawat, 'Building Strategy on the experience curve', *Harvard Business Review*, Mar–Apr 85, pp. 143–9 (with permission).

FIGURE 4.9
Umbrella pricing and the characteristic unstable pattern between price and cost decline which follows[17]

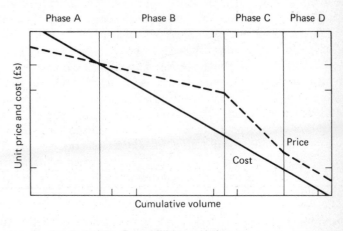

Source: Boston Consulting Group. With permission

competitors are attracted into the market which then forces down the unit price as shown in Phase C. In this phase, price decline is at a rate greater than cost decline and the resulting competition brings about a shake-out period in the industry. At the end of this period, the stable relationship between price and cost is established (Phase D). If this did not happen then the severity of the market shake-out would be heralded by a situation, for a time at least, where margin was squeezed even to the point of creating a loss-making position. Eventually, either the equilibrium between price and cost decline will be established or the unstable pattern of Figure 4.9 would be repeated.

Examples of umbrella pricing are again provided by the Boston Consulting Group in their book *Perspectives on Experience*; the US industry examples provided include silicon transistors, low density polyethylene, polypropylene, polystyrene, monochrome television receivers and free-standing electric ranges.[18]

4.5   Areas of Activity which will Affect the Rate of Cost Improvement

Experience curves are an observable phenomenon. For whatever the reasons, they happen. The important question to address from a corporate point of view is, therefore, how through managerial action do you ensure that the rate of cost improvement is achieved, maintained and reflected in improved competitiveness? As the forces underlying the experience curve phenomenon are based upon organisational improvement then the sources of activity to achieve this improvement involve several major and related areas of managerial action. Although production functions will be towards the top of such a list, the size of overhead costs in many manufacturing companies will provide substantial opportunity to address major areas of non-manufacturing costs. The various activities and areas of principal attention which will affect the rate of cost and, therefore, competitiveness improvement are now considered.

Product redesign, substitution and standardisation

The growing size of direct materials as a percentage of total costs is the key to the importance of material cost reductions through redesign, substitution and standardisation. In many manufacturing companies, material costs will be on average some two to four times greater than direct labour content. It is most important, therefore, that companies allocate time, resources and management effort to the areas of large cost. Currently, however, many businesses in line with past tradition, still divert relatively large resources to the control and reduction of direct labour costs and relatively small resources to the areas of purchasing, value engineering and value analysis. These latter activities concern the effective procurement of materials and the systematic evaluation of the proposed or current design of a product. The purpose is to assess opportunities for cost reduction through redesign, material standardisation, or substitution and a review of the value provided and the costs incurred.

Labour efficiency

Labour's contribution to the experience curve effect falls within the province of the learning curve. The early studies on aircraft manufactures before the Second World War showed a cost reduction of some 20 per cent over the years reviewed. Further investigation into production plants with the same high labour content revealed similar gains. Naturally, many observers concluded that the experience effect is related to labour. However, it is now recognised that this experience effect extends beyond direct labour's contribution to include support staff throughout the organisation, besides the many others discussed later, particularly in companies which do not have a high direct labour cost element.

However, whilst this is so, reductions in labour cost are an important contribution to overall cost improvement. Bodde[19] argues that the achievement of these learning effects depends upon effective management in three areas

1. *High quality and stability* in the labour force are necessary to achieve the learning effects. This is due not only to the on-costs of training and turnover, but that the very essence of the learning curve is underpinned by the quality of the labour force to achieve the cost reductions and their experience in the job concerned. Macklin in an article on the Douglas Aircraft Company[20] emphasised that it was the company's failure to meet the cost improvements on which the price of the DC-9 had been based which ultimately forced a merger with McDonnell. One of the critical reasons for this was their inability to attract the required skilled people in the mid-1960s due to a general upsurge in the economy. This, coupled with a higher-than-expected demand, forced Douglas into a massive recruitment and training programme. However, of the 34 703 staff recruited in the 18 months from the beginning of 1965, a little over 12 000 were lost. As a result, the anticipated 85 per cent learning curve on which prices had been based was not achieved.

2. *The payment system* and its link to productivity is also strongly argued. Almost all industrial situations will reveal their own examples of this source of labour productivity gains. 'Output pegging', the systematic erosion of 'standard output' by gaining allowances for all categories of excesses and the pressure applied to 'loosening' labour standards are unfortunately the classic hallmarks of wage drift and the corresponding fall in or holding back of productivity achievement. Many payment systems are designed or applied which unconsciously discourage rather than encourage performance improvements. It is most important that payment systems facilitate further improvements whilst recognising that there is a need to be aware of

the classic ways in which payment systems can be undermined.[21] The development of payment systems is also one of the areas addressed in Chapter 6, 'Manufacturing Infrastructure Development'.

3. *Work structuring* is the third feature which is highlighted as making an important contribution to labour efficiency improvements. Experiments in alternative forms of structuring work have been extensively documented. Professor R. E. Walton's data on experiments in the US[22] together with the Volvo experiments at Kalmer (Sweden), and the radically different approaches adopted by Japanese management, both at home and in overseas plants in the UK, US and elsewhere suggest that these changes have been very successful.[23] This aspect is dealt with in some detail in Chapter 6.

Economies of scale

The experience effect is in part the outcome of increased volumes. Hence, the economies of scale are linked to growth which in turn requires additions to capacity. Each increment in capacity, however, usually requires a correspondingly lower investment. In process industries, for instance, an approximate effect of scale is to only increase capital costs by the sixth-tenth power of the increase in capacity. This is based on the recognition that to double capacity, for instance, would not require a twofold increase in investment. Thus, if a 100 per cent increase in capacity led to a 55 per cent increase in capital costs then the total capital would be 155 per cent for a 200 per cent capacity achievement. The average would then become 155/200 or 77 per cent of 100 per cent. In addition to this reduction, the labour and other cost reductions associated with the investment would also accrue thereby adding to the scale effects and its contribution to moving down the experience curve.

Improved processes and methods

The experience gains derived from process and methods are particularly important in businesses in which the direct labour content is small. In such instances improvements in processes are much more important sources of cost reductions. The classic example of this is found in the electronic semiconductor industry where process technology improvements have led to significant cost reductions over time despite the relatively low potential for labour efficiency gains.

4.6   Experience Curves and Manufacturing Strategy

The experience curve is a long-term strategic rather than a short-term tactical concept. It combines the effects of numerous factors relying on a competent and effective management team to systematically exploit the experience cost opportunities which exist. Because the gains slow down and eventually yield less it is of paramount importance to the business that this opportunity to reduce costs is unfailingly pursued over a long period of time, where cost-reduction is essential to the manufacturing strategy. Although low-cost manufacturing may not be, in some instances, the most important order-winning criterion, for many products it provides a very powerful facet of manufacturing's support for the market-place.

The experience concept within strategic decision-making is based upon the association between market share, cumulative volumes, low cost and profitability. Some of the basic marketing strategies adopted by businesses are, in part, underpinned by the experience effect. For instance, building and maintaining market share. Evidence suggests that a firm needs a minimum market share to become viable. Such build-ups of market share are achieved slowly, and need the inherent experience gains to be fully exploited to help in this achievement.

Examples where companies have used cost reduction based upon experience include Ford and its approach to Model T production referred to earlier (see Figure 4.7). Texas Instruments provides a second example of a company using a cost minimisation manufacturing strategy to great effect. In its First Quarter 1973 Report, the company outlined its proposed corporate strategy based upon the experience phenomenon and its intention of keeping ahead of the competion as it raced down the appropriate curve.[24]

Figure 4.10 shows Company A over a four-year period, its relationship to Company B and illustrates that where market share is maintained then so are relative percentage costs.

However, changes between competitors' positions will result in other market situations depending upon the experience curve achievement of the companies involved. Figure 4.11 illustrates two competitors A and B and their relative experience curve achievement over a number of time periods in relation to the industry price. In this example, Company A is operating at breakeven (P_1), maintains market share over P_2, P_3 and P_4 but does not reduce costs at the same rate as Company B. The situation can now arise where the market price could be set more

FIGURE 4.10
The relationship over time between market share and relative costs

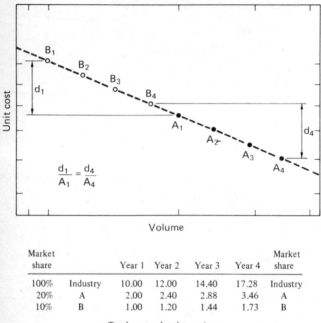

Market share		Year 1	Year 2	Year 3	Year 4	Market share
100%	Industry	10.00	12.00	14.40	17.28	Industry
20%	A	2.00	2.40	2.88	3.46	A
10%	B	1.00	1.20	1.44	1.73	B

Total accumulated experience

Source: Boston Consulting Group. With permission[25]

in line with either Company A or company B's experience curve (S_1 or S_2 respectively) or somewhere in between (e.g. S_3 or S_4). However, for Company A only S_1 would create a situation of profit in the longer-term.

Where two companies maintain the normal rate of cost decline within a segment of the market, then the company with the greater cumulative experience will always be ahead of its competitor. However, as Figure 4.12 vividly demonstrates, if Company A initially ahead (A_1) loses market share then Company B, moving down the experience curve at a faster rate, will displace Company A as illustrated in B_2 and A_2 respectively.

FIGURE 4.11
Experience curve decline and survival

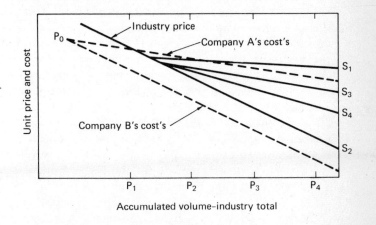

FIGURE 4.12
The effect of market share on cost differentials where companies main-tain the same level of cost reduction

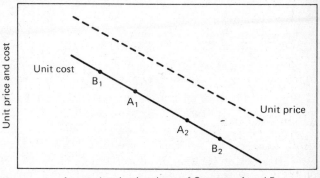

4.7   Limits of the Experience Curve

Although claims are made that the experience curve effect is ever-descending, without limit, most evidence suggests otherwise. The most important reason concerns product obsolescence. Development based, in part, on rapid advances in technology will lead to replacement products being introduced long before the lower limits of the experience curve of existing products have been reached. Furthermore, to pursue experience curve advantages in isolation of the other factors pertinent to sales and markets can lead companies into a myopic spiral with potentially catastrophic consequences. Perhaps the best example of this is the experience of the Ford Motor Company and its Model T.

Figure 4.7 was cited earlier in the chapter as a company-based example of a stable pattern between price and cost reduction. This illustrates the outcome of the Ford strategy during the period from 1909 to 1923, during which time company profits increased despite the lower margins accrued on each sale. Abernathy who has well-documented the Ford approach, outlined the way in which the company systematically pursued each area of potential cost reduction in order to help maximise sales volume.[26]

As a result of this strategy, Ford dominated the car market over this period. To achieve these productivity gains Ford integrated backwards into raw material supplies such as steel and lumber together with the railroad to haul them.

Product stability was increased mainly by offering minimum product variation and labour specialisation was resolutely achieved. However, by the early 1920s market demand was beginning to move from a need to supply low cost transport, with new car buyers switching to closed-body designs which offered greater comfort. In order to compete, Ford was forced to add features to the Model T. However, the sole pursuit of cost reduction carried with it the inherent inflexibility which was to prove the basis of the company's downfall. By the mid-1920s, the Model T was uncompetitive in terms of engineering design. Faced with increasing consumer preference for the new designs, Ford stopped production in May 1927. The result was devastating both in the short and longer-term. Locked into large capital investment, fixed processes and high levels of vertical integration, Ford lost $200m in the year it took to change over to its Model A design. It had to replace 15 000 machine tools, rebuild 25 000 more and laid off 60 000 workers in Detroit alone.

In the longer-term, although Model A was initially well received, market leadership in the car industry passed to General Motors.[27]

The story of Ford's Model T strategy also provides a vivid illustration of the failure to recognise that there are several ways in which products win orders in their market and these might well change over time, creating a breakdown of one market or market segment into further segments. A clear understanding of which segment(s) and the pertinent order-winning criteria in each segment is an essential prerequisite on which to base an appropriate manufacturing strategy. For instance, whereas Texas Instruments successfully pursued the gains associated with a cost-reduction strategy to displace Bowmar as the market leader in the hand-held calculator market, Hewlett-Packard (HP) adopted a different approach with equal understanding and success. Whilst still exploiting the gains associated with accumulated experience, HP pursued a policy of gaining competitive advantage through developing innovative products in the high price segment of the market. Its 'success is a classic illustration of technology-orientated market strategy at work'[28] As HP's technology became less expensive, the company had a choice between cutting prices or adding performance features. But, HP's policy was not to compete in the high volume, low price end of the market but to retain its price advantage by adding features to its products which were not already available.

4.8 Experience Curves and Focus

Management's contribution is an essential prerequisite in order to achieve the gains associated with cumulative volumes. The experience curve is important, therefore, because it provides:

1. A yardstick against which cost reductions can be measured and a basis on which future reductions can be predicted.
2. Some tangible measure of the degree of specialisation or orientation that has been or is being built into the process, which leads to the general concept of focus.

The company referred to earlier (pp. 108) which manufactured products for the telecommunications market, showed significantly different cost patterns on the units which went into its electronic products. With the increased output levels of Product B, corresponding investment in the manufacturing process was made to increase the level of automation and achieve reductions in costs. It would have been expected, therefore, for unit costs to be consistently reduced. Figure 4.13 shows the experience curves for the four units which, in a number of different combinations, comprised Product B.

FIGURE 4.13
Experience curves for Units 1 and 2, and Units 3 and 4 for Product B

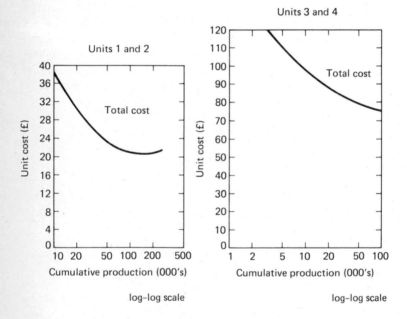

Source: T. J. Hill and R. M. G. Duke-Woolley, 'Progression or Regression in Facilities Focus'.[29] With permission.

As expected, the curves show a cost-reduction particularly over the initial years. However, it is most noticeable that in the case of Units 1 and 2 the rate of decrease not only slowed (as with Units 3 and 4) but it also showed an upward trend in the later period. On looking into the causes of this unexpected change it was established that the processes used to make Units 1 and 2 for Product B were also being used to make Unit 1 for Product C. Hence the initial 17 per cent experience curve gain had now been completely lost. The impact on costs of attempting to accommodate both a process focus for Product B and a product focus for Product C was there for all to see. The experience curve for Units 3 and 4 which were only used on Product B showed an initial 10 per cent unit cost reduction which had flattened out to almost 7 per cent.

These facts now allowed the company to recognise that the level of initial gains was lower than could be expected whilst their slowing down was premature. Thus, the lowering of costs with each doubling of cumulative production had not been maintained. In the case of Units 3 and 4 the deceleration, though slight, indicated that the necessary focus and concerted management effort had, on the whole, not been maintained. In contrast to this, the cost pattern for Units 1 and 2 was both marked and disconcerting. Marked in that the initial 17 per cent cost reduction had been more than lost and disconcerting in that these units were important to both the short-term (Product B) and long-term (Products B and C) success of the business.

Compare this example, however, to the one which follows and provides an illustration of a company's experience curve gains with increased plant focus. The information in Table 4.3 is for the five-year

TABLE 4.3
Changes in product range and volume at one company in the period 1971–5[30]

Year	Number of models	Volume per model	Plant volume
1971	20	90	1800
1972	16	130	2080
1973	15	210	3150
1974	9	360	3240
1975	6	550	3300

Source: Boston Consulting Group, unpublished data. With permission.

period from 1971–5 and shows the changes in the number of models in the product line, the volume per model and the total plant volume.

In Figure 4.14, the reductions in the standard cost per unit are plotted against the volume per model and show the characteristics

---

FIGURE 4.14
The impact of focus on standard cost per unit

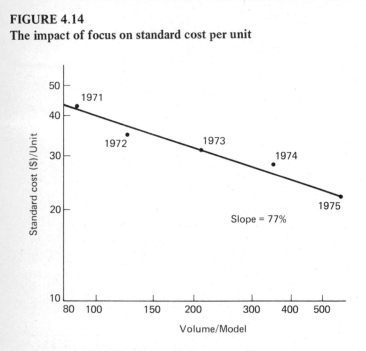

Source: Boston Consulting Group. With permission[31]

---

associated with experience curves. This shows that standard cost per unit decreased by 23 per cent (in constant S) with each doubling in the cumulative unit volume per model. Whilst this decrease was in part attributed to increased capacity utilisation over the period, other evidence collected confirmed that the 'focusing of the product line was the most significant factor behind the reduction in costs'.[32] Data to illustrate some of the gains of focus which contributed to this reduction in standard cost/unit are provided in Figure 4.15 and 4.16. These show a 76 per cent reduction in overhead cost/unit as the number of models

FIGURE 4.15
The impact of product line focus on overhead cost/unit for the company illustrated in Table 4.3

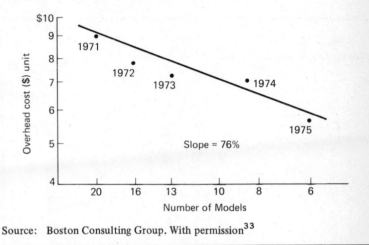

Source: Boston Consulting Group. With permission[33]

were reduced and the impact of product line focus on inventory turn-over respectively.

Further empirical evidence to show the impact of focus on corporate performance is also provided by the Boston Consulting Group.[34] Their work compared several firms in the same industry. Figure 4.17 shows the operating margin and 1977 sales ($m) for each of eleven companies (A to K). The relationship shown here does not reveal a close fit between the two sets of information. However, Figure 4.18 relates operating margins to the number of product lines produced by each company – shown in brackets after each company reference. This now clearly identifies the increase in margin associated with each number of product lines produced. The circle is then completed by presenting the three sets of information and determining the relationship between operating margin, sales ($m) and the degree of focus as represented in the number of products/processes. Figure 4.19 thereby separates the more focused from the less focused companies.

FIGURE 4.16

Impact of product line focus on inventory turnover in the period 1971–75 for the company illustrated in Table 4.3

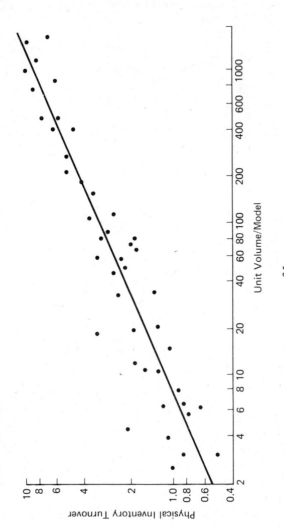

Unit Volume/Model

Physical Inventory Turnover

Source: Boston Consulting Group. With permission[35]

FIGURE 4.17
Profitability and the size ($ turnover) of eleven companies in one industry.

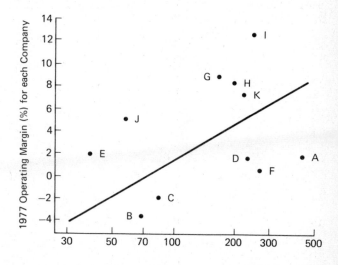

Source: Boston Consulting Group – unpublished data. With permission[36]

This gives a much better fit between profitability and size; the more-focused firms and facilities experiencing substantially higher profitability by as much as eight to twelve percentage points in operating margin than similarly sized, less-focused operations. Additionally, for this industry, focus appears to increase in value as the size of the firm increases. This may be due to the fact that with larger operations, facilities (and their production processes) can be even more narrowly focused than would be the case for smaller operations.[37]

This type of industry analysis has a further advantage when evaluating the impact of focus on a company's competitive position. Compared to the data over time for a single firm, this analysis holds changes in the competitive environment and general business conditions constant for all companies. In this way, therefore, it limits the possible explanations for differences in performance.

FIGURE 4.18
Profitability related to the number of product lines manufactured by eleven companies in the same industry

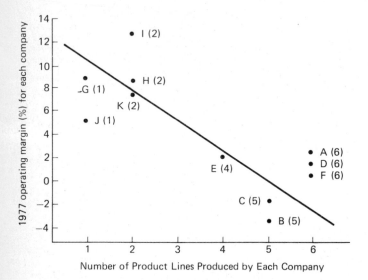

Source;   Boston Consulting Group – unpublished data with permission[38]

4.9   Conclusion

Achieving and maintaining focused manufacturing needs to be an overt corporate activity. Focus does not occur naturally and, in fact, there are normally forces at work which militate against it. These need to be recognised so that action may be consciously taken to ensure that improved focus is not inhibited due to corporate neglect or traditional views of what is best for the business.

1. *Marketing* often stimulates the desire to create and maintain a broad product line. This is largely because it is and has been for some time, an integral part of its own strategy. It has thus become a felt need

FIGURE 4.19

The impact of the degree of focus (number of product lines produced) and operating performance for eleven companies is one industry

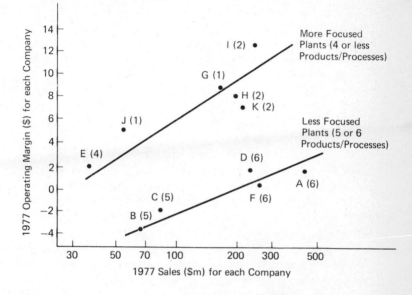

Source: Boston Consulting Group – unpublished data with permission[39]

with overtones of image and, frequently, constitutes an important measure of functional performance.

2. *Sales* holds the understandable view that it is easier to sell a broader line, a fact which is reinforced by commission schemes for salesmen, normally being based upon total sales value (£s). This implies, therefore, that sales of all products are of equal value to the business and thus fails to recognise the need to differentiate one product sale from the next. This function will also argue that a review of total competition reveals a wide variety of features on offer thus affording wider selection for the customer. It follows, therefore, that as

customers' preferences vary then a wide range better meets the total diverse needs. However, although this may well be true for some of the time, it does not usually hold true for all the time. Often customers' preferences are based upon unsubstantiated and/or non-technical rationale. In these circumstances it is much harder to sell to customers a product which meets their actual as opposed to their perceived needs.

Finally, in businesses experiencing seasonal or cyclical demand, there is often a strong argument to increase variety to help smooth out such patterns.

3. *Manufacturing* also inhibits focus for reasons such as precedent, being bound by past union agreements on work, the high investment costs associated with the purchase and movement of processes and the risk of uncertain benefits.

4. *Accounting and finance* similarly stimulate forces which work against focus. These include capital restrictions and capital rationing, the overriding emphasis on short-term earnings and the prevalence of cost information which distorts reality by failing to provide data which allows sensitive insights to be gained.

5. *Corporate* forces also limit the steps taken owing to a general resistance to include the manufacturing perspective in the corporate strategic development and a reluctance to increase the interaction between marketing and manufacturing. The reason for this trend is based largely on the divisions within management between specialists and executives and the predominance, at different times, of a single function in formulating strategy. The background and perspectives brought to strategy discussions by key managers, therefore, have been too narrowly based. This leads to corporate imbalance in the first instance and insufficient breadth in the second on which to base appropriate revisions. The changed economic circumstances of the late 1970s to mid-1980s has only now forced the corporate hand to arrive at strategy decisions based upon what is best for the business as a whole. This change has been brought about by the increased level of corporate consciousness within the business as a whole. Strategies developed out of a single functional perspective, which were then superficially overlaid by particular perspectives as and when they arose, are rapidly being replaced by genuine corporate debate. However, until that happens, corporate forces will drive out focus and other manufacturing strategy arguments, placing these functional perspectives in their customary reactive position.

Ways forward – halting the drift into unfocused manufacturing

The development of a manufacturing strategy as outlined in Chapter 2 provided one overriding advantage: it offers a meaningful and realistic way for manufacturing to communicate with the rest of the business. By doing this, therefore, it provides the base on which to build thereby creating a positive move to halt the drift into unfocused manufacturing.

The first step is to concentrate management attention and effort on to the core business areas. As a company adjusts to market-place changes, then product lines, customer characteristics, customer preferences and order-winning criteria all change. There must, therefore, be a reference point from which, or around which, to build the corporate strategy. This reference is the existing core of the business in which a company has a clear competitive advantage. Attention by both production and marketing on the core business is essential. However, there are several aspects both general and specific which need to be addressed and these are outlined below.

Overall it is important to use the opportunity created by the strategic development procedure to redress some of the general inhibitors detailed earlier. The development of an appropriate manufacturing strategy will in itself induce a corporate strategy which embodies both the marketing and manufacturing perspective. In so doing it will get both these functions to pull in the same corporate direction by matching production and marketing with the corporate need and measuring the achievement of both against the same corporate yardsticks. Similarly, capital budgeting needs to be couched within the long-term corporate plan and each expenditure measured in terms of the agreed focus. Revisions need also to be made in the accounting system in order to provide data which is more relevant to these decisions and so provides the necessary information on which to base them and to monitor future performance.

Now that some of the important background issues have been attended to, it is time to consider the tasks essential to achieving focused manufacturing. The fundamental purpose behind focus is to establish a plant mission based upon the development of an appropriate manufacturing strategy. In many instances, it will result in a split of existing facilities in terms of both processes and infrastructure and the establishment of plant-within-a-plant configurations. Where these steps are principally to do with refocusing existing plants it is also important for manufacturing to establish and agree an optimum plant size. By doing this, not only will it restrict the task to what is meaningful and manageable, but also it will limit the future potential for focus regression. But, this in itself is not enough. Manufacturing's task is to ensure that focus progression becomes an integral part of their strategic task, and this is facilitated in two ways. The managerial consciousness of the importance and strategic strength derived through focus and an annual programme to give direction to ensure its achievement.

Notes and References

1. Brought to prominence in E. F. Schumacher's book, *Small is Beautiful* (Blond Briggs, 1973).
2. W. Skinner, 'The Focused Factory', *Harvard Business Review*, May–June 1974, pp. 113–21.
3. Skinner, 'The Focused Factory', p. 114.
4. Ibid., p. 118.
5. R. W. Schmenner, 'Every Factory has a Life Cycle', *Harvard Business Review*, Mar–Apr. 1983, p. 123.
6. Skinner, 'The Focused Factory'.
7. R. H. Hayes and S. C. Wheelwright, *Restoring Our Competitive Edge – Competing through Manufacturing* (Wiley, 1984) p. 91.
8. Product and process-focused plants are examined by R. H. Hayes and R. W. Schmenner in their article, 'How Should You Organise Manufacturing?' *Harvard Business Review*, Jan/Feb. 1978, pp. 105–18 and R. J. Mayer and K. U. Agarwal in their article 'Manufacturing Strategy: Key to Industrial Productivity', *Outlook*, Fall/Winter, 1980, pp. 16–21.
9. The company example described in this section together with Figure 4.1 was first detailed in an article by T. J. Hill and R. M. G. Duke-Woolley, 'Progression or Regression in Facilities Focus', *Strategic Management Journal*, vol. 4 (1983) pp. 109–21.
10. This concept was first introduced in Hill and Duke-Woolley, 'Progression or Regression in Facilities Focus', p. 118.
11. The computation of an experience curve is clearly detailed in the Harvard Business School Paper 9–675–228 (Revised 7/75), 'Experience and Cost: Some Implications for Manufacturing Policy'; and in Appendix 8A in Hayes and Wheelwright, *Restoring Our Competitive Edge*.
12. Boston Consulting Group Perspective, 'The Experience Curve Reviewed: V. Price Stability'.
13. Boston Consulting Group, 'Perspectives on Experience' (1972) p. 12.
14. This is also described in 'Perspectives on Experience', pp. 19–22 and Hayes and Wheelwright, *Restoring Our Competitive Edge*, pp. 240–1.

15. This example whilst being one of a number of examples in the 'Perspectives on Experience' was updated in the Boston Consulting Group Perspective 149, 'The Experience Curve – Reviewed: V. Price Stability'.

16. W. J. Abernathy and K. Wayne, 'Limits of the Learning Curve', *Harvard Business Review*, Sept.–Oct. 1974, pp. 109–19.

17. Boston Consulting Group, 'Perspectives on Experience', provides details of volumes and prices (£ constant) for a number of umbrella pricing examples.

18. 'Perspectives on Experience', Exhibits 15, 24, 26, 31 and 33 respectively.

19. D. L. Bodde, 'Riding the Experience Curve', *Technology Review*, Mar.–April 1976, pp. 53–9.

20. J. Macklin, 'Douglas Aircraft's Stormy Flight Path', *Fortune*, Dec. 1966.

21. For a fuller explanation of payment systems and their development refer to Chapter 13 in Terry Hill's book, *Production/Operations Management* (Prentice-Hall International, 1983).

22. R. E. Walton 'How to Counter Alienation in the Plant', *Harvard Business Review*, Nov.–Dec. 1972, pp. 70–81 and 'Work Innovations in the United States', *Harvard Business Review*, July–Aug. 1978, pp. 88–98.

23. These include R. T. Johnson and W. G. Ouchi, 'Made in America (under Japanese Management)', *Harvard Business Review*, Sept.–Oct. 1974, pp. 61–8; W. B. Scott, 'Participative Management at Motorola – the Results', *Management Review*, July 1981, pp. 26–8 and N. Hatvany and Vladimir Pucik, 'Japanese Management: Practices and Productivity', *Organisation Dynamics*, Spring 1981.

24. Texas Instruments Inc., First Quarter and Stockholders' Meeting, 18 April 1973.

25. 'Perspectives on Experience', p. 17.

26. W. J. Abernathy, *The Productivity Dilemma* (Johns Hopkins Press, 1978).

27. Interesting accounts of the Ford Experience are provided in W. J. Abernathy and K. Wayne's article, 'The Limits of the Learning Curve' *Harvard Business Review*, Sept.–Oct. 1974, pp. 109–19; A. P. Sloan Jr, *My Years with General Motors* (Anchor Books, Doubleday (New York), 1972) and Abernathy, *The Productivity Dilemma*.

28. 'Hewlett Packard – Where Slower Growth is Smarter Management', *Business Week*, 9 June 1975.

29. From Hill and Duke-Woolley, 'Progression or Regression in Facilities Focus', p. 117.

30. This example is derived from unpublished data provided by the Boston Consulting Group and is also used in S. C. Wheelwright, Research Paper No 517, 'Facilities Focus: a Study of Concepts and Practices Related to its Definition, Evaluation, Significance and Application in Manufacturing Firms', Stanford University, 12 Dec. 1979.

31. This is from unpublished information provided by the Boston Consulting Group and is also used in Wheelwright, Research Paper No. 517, pp. 14–16 and 21.
32. Hayes and Wheelwright, *Restoring Our Competitive Edge*, p. 113.
33. This is from unpublished data: see ref. 31.
34. Ibid.
35. Ibid.
36. Ibid, p. 22.
37. Wheelwright, Research Paper No. 517, p. 22.
38. Boston Consulting Group and Wheelwright Research Paper No. 517, pp. 14–16, 21.
39. Ibid.

Process Positioning

An important facet of a company's manufacturing strategy concerns the question of 'process positioning'.[1] This comprises the width of a firm's internal span of process, the degree and direction of vertical integration alternatives and its links and relationships at either end of the process spectrum with suppliers, distributors and customers. The process positioning decision, therefore, has major ramifications within the business itself. As an integral part of corporate strategy it can, on the one hand, be crucial to survival as in the Texas Instruments and Bowmar example referred to in the last chapter. On the other hand, however, it can restrict a company's ability to change direction in the future due to the investment involved in earlier integration moves, often justified on the short-term rationale of profit return.[2]

5.1 Reasons for Choosing Alternative Strategic Positions

Although in theory, every item is a candidate to be made or bought, in reality the choice is far more restricted. Many businesses, however, when taking stock find that rarely has their current position been arrived at as part of some strategically based set of arguments over time. A review of current process positioning will often reveal a number of reasons which have persuaded a company to change its process position or which have contributed to its current stance. Some of the reasons are now outlined. They have been chosen to reflect not only important factors but also to illustrate the different levels of corporate awareness involved.

Core elements of the business

Most companies choose to keep in-house those processes which represent the core elements of their business. For instance, in the situation where a company manufactures its own finished items then it will invariably retain the assembly onwards end of the production process. The reasons include the wish to retain product identity within its own immediate control, design security, to enable it to exercise final product quality and to provide control over the penultimate link with its customers.

Strategic considerations

Ideally process positioning is chosen in response to the strategic requirements of the business. This decision will include a manufacturing strategy input concerning aspects such as lower cost and improved control. It will also take into account non-manufacturing arguments concerning the market-place and the competitive conditions in which a business operates.

Span of process and product technology

Often, a significant increase in product technology can lead to a corresponding decrease in the internal span of process. This arises where a company applies technology changes to its existing products or on the introduction of new or similar products within its range. Not having the process capability in-house to meet all of the new and more complex product technology requirements, it takes the practical step of buying-in the technology in the form of components. Normally, this narrowing takes place in the earlier stages of the process where the new technology developments are the most radical, the later stages of the process being kept in-house. This is due to the fact that the technology associated with these later processes is more in line with existing manufacturing expertise and is closer to the final product itself. Figure 5.1

FIGURE 5.1

To illustrate (not to scale) the reduction in span of process with increases in the technology of the product

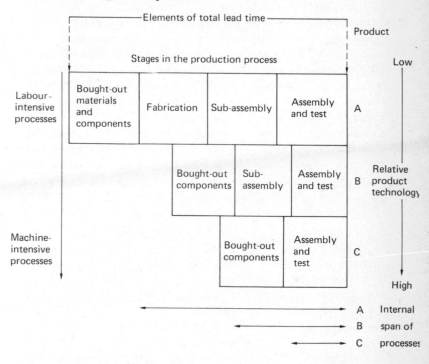

Source: T. J. Hill and R. M. G. Duke-Woolley, 'Progression or Regression in Facilities Focus'.[3] With permission.

provides an example of this in the strategy adopted by the telecommunications company referred to in Chapter 4 (Table 4.2). When the company only produced Product A, it had developed the in-house processes necessary to complete most of the manufacturing involved. However, the advent of Product B and later Product C heralded a distinct product technology change from mechanical (Product A) to electro-mechanical (Product B) and electronic (Product C). Not having the manufacturing process capability to provide these new requirements, the company bought them in from outside in the form of components. The narrowing of the internal span of processes which resulted is shown in Figure 5.1.

In these situations, the decision on when and by how much to widen the span of process after the initial narrowing is a significant strategic issue, whereas in practice it is often treated as an operational decision. The example in the last chapter concerning hand-held calculator manufacturers provided an example of how Bowmar, one-time market leader, failed to successfully integrate backwards into integrated circuit production and eventually withdrew from the business. Whereas Texas Instruments (TI) successfully integrating forward into calculators, took over the market leadership. One major reason for TI eventually displacing Bowmar was that its comparative process position gave it more opportunity to reduce costs and exploit the potential experience curve gains. And that is what it did. Bowmar, restricted to assembly cost gains, was limited by its suppliers' price reductions for a large part of its costs. TI, on the other hand, had no such limitations. In a related example, *Business Week* in 1974[4] provided a survey within the calculator market. Part of this concerned the stated strategy of Commodore at this time; one which was to change within a couple of years. It quotes Commodore's President arguing that backward integration was neither necessary nor desirable. To retain the ability to get into and out of a technology as and when necessary was considered by Commodore to be well worth the higher component costs associated with this strategy. However, in 1976 Commodore's purchase of MOS Technology, an ailing manufacturer of calculator chips 'is sometimes credited with Commodore's later success in small computers'.[5]

Product volumes

Where companies are faced with the different tasks involved with manufacturing high and low volumes the strategic decision of adopting a plant-within-a-plant alternative has already been reviewed in Chapter 4. A company may also consider buying out those products with a low-volume demand, for instance, which would, in turn, normally lead to a narrowing of the internal span of process. An example of this decision involved a manufacturer of engine parts for agricultural and diesel trucks. When the low-volume spares demand was reached in a product's life cycle, the company increasingly subcontracted component manufacturing where the machining processes involved were only used on operations for components for that product or products with similar low volumes. In that way it reduced its span of processes and kept the manufacturing task within agreed bounds.

Yesterday's strategies

It is not unusual for companies' process positions today to be a direct result, at least in part, of yesterday's strategic decisions. Reduction in product life cycles, changes in product and process technology development and an acceleration in world-wide competition over the last fifteen years have all contributed to companies taking their eye off the ball. Unless periodic revision is made of this important strategic area, the impact on costs and manufacturing complexity will go unnoticed until a radical overhaul is necessitated. The damage meanwhile, especially in times of accelerating change, can be irrepairable.

Shedding difficult manufacturing tasks

In the UK and USA over recent years the trend involving corporate responses to difficult manufacturing tasks has been to shed them by subcontracting or divestment. The area of concern is that many companies approach this decision with an eye more on the difficulties embodied in the task rather than the strategic consequences of the make or buy decision they are about to take. Short-term gains taken on their own look most attractive. However, the accompanying loss of skill and essential manufacturing know-how and infrastructure may limit a company's ability to respond in the future. A maxim to bear in mind is that if the manufacturing task is easy, then any company can do it! The key to manufacturing success, therefore, is resolving the difficult manufacturing issues, for this is where high profits are to be made.

5.3   Issues Involved in Process Position Changes

While in the past, process position changes have principally been associated with the widening of a company's initial span of process, more recently the decision to reduce process spans has been a necessary option to be considered by many businesses. Faced with a decline in demand and the associated reduction in capacity requirements, companies have, possibly for the first time in their recent histories, been confronted with the necessity to decrease parts of their span of processes and often on many major business fronts.

However, when repositioning whether for growth or contraction, it is essential for a business to fully assess the issues involved. Particular attention needs to be given to ensure that the real costs and investments in both process and infrastructure have been fully assessed on the one hand, and will be achievable on the other. Additional, quite sizeable, investments are often incurred after the event which, although not included in the original decision, form an integral part of securing the benefits of the original undertaking. In the same way, cost and investment reductions assumed to accrue from divestment may well not be achieved when anticipated, and sometimes not at all. An illustration which typifies this concerns the support functions within a firm's overhead structure. Often, the extent of overhead support necessary to effectively sustain the new process investment and/or growth into new products is understated whilst the anticipated reduction in overheads associated with a narrowing of a firm's internal span of process is generally overestimated.

It is also necessary to separate the issues involved in these decisions between those which essentially support strategy and those which do not. To ensure that span of process decisions are consistent with key corporate objectives (or if not, are recognised as not being consistent) is an important management task. Decisions can all too often be taken without this appropriate level of clarity. This differentiation of issues provides the opportunity to review these critical manufacturing decisions in the light of relevant corporate strategy considerations, by allowing comparisons between options to be made on the basis of appropriate information. Separating the strategic arguments into their functional derivatives will add further clarity to the corporate understanding of the basis on which these important manufacturing decisions need to be addressed.

Recognising that particular issues will differ from one case to another and that the level of importance of issues will vary, some of the more important advantages and disadvantages are listed here. How effectively a business is able to achieve the mix of benefits and risks involved and yet offset costs wherever possible depends upon a functionally capable and alert management team together with the level of understanding and agreement they have reached on the strategic issues involved.

Costs and investments

One of the fundamental sets of trade-offs involved in span of process decisions concerns costs and investments. The level of investment will determine the width of process internal to the business and in so doing will have a direct bearing on the levels of cost involved. (The link between span of process and experience curves was discussed in Chapter 4.) The principal areas of cost associated with span of process decisions are:

- Transaction costs concerned with the buying, selling and physical handling activities involved in the supply of materials throughout the relevant processes.
- The costs associated with improving the co-ordination between the supply, production and distribution activities.
- The combination of similar overhead activities is afforded where firms widen their span of process. However, where centralised activities exist, it is really difficult to achieve the apparent overhead gains where internal span of process is narrowed. In these situations, companies need to be aware that unless the *vertical slicing* into those overheads attributable to a proposed reduction in span are in fact achievable then the cost rationale for this decision will need to be reassessed (see Figure 5.2).
- The investment linked to span-of-process changes not only involves the hardware but also the controls, procedures and other relevant infrastructure requirements. Although the tangible costs of plant and equipment are both readily identified and at least in principle agreed to, the costs resulting from changes in the less tangible areas are not as apparent and do not lend themselves to be as easily quantified. In turn, they become the decisions which are subject to judgement, often have to bear the brunt of close vetting, and invariably become the areas where projected costs are cut on the assumption, or based on the argument, that the existing infrastructure can or will have to cope.

In situations of process widening, many companies neither clearly identify all the investment and associated requirements involved, nor hold a shared view of the strategic relevance of the proposed span-of-process changes. Invariably in these circumstances, sufficient allowances will not have been provided or the necessary allocations will be squeezed out of the proposals as a result of the apparent conscientiousness of those involved. The outcome will be an under-estimate of the

FIGURE 5.2

A diagram to illustrate the corresponding overhead support to the process under review which will form part of the corporate decision on process narrowing – known as *vertical slicing*

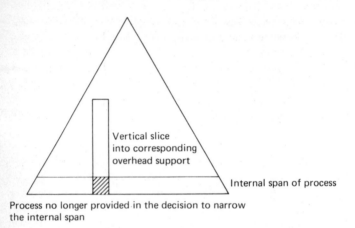

Vertical slice
into corresponding
overhead support

Internal span of process

Process no longer provided in the decision to narrow
the internal span

investment needs in the short-term which will normally result in a number of further investments in the future. The final tally will sometimes be well in excess of that on which the initial strategic decision was based.

Two further important ramifications of widening the internal span of process concern a company's ability to adopt different options. On the one hand, the capital used up in these moves prevents its use elsewhere. On the other hand, the implied commitment to a market and the product and process technologies and life cycles involved can verge on the highly risky. The inherent inflexibility which is accumulated in these strategies may result in a sluggish response to change, high levels of unplanned capital expenditure and often sizeable write-offs.

Strategic considerations

Although decisions on process repositioning usually embody their own set of specific strategic considerations, there are some important general considerations which help form the basis for strategic action.

- *High entry barriers.* In industries where a wide span of process brings with it a set of distinct advantages, then increasing the internal span will raise the financial and managerial resources required to enter and compete effectively with existing businesses. Established companies may, therefore, raise the stakes thus discouraging new entrants.
- *Supply assurance.* The supply of critical materials may well be of such importance to a company, that this gain alone will be the basis for the investment involved. However, as with all forms of backward integration, the issue of whether or not a company aims to keep the supply capacity solely in balance with its internal needs raises its own set of advantages and disadvantages.
- *Secured outlets.* In the same way as supply can be assured by integrating backwards, securing outlets can result from integrating forwards. Additional advantages also accrue with this move from improved feedback which leads to the position of being more aware of demand changes and provides the opportunity to increase the accuracy of forecasts.

The managerial task

Changes in span of process will invariably lead to a change in the total management task within the business. These come under three broad headings:

- *The level of complexity.* One important consequence which invariably comes from a widening of process span is the increase in complexity and the hidden costs associated with these incremental uplifts. The associations of synergy are probably more apparent in the level of complexity than elsewhere. Here, one and one really are greater than two.
- *The question of balance.* When companies increase their span of process they face the questions of the trade-offs involved between whether or not to keep the supply or outlet in balance with the rest of the business. A large group of manufacturing companies, deciding on a policy of expansion, asked the individual companies involved to put forward proposals relevant to their own business. One such company, a cable-maker, put forward a proposed strategy of integrating backwards into wire-drawing. In order to limit the investment involved it purchased a local site and installed capacity roughly

in line with its own needs. With the high price of copper, neither part of the business wanted high material inventory. As a consequence, the production runs on which the drawn wire cost structure had been based and which also sustained the investment rationale could not be maintained. This was due to the programme changes necessary to meet cable sales and the low inventory planned for in the overall investment. As one part of the business was not adequately decoupled from the next, even shorter runs and overtime working in the wire-drawing plant could not prevent cable delivery dates being missed. Eventually, issues of capacity balance and decoupling inventory levels had to be re-examined.

- *The manufacturing task.* Span of process changes bring corresponding changes in the manufacturing management task. The cable-making/wire-drawing example had one further important rider. The management team assumed that their knowledge of cable-making together with existing internal organisational and control systems would be sufficient to anticipate likely difficulties and to cope with any that were unforeseen in the processes involved in drawing wire. They under-estimated the change in the manufacturing management task which partly contributed to the wire-drawing unit's failure to break-even in the first twenty months let alone meet the projected return on investment.

The traditional argument for ownership has been based, at least in part, on the economies of large scale. In the last two or three decades this argument has been a major thrust within existing accounting perspectives. Based on inadequate analysis of what the new reality would bring, the economies of large scale rationale has often been the principal distorting factor in these critical decisions. In many companies the impact has been further disguised by the build-up of complexity associated with incremental process widening. In most situations, it is not the technology considerations but the control and other infrastructure features of the manufacturing task which are affected.

5.3 Alternatives to Widening Internal Span of Process

The discussion so far has implied that the choices to be made also presented an ownership or non-ownership option. Either a company invested in the process through ownership or it bought out its requirements from suppliers. Many companies, faced with what they perceive to be as only two viable options, would consider that, in many situations, they had, in fact, Hobson's choice.* Being reliant on suppliers was not considered a feasible alternative.

Given this background and where greater 'control' is considered necessary alternatives to widening the internal span of process need to receive serious consideration by manufacturing companies. To help in the assessment of whether the preferred decision should be by investment or not, it is essential to separate strategic from tactical issues and also to trace the strategic arguments to their functional source. Only in this way will a business be able to clearly establish whether or not a decision has to be through investment ownership.

The two principal alternatives are based upon an appropriately high degree of liaison between those involved. The first of these is based upon a legal agreement or arrangement of some kind. The second springs from the recognition that it is in the best interests of all concerned to generate mutually beneficial links in order to exploit the combined opportunity.

Joint ventures and long-term contracts

Companies can often find themselves needing to exploit opportunities particularly in areas such as applied technology and research. Where there exists a similar need in another company and mutual benefits from joining together exist, then joint ventures suit both parties' needs. In this way, not only is the investment shared but, often more importantly, a direction for these activities is created. Identifying the areas in which to focus attention and with the knowledge that the developments will have a commercial outlet can give substance to this decision. Reducing risk in this way, whilst also limiting the investments required to bring the activity to fruition is an ideal solution. Joint venture arrangements provide this mix and hence provide a sensible alternative to the owner/non-owner options.

Where technologies have already been established, many companies prefer to arrange long-term contracts with suppliers. For both parties involved, such an agreement provides added predictability and increased

---

*Thomas Hobson, a Cambridge carrier, had a policy of letting out his horses in rotation, without allowing his customers to choose among them. Hence, they had to take or leave the one on offer.

assurance which helps when establishing long-term plans. The key trade-offs here are between flexibility (both in terms of volume commitment and sourcing) and the classical set of gains to do with price and delivery. In this way, a customer can enhance the commitment of suppliers to meeting its needs and requirements whilst providing increased stability for the supplier itself.

Customer/vendor relations

Traditionally, UK and US companies have restricted themselves to either an owner or non-owner position. Furthermore, the prevailing attitude towards suppliers has been to exercise the more extreme positions within the two alternatives. At the non-owner end, companies choose to exercise the arms-length, free market philosophy towards their suppliers. The consequence is that customer/supplier relationships are based upon short-term agreements which are invariably multi-sourced. In this way, added leverage is gained by playing one supplier off against another as part of the drive to achieve better terms especially concerning price.

This perceived need, especially by larger companies, *to control their own destiny* by either ownership or retaining the power over supplies through multiple sourcing, characterises the current view of how best to manage these relationships. The 'you need us more than we need you' syndrome is employed by many companies as a way to threaten their suppliers. Typical of this approach is that displayed by the UK motor manufacturers towards the automotive component industry. Ford's review of the Japanese threat referred to in Chapter 1 illustrates the classic position. Faced with the realities of tough foreign competition, Ford's message to its suppliers, through a series of presentations, was to show them what they had to achieve in order to make Ford and hence their own businesses viable. The one aspect that was not mentioned is a most critical ingredient to Japanese companies' success: the customer/supplier relationships engendered by the Japanese motor manufacturer. Throughout the 1980s the picture has been the same, culminating in mid-1984 when British Leyland invited suppliers and would-be suppliers to discuss the future. The venue amongst other things housed displays of bought-out components and the underlying message was clear: the complete range of bought-out parts was open to all-comers.

How to assess which alternative is the better needs to be based on the view of what constitutes the business. The apparent misconception which separates the two approaches is that the Western European and American truck and automobile companies consider that the competition is between car makers, whilst the Japanese realise that it is a car maker and its suppliers versus another car maker and its suppliers (see Table 5.1).

TABLE 5.1
The role of customer/supplier relations in a company's competitive stance

The company's country of origin	The perceived base used for competitive analysis		
West European and USA	Car maker	versus	Car maker
Japan	Car maker and its suppliers	versus	Car maker and its suppliers

---

Significantly out-performed, many companies are highlighting areas where comparative supplier performance is low. But it appears that they often fail to differentiate between symptoms and causes or to appreciate that these results emanate from a comprehensive approach in which all parts are needed to make a successful whole.

These approaches, however, are in many ways much more difficult to manage than those based on the relatively simple premise of power or legal agreement. Ownership, open market strategies or contractual arrangements all provide a power base for the customer. Losing their power base presents a much more demanding task. Japanese companies, however, tend to look upon their key suppliers as partners in a joint venture. While this is not based upon a legal agreement, it is constituted on the shared understanding that it is a long-term relationship, to the benefit of both parties. Furthermore, it is not limited to a prescribed set of issues as is often the case in joint ventures and invariably so in long-term contractual arrangements. For this to work it requires three important conditions to be made:

1. It is necessary that both organisations have a shared understanding of the long-term nature of what constitutes a mutually beneficial

relationship. This does not, however, imply that the customer/ supplier relationships are not rigorous. The essential characteristic which underlies this liaison is that their fortunes are interlinked. The Japanese capture the essence of this by using the term 'co-destiny'. But to make this happen requires two other important conditions.

2. As both customers and suppliers are interlinked and as such form part of the same business they must each achieve the level and nature of the commitments involved. At the operational end of the business the elements of quality, delivery and price must be met by the supplier in line with the customer's agreed needs. Similarly, the customer must fulfil the scheduling, payment and volume agreements on which the suppliers have based their commitment.

3. Finally, it is essential for a company to recognise that not only is the quality of purchased materials and components rooted in the processes of its suppliers but also, the basis for cost reduction. To design components without an understanding of the process capabilities of its suppliers is a common approach in UK and US manufacturing industries. To trade with a supplier and yet not systematically discuss how best to make changes for the common business good of both parties is difficult to explain away. An example comparing two approaches serves to highlight the differences involved. The procedure by which Ford and British Leyland will incorporate changes to components or assemblies is time consuming (normally several years) and provides little incentive to suppliers. However, the Boston Consulting Group's report on the British motor cycle industry exemplified a basic difference when it summarised the approach adopted by a Japanese producer.

Honda in 1974 informed some parts suppliers that it did not want a parts' price increase for the next five years. Having stipulated this, however, Honda is now currently working closely with the suppliers to help them rationalise and modify parts designs. Honda is also suggesting new production methods and technology to the suppliers.[6]

The essential difference, therefore, springs from the approach used by these organisations in encouraging and facilitating its suppliers to help satisfy its own requirements and strengthen its own competitive position. In the UK examples price reductions are limited or even reduced by the leverage exercised by a customer. In this way the contributions to the necessary drive on costs are isolated to those basically provided by the supplier itself. Honda, on the other hand, widened the contributions towards keeping prices low from a supplier-only position to one which included not only its own contributions, but also the joint contributions arising from the customer–supplier relationship it had forged.

Just-in-time production

Although dealt with more extensively in the next chapter, the just-in-time (JIT) production concept is an essential facet of the management of some Japanese manufacturing and productivity improvement. JIT is based on a simple principle. The idea is for all materials to be active in the process at all times thereby avoiding situations of cost without appropriate benefit. The concept is neatly summarised by Schonberger as the aim to 'produce and deliver finished goods just in time to be sold, sub-assemblies just in time to be assembled into finished goods, fabricated parts just in time to go into sub-assemblies, and purchased materials just in time to be transformed into fabricated parts'.[7] However, for this to work efficiently requires effective co-operation and co-ordination between the various parts of the process. Where these are not owned, then only sound supplier/customer relations will enable this to work. The gains, however, are considerable. Toyota can point to an inventory turnover of 70 times on purchased parts and work-in-progress and 16 times if finished goods inventory is included.[8]

5.4 Conclusion

The different factors which motivate companies to change their span of process need to be carefully assessed. In the past, and carried on the winds of growth, many companies repositioned their point on the process span as a matter of course. Often born out of the belief that the company could manufacture anything, decisions to widen process span were taken without adequate understanding of their strategic fit and the tactical consequences involved. In times where decisions to narrow process span need to be addressed, a similar strategic and tactical analysis needs to be completed.

With this to provide the basis for assessing the true extent of the process and infrastructure investments to be made, a company is now able to establish the key points on which to make its decision. In this way, it will be able to consider the benefits to be gained from the proposed repositioning whilst clearly taking into account the trade-offs involved between the alternatives. Besides the strategic issues involved, span of process repositioning will enmesh a firm in a series of organisational issues that will require a careful reappraisal of its infrastructure. The extent of the change will itself establish the level of change involved. Increasingly, however, companies are becoming aware of the fact that single systems are inadequate to meet the varying needs of manufacturing functions. Changes in markets and their impact on the manufacturing task were the subject of Chapter 2. In the same way, span of process changes will make a significant impact on manufacturing.

The key manufacturing issues are, therefore, related to the size and nature of the manufacturing activity. Many UK industrial firms are faced with increased problems in terms of manufacturing control. For most, the response is to spend money on solving the control problem. Few start with the appropriate step of deciding what should or should not be retained as an integral part of an appropriate manufacturing strategy. Determining the size of the manufacturing task, therefore, is the necessary first step. This needs to be completed before investing in the manufacturing infrastructure to ensure that the time and money spent is both necessary and appropriate to the key manufacturing aspects involved.

Notes and References

1. First used by R. H. Hayes and S. C. Wheelwright in their book, *Restoring Our Competitive Edge: Competing Through Manufacturing* (Wiley, 1984) p. 275.
2. R. H. Hayes and J. Abernathy, 'Managing Our Way to Economic Decline', *Harvard Business Review*, July–Aug 1980, pp. 67–77.
3. From T. J. Hill and R. M. G. Duke-Woolley, 'Progression or Regression in Facilities Focus', *Strategic Management Journal*, vol. 7, pp. 109–21 (1983).
4. 'Why They're Integrating into Integrated Circuits', *Business Week*, 28 Sept. 1974, p. 55.
5. Hayes and Wheelwright, *Restoring Our Competitive Edge*, p. 291.
6. 'Strategic Alternatives for the British Motor Cycle Industry', A report prepared for the Secretary of State for Industry by the Boston Consulting Group (HMSO, July 1987) p.34.
7. R. J. Schonberger, *Japanese Manufacturing Techniques: Nine Hidden Lessons in Simplicity*, New York: (Free Press, 1982) p. 16.

8. Taken from G. O'Donnell, 'How Australian Industry Points the Way on Kanban', *Production Engineer*, July–Aug. 1984, pp. 19 and 20.

Further Reading

Armour, T. J. and Teece, D. J., 'Vertical Integration and Technological Innovation', *The Review of Economics and Statistics*, vol. 62, no. 3, Aug. 1982, pp. 470–4.

Arrow, K. J., 'Vertical Integration and Communications', *Bell Journal of Economics*, vol. 6, no. 1, Spring 1975, pp. 173–82.

Blois, K.J.,'Vertical Quasi-integration', *Journal of Industrial Economics*, July 1972, pp. 253–72.

Buzzell, R. D., 'Is Vertical Integration Profitable?' *Harvard Business Review*, Jan–Feb. 1983, pp. 92–102. Offers an analysis based on the PIMS (profit impact of market strategies) data to assess a number of relationships including vertical integration and profitability; vertical integration, investment intensity and return on investments and vertical integration, relative market share and profitability.

Gale, B. T., 'Can More Capital Buy Higher Producitivty?' *Harvard Business Review*, July–Aug. 1980, pp. 78–90.

Kraljic, P., 'Purchasing Must Become Supply Management', *Harvard Business Review*, Sept.–Oct. 1983, pp. 109–17.

Porter, M. E., *Competitive Analysis* (New York: Free Press, 1980) ch. 14, provides an extensive discussion of the potential benefits and limitations of vertical integration.

Schmalensee, R., 'A Note on the Theory of Vertical Integration', *Journal of Political Economy*, Mar.–Apr. 1973, pp. 442–9.

Williamson, O. E., 'The Vertical Integration of Production: Market Failure Considerations', *American Economic Review*, vol. 61, no. 2, May 1971, pp. 112–23.

Manufacturing Infrastructure Development

The need for a business to resolve the issues of process choice in line with the manufacturing strategy requirement has been paramount in the book so far. This emphasis is owing to the fact that it is necessary to clearly understand which manufacturing processes can best meet the needs of the market-place or how well existing processes provide the order-winning criteria for each product family. However, the task facing manufacturing is not a simple one based upon the choice and workings of the hardware dimension. When this has been analysed and the trade-offs reconciled the emphasis shifts. It now becomes equally important to ensure that the structure and composition of the component parts or functions which provide the necessary systems and communications within a manufacturing company are also developed in line with the manufacturing strategy requirement. Process choice concerns the features of hardware, the tangible ways in which the products are manufactured. But the task is more than this. The supporting structures, controls, procedures and other systems within manufacturing are equally necessary to successful, competitive manufacturing performance.

These structures, controls, procedures and other systems are collectively known as the *manufacturing infrastructure*. It comprises the inner structure of manufacturing including the controls, procedures, systems and communications combined with the attitudes, experience and skills of the people involved. Together they form the basis of the manufacturing organisation charged with the task of providing the necessary support functions to the areas of responsibility involved.

Without the appropriate processes, mismatches will result similar to those reflected by the dog-leg type analyses shown in Table 3.2. They lead to an essential conflict between what the business needs and what manufacturing can best provide. Although the provision of appropriate manufacturing infrastructure will help minimise this fundamental difference if will not resolve it. However, a hardware fit on its own is also not enough. Without the appropriate infrastructure, effective links will not be provided between manufacturing and marketing strategies and between manufacturing and the support systems within a business. Furthermore, this will usually lead to a situation where the basis for future development to meet the dynamic properties of a business will not be forthcoming. The result, at best, is a manufacturing organisation becoming increasingly out of line with a changing business. The static nature implied by, and the inertia sometimes created by these conditions leads to situations where those responsible for the realignment of the essential components of manufacturing infrastructure are unaware of or unable to respond to the growing need to make the necessary and appropriate changes. One underlying message in Peters and Waterman's *In Search of Excellence*[1] was that the essence of success depended much on the awareness factor. Building the infrastructure on a manufacturing strategy base does just this. It gives appropriate direction and allows appropriate choice between alternative sets of trade-offs to be made. The company then has a shared awareness of what is required in manufacturing if it is to best support the current and future need of the business. A commonly held recognition of the necessity to link manufacturing through its process hardware and organisational software to the market-place is thus established. Showing them together and inexorably linking them together (see Figure 6.1) binds the prerequisites of manufacturing strategy to give them both coherence and synergistic purpose.

The infrastructure, therefore, represents part of the complexity inherent in manufacturing. If it is to effectively support manufacturing then it is necessary to get into the complexity within this part of the infrastructure of a business in order to understand and then develop it appropriately. This comprises two important dimensions. The first highlights the need to address the issues of how the company is structured internally and why it has evolved that way. The second concerns

FIGURE 6.1
The inexorable link between the components of manufacturing strategy with each other and with the business needs

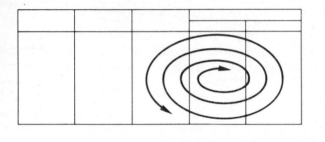

recognising some of the key perspectives to be taken into account when developing the important areas which comprise infrastructure.

By themselves, most elements of infrastructure do not require the same level of investment nor do they have the same impact on manufacturing's strategic role as does process choice. But, taken collectively they do. Together their importance in providing the strategic support for the business cannot be overstressed. Similarly, the difficulties experienced through the interaction of inappropriate systems and the costs involved in effecting major changes can be of the same order of magnitude as those decisions involving manufacturing hardware. Transforming over time the support for the market-place into an appropriate collection of facilities, structures, controls, procedures, and people comprises the manufacturing strategy task. Hayes and Wheelwright conclude that

> **it is this pattern of structural [*process*] and infrastructural decisions that constitutes the 'manufacturing strategy' of a business unit. More formally, a manufacturing strategy consists of a sequence of decisions that, over time, enables a business unit to achieve a desired manufacturing structure [*process choice*], infrastructure, and set of specific capabilities[2]**

In relation to corporate strategy they recognise that 'the primary function of a manufacturing strategy is to guide the business in putting together the set of manufacturing capabilities that will enable it to pursue its chosen competive strategy over the long term'.[3]

6.1 Manufacturing Infrastructure Issues

Manufacturing infrastructure comprises a complex set of interacting factors. Companies in Western economies have traditionally coped with this by breaking the infrastructure into appropriate sets of responsibilities or functions and deploying people to provide the necessary support. For this to work effectively it requires a high degree of co-ordination linked to manufacturing's strategic tasks. However, the reality does not bear out the theory. The way it tends to work is that these parts or functions are managed separately and come together primarily at the tactical or operational interface. Typically, developments within infrastructure are given the level of detailed attention they require at the points of application. It is at these levels where meaningful, in-depth discussion takes place, no doubt stimulated by the real need to make the particular area of infrastructure development work effectively. However, the merits of the individual parts and how they fit together are rarely encompassed by any strategic overview. For this reason, piecemeal developments, propounded in the main by specialists, lead to an unco-ordinated approach to infrastructure design.

The essential requirement is for the basic parts of the organisational framework to reinforce and support the manufacturing task. This enables the company to get away from functionally based arguments and perspectives in terms of what is appropriate and important. The only way to achieve this is to concentrate on the business: to replace functional argument by the corporate resolution between alternatives; to replace unilaterally stimulated argument of what is best for the business, by corporate based argument of what is best for the business. This then provides a base on which to develop a comprehensive, co-ordinated and directed infrastructure to meet the firm's current and future needs. It not only enables a company to get its orientation right but will also enable it to avoid being saddled, in organisational terms, with the existence of functions which are no longer required or are inappropriately weighted when related to the business needs. Changing the *status quo* is difficult unless the firm knows why and how it wants or has to change. Only then is it able to move from subjectively based to objectively based analyses and decisions. In business terms this requires a very clear statement of what constitutes the manufacturing task – the manufacturing strategy appropriate to the company. Once this is understood and appreciated by the functional managers, a company can take the *status quo* and reshuffle it. It is then in a position to avoid situations where vested interests argue for the retention or growth in capabilities/capacities for their own sake rather than for their relative contribution to the current and future success of a business.

Questions which stem from these views concern the reasons why functions hold on to their current level of size and why they argue for their own retention and growth. In many instances they do so because it is the best perspective they have. Only when a business orientates functions towards the outside (i.e. what the market requires) can it provide the opportunity for alternatives to be measured against corporate related criteria. It is the provision of a common, relevant base which enables functional arguments to be put into perspective. It shifts the evaluation of proposals from the use of subjective to objective criteria. It gives appropriate direction to which all infrastructure development must aspire, whilst also providing the detailed checklists against which developments can be evaluated. In this way it ensures that it is the manufacturing strategy requirement rather than a functional or specialist perspective which will be met by these costly developments. Furthermore, by looking outward and forward, developments will be made with a knowing eye on future competition and thus become more likely to incorporate the manufacturing needs of tomorrow.

In this way, the functions which are charged with making effective infrastructure provision are given strategic direction. Without this, there is the real possibility that specialist support functions will pursue their own point of view, an underlying problem which many businesses experience today. Firms need the function and specialist capabilities to make sense of the complexity. Without these inputs firms cannot reach the level of effectiveness necessary to meet today's competitive pressures. However, the difference between providing an infrastructure based upon a number of specialist views and one which is co-ordinated to meet the needs of a business by an appropriate strategy is significant for most firms and critical for many.

The review and incremental development of infrastructures within the strategic context of manufacturing is equally important – it concerns altering the balance or changing the focus of development so that it is in line with the manufacturing task and hence forms an integral part of manufacturing strategy. A firm's ability to back-track on its decisions is also at times important. This activity, however, is often thwarted by the difficulties presented by specialists, highly analytical people capable of arguing their case with great clarity and strength protecting their own views and areas of responsibility in a vacuum. Again, the existence of a manufacturing strategy provides the parameters for analysis and debate to either reconcile arguments or views or redirect development work.

6.2 Infrastructure Development

Strategy comprises the development and declaration of a shared view of business direction. Therefore, unless a business regularly and frequently updates its strategy not only will change go unnoticed, but the individual interpretations of strategy will become fact rather than the strategy statement itself. In both instances, fragmentation will occur and the necessary cohesion will diminish.

Approaching the successful development of infrastructure must also be done with care. Many companies have adopted a piecemeal approach by resolving one facet at a time, as often stimulated by the apparent need of the moment as by a carefully selected priority. Picking off one area makes sense as a way of coping with the complexity involved. However, many organisations even in these situations do not undertake the essential analyses which must precede and then determine the area for development. This preliminary analysis need not become a complex debate; Figure 6.2 points to the essential issues – the need to determine the process position and to define the size of the manufacturing units. Thus, rather than investing money, time and effort in resolving the current complexity, a company should define the level of complexity it wishes to handle. Only then is it able to decide how best to manage the chosen level, and only then is it able to resolve the infrastructure appropriate to its needs. For, once a company understands both its manufacturing task and organisationally what it needs to be (its *organisational profile*), the direction and content of any infrastructure development will then be clear and comprehensible.

However, what many companies have done in the past is to pursue the economies of large scale without fully evaluating the net gains involved. A classic approach to achieving these apparent gains has some-

FIGURE 6.2
The need for a company to develop the level of manufacturing complexity involved before it attempts to approach its infrastructure development, as part of the manufacturing strategy approach

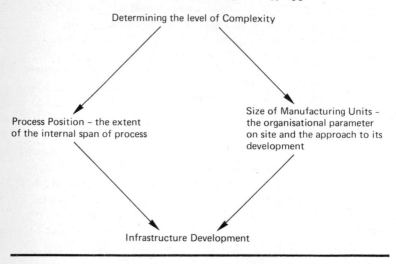

Determining the level of Complexity

Process Position – the extent
of the internal span of process

Size of Manufacturing Units –
the organisational parameter
on site and the approach to its
development

Infrastructure Development

times been to centralise both at corporate and plant levels. This had led to centralised functions being created throughout the organisation. Uppermost among the counter-arguments is the increased complexity involved in large organisations and the difficulties of reshaping them in times of change. In many instances, the anticipated gains of centralised functions have proved to be an organisational El Dorado.

The theme of the chapter so far has been to emphasise the importance of appropriately developing manufacturing infrastructure and stressing its significant contribution to providing the necessary manufacturing support to the market-place. However, before discussing some of the key areas of infrastructure design, it will be worthwhile to highlight three practical, but general considerations.

1. It is most important to determine and agree the important areas of infrastructure within manufacturing. The need to adopt a discretionary approach to change is essential in order to utilise scarce developmental resources in line with those areas which will yield the

best returns. Emanating from the concept of the 80/20 rule* this point emphasises the fact that the approach to change must reflect those areas which will have the most strategic impact.

2. As with process choice, it is necessary to establish and then choose between the sets of trade-offs which go hand-in-hand with each decision. The criteria, however, against which to measure the trade-offs must be concerned with manufacturing's strategic role.
3. The essence of sound infrastructure design is that it must respond to the dynamics of reality. To do this requires recognition that there are areas of incremental and major change, but that much of the necessary change can be achieved incrementally. Once this distinction has been drawn, it is essential that areas of manufacturing infrastructure are reviewed on a regular basis in order to effect the necessary developments including the simplification and even withdrawal of controls, systems and procedures. It is most important, on the other hand, to avoid wherever possible the need for major change. In many cases where major change is required it reflects the degree of mismatch between need and provision which has developed incrementally over time within the relevant area of infrastructure, and indicates the size and length of disruption which will take place to put things right.

6.3 Important Infrastructure Issues

A company which fails to develop its infrastructure as part of its response to meeting the needs of its market-place is likely to experience two separate but linked consequences:

1. A worsening business position, because amongst other things, the systems and controls will fail to give executives the accurate and timely indicators necessary to help them to manage the business and initiate the necessary developments as required.
2. The key components of infrastructure necessary to help reshape or rebuild the business may not be in place at the time when they are most necessary and most urgently required.

*The 80/20 rule reflects the implied relationship between two sets of data or consequences. In this instance, it illustrates the fact that 80 per cent of the total strategic benefit to be gained from infrastructure development will arise from 20 per cent of the areas of application. The use of the figures 80 and 20, however, are illustrative of the relationship implied in the selected phenomenon and not intended to be definitive.

The approach to developing the separate parts of a manufacturing company's infrastructure involves two integrated steps. The first is determining the market-place or competitive requirements; that is, the way in which products win orders needs to be the factor around which each aspect of infrastructure is built; the controls, systems, procedures, attitudes and skills involved will then be orientated towards those manufacturing tasks which are pertinent to the different products in terms of their relevant order-winning criteria. The second is the need to ensure that the necessary level of coherence and co-ordination exists in the various but related parts of manufacturing infrastructure. In this way, not only does the software pull in the same, appropriate, corporate direction but the company releases the synergy inherent in this substantial investment.

Those involved also recognise the symptoms of coherent direction and feel the facilitating and motivating benefits which occur as a consequence.

Selecting for specific discussion those infrastructure issues from the many which could warrant attention has not been easy. Although the factors of relevance and importance have been paramount in this procedure, there is embodied in that evaluation more than a small slice of subjective opinion. However, in many ways that factor is not so important here, because relevance will change between businesses, and the examples themselves are primarily being provided to explain the principles of infrastructure design and development, rather than as a comprehensive statement on manufacturing infrastructure.

The areas discussed in the rest of the chapter concern a number of organisational issues and some of the key areas of operational control. The other important aspects of infrastructure not covered here will need to be similarly developed using the same elements and procedures described in the following sections.

6.4 Some Organisational Issues

The development investment and running costs required to maintain the support functions within a manufacturing business are high. The rationale for this high cost provision is based, in part, on providing adequate and appropriate support for manufacturing in order to make this activity both more effective and more efficient. It is essential, therefore, to ensure that this is achieved. However, for the most part, the approach to developing relevant support for manufacturing has been treated by most organisations as an operational and not as a strategic issue. The consequence of this has been that in many businesses the approach to critical aspects of organisational design has not been based on the necessity to support manufacturing's strategic role. Some of the consequences of this are now discussed.

6.5 The Role of Specialists

Most UK and US manufacturing firms make an extensive use of specialists in running a business. The approach adopted by companies in the past has been to create functions comprising specialist staff to supply expert advice, guidance and activity in various relevant areas. The intention has been to provide the major line functions with the necessary help in terms of infrastructure provision within the organisation. In the last three or four decades this trend towards the employment of specialists has been a growing feature of manufacturing and other sectors of the economy.

It is important especially in terms of increasing world competition, that companies reassess this development both in terms of its extent and the appropriateness of its direction. Before discussing alternatives to the typical pattern of specialist provision currently used in most firms, it would be helpful to review some of the ways in which this concept of control has tended to evolve as a method of examining the current position whilst providing some possible insights into the ways forward. The emphasis throughout will be towards the manufacturing function although the points raised and suggestions made may well prove pertinent in other line areas.

1. The rationale underpinning the concept of control by specialists is to bring together staff to provide a level of capability, support and development which is deemed necessary to help line functions meet the needs of a business. The placement of these groups has traditionally been on a functional basis. Eventually, though often not initally, they have been positioned in a reporting structure which has been outside the main line functions.

   The consequence of this is that several major difficulties are experienced by many of the companies adopting this concept of control. One of the principal outcomes is that it is not highly effective. This is wrong to a number of reasons, including:

- *The question of ownership.* The lack of detailed understanding shared by both line and staff functions of the important perspectives of each other is legendary. To redress this in the last few years, words such as 'user-orientated', 'user-sensitive' and 'user-friendly' have become part of the standard approach in an attempt to overcome the inherent difficulties created by this organisational arrangement
- *Role clarity.* The roles and relationships shared by line and staff functions within the common decision procedures in which they are involved has led, in certain instances, to a large measure of misunderstanding and criticism leading even to periods of acrimony and derision. This is due, in part, to the people themselves, the different salary, reporting and working structures involved, the implied criticism of the specialist's activity, the high level of failures, apparent lack of interest or time allocation by specialists in the post-implementation period and the relative inexperience of specialists both in organisational and personal terms, which leads to a failure to appreciate that the only hard task in management is managing. However, the perceived roles of the line and support functions within the whole of these areas of development or day-to-day support procedures are too often not clarified either at the organisation or operational levels.

    Line managers invariably see the specialist function as a means of improving an area of operational weakness. As busy executives, and not owning, in organisational terms, the time or control of the specialists involved, there is too often a tendency for line managers to take a reactive role in the key periods of the development programme. But, given the fact that it is they who have to make the final decisions or to make the development effective, all that happens is that the time involvement is delayed until later on when the problems invariably arise. The results are far from effective.

2. In many organisations, the role and area of responsibility attributed to specialists has grown. However, this growth has been determined more on the basis of perceived organisational neatness than to make best use of the specialists' contribution and to meet the needs of the business. Typically, as illustrated in Figure 6.3, the areas of responsibility, once within the province of the line functions, have been

drawn into the authority sphere of specialists (Phase 1). Classically, this then leads to an independent reporting structure evolving (Phase 2). The result is that key sets of responsibilities which need to be integrated into the line activities have now been separated and the inherent difficulties associated with this structure when trying to

FIGURE 6.3

Typical phases in the evolution of specialist functions in an organisation

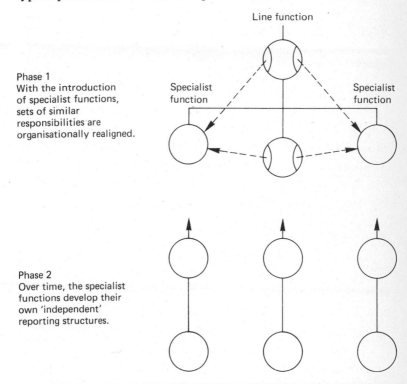

Line function

Phase 1
With the introduction
of specialist functions,
sets of similar
responsibilities are
organisationally realigned.

Specialist
function

Specialist
function

Phase 2
Over time, the specialist
functions develop their
own 'independent'
reporting structures.

redress the lack of necessary integration are now apparent in many companies.

3. In addition to the difficulties outlined or implied earlier, this concept of control by specialists has also led to other trends inside manufacturing organisations. The first concerns the exercise of

control over manufacturing companies by financial analyses and reporting systems which have been developed without an adequate knowledge of the business itself. This increasing tendency has been brought about, in part, by the belief that effective management can be maintained at a distance, using controls, systems and feedback which have been developed by specialists. The result has led to situations where the hands-off controls being used have failed to reflect key trends in themselves while those responsible for exercising and monitoring control have lacked the level of knowledge of the business under review to detect changes and to ask penetrating questions at the opportune time. At best, the consequence has been to contribute to the decline in performance, whilst at worst it could accelerate this decline by emphasising for instance, short-term performance improvements at the expense of medium- and long-term strategic requirements. Having gathered momentum in the 1970s, companies are now reassessing the practice of reviewing performance in this way. Stimulated and given credence by the predominant role of specialists inside an organisation, companies are reconsidering the value of leaning too heavily, sometimes solely, on the views and contributions of these functions.

4. Companies need to reflect the relative importance and contribution of executives to a business by the level of remuneration and opportunity for advancement provided. Attracting able people into key jobs, therefore, needs to correspond to the reward system in the organisation. Many companies, unfortunately, have failed to differentiate between executives' roles and the direct impact they will have on the success of the business. What has unduly influenced salary structures and the opportunity for promotion are factors such as apparent scarcity, assumed contribution and market rates for salaries. The consequence has all too often been that higher salaries have been offered to those whose influence falls in the 20 per cent of the 80/20 rule. The result has been that the more-able people have been attracted away from those line functions whose performance affects the 80 per cent of what constitutes business success.[4]

Too many layers

Invariably, one consequence of this approach is that companies evolve into organisations with too many people and too many layers of management. At head office, corporate staff turn into expensive bureaucracies. At plant level, divisional staffs, built up by middle management as they get promoted, have been retained by their successors. Steward (McKinsey & Co) claims that 'ever since the 1960s, when we started to believe that a professional manager can manage everything, we've been on the wrong track'. The random rotation of managers, based upon this belief, led to 'the new managers, unfamiliar with the businesses they were expected to run, hired staff to advise them. When they moved on, a new manager repeated the cycle. . . . The problem was compounded when companies started going international'.[5] The economies of large scale organisations has made its own unique input into this problem. 'Along with bigness comes complexity. . . . And, most big companies respond to complexity in kind, by designing complex systems and structures. They then hire more staff to keep track of all this complexity . . .'[6]

The way forward is to reduce the layers and cut out the fat. The question to be answered is, 'Which is the best approach to take?' For many companies, the classic response has been to implement across-the-board reductions. Having cut the workforce and dispensed with the 'frills', managers would then be requested to reduce all round by an appropriate percentage. But these haphazard cuts left most corporate or central staff intact, the divisional ratios between managers and workforce rising, and organisations which became more sluggish and less profitable. For instance, in 1981, 'the salaried staff costs for Ford's North American automotive operations were $4 billion'.[7] This comprised *twelve* layers of managers compared with Toyota's *seven*.

But this approach smacks of the specialist's view of an organisation. To make the bottom line come right, just change the figures around! However, this assumes that the structure which exists will be appropriate in a reduced form. Many businesses are realising that the one thing they must not do is to take an axe to the job. Reshaping an organisation requires careful surgery with reductions in line with the business. It needs to start, therefore, with the business and build up from the bottom as well as down from the top. Many organisations in the past have only built top-down without an assessment of the contribution of each part to the business as a whole. This has merely added to the layers. However, reshaping an organisation needs to take into account the role of functions, establish the responsibility for decisions and boundaries of authority and agree the appropriate level and reporting structure between the line and support functions involved. It helps clarify, therefore, that the line functions will in many instances always make the decisions of importance due to the authority/responsibility link which needs to exist. Such a review will also reveal that support functions in many instances provide a clerical/administrative back-up, filtering service or front position. For example, in recruitment their role is advisory and usually, and quite rightly, only consists of drawing-up a short-list. In industrial relations negotiations, the specialist provides a first negotiating line to allow those with prime responsibility to take any necessary fall-back position.

The business related approach, therefore, enables a company to grow its organisation in line with its needs and it also provides the opportunity to change the perception of roles at all levels in the organisation from top to bottom. Finally, not only is this procedure based on the business but it also blocks-off any functional or personal bolt-holes which tend to be prevalent in many companies.

6.6 Operational Effects of Structural Decisions

A significant consequence of the decision to extensively use specialists within a business is the effects it has at the operational level. One important issue which derives from this approach concerns role definitions on the shop-floor.

The concept of an operator's job

The concept of an operator's job as perceived in most UK and US manufacturing companies is that of a doing task (e.g. operating a machine or assembling a product). For this reason, when there are no appropriate doing tasks to be completed, the dilemma facing the shop-floor supervisor is between recording a labour excess and completing work which is not required in the current period (i.e. creating inventory). This problem is made even worse by process investment. In their efforts to reduce the skill and input requirements of the doing tasks within manufacturing, management also reduce the job skills and the work involved when they invest in plant and equipment. In order, therefore, to redress the reducing job interest and to capitalise on the opportunity to use the time released in an effective way, it is first necessary to change the concept of work.

The premise on which this change should be built revolves around the fact that work, in effect, comprises not only the doing task, but also the tasks of planning, and evaluating.[8] In many companies, however, work has been separated into these three components, with each part completed by a different function. The rationale for this is a by-product of the use of specialists and the development of support functions within an organisation. Figure 6.4, therefore, is an extension of

FIGURE 6.4

The separation of the three facets of work and the gap between them created by the organisational structure

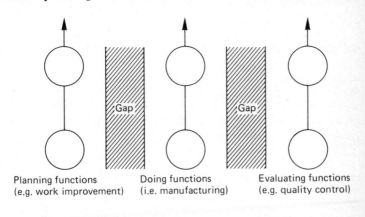

| Planning functions
(e.g. work improvement) | Doing functions
(i.e. manufacturing) | Evaluating functions
(e.g. quality control) |

Phase 2 in Figure 6.3. It illustrates a typical structure, the separation of important activities at the operator level and the inherent gap created by the structure between these three intrinsic parts of work. This has resulted from the development of organisational structures which have emanated from the use of specialists and the growth of functional reporting procedures. It has led to a situation where the inherent contribution of operators to work improvement activities has been lost and the essential link between the responsibility for manufacturing and quality has been severed.

6.7   Strategy-based Alternatives

For many companies, the current organisational structure comprising line and support functions is proving less than effective. Any evaluation of structures and detailed roles, however, needs to be based on the premise: will it meet the requirements of the business? The areas of suggested change which follow are intended to more accurately reflect existing responsibility structures or designed to facilitate an appropriate and relevant contribution being made by people throughout the organisation. If firms are to compete effectively in world markets then their structures need to be both dynamic and designed to tap the relative potential of all their employees.

Functional teamwork concept

One important change which UK and US companies need to consider is to break down the currently held view of line and support functions. The alternative is to consider a move to build specialist functions back into the line and for them to report within that authority/responsibility structure. The principal consequences of this would be:

- Changing the reporting structures removes the problem of the line management/specialist interface not working.
- It clarifies the current role of specialists into those areas which (a) are primarily within the scope of the specialism – for example, quality assurance, the development of robotics within productivity improvement and production planning, (b) should be under the auspices of the line management function – for example, quality control, internal efficiency activities and production control, respectively.

This, therefore, enables an organisation to build its structure around sets of coherent, interrelated activities rather than, as at present, around activities which have similar names. This does not *per se* lead to reductions in people and, in fact, will sometimes lead to increases of staff in certain functions. Although pushing decision-making activity from the centre to the plant and from specialists into the line may not change staffing levels, it will dramatically change the relevance of activities undertaken and assignment priorities established. The benefit, for instance, for a manufacturing manager to have the opportunity to

generate cost analyses in line with his own perspectives and requirements and in line with his contribution to corporate decisions has to be
seen to be believed.

The structure of work

As implied by the comments on what constitutes work, organisations
need to build back into the doing task aspects of planning and evaluating. Enhanced by the *functional teamwork* concept described above,
and as part of the rationalisation of work and relative contributions by
different employees, Figure 6.5 suggests how parts of those planning

---

FIGURE 6.5
**The doing task which now incorporates appropriate planning and evalu-
ating steps, so much an intrinsic part of work**

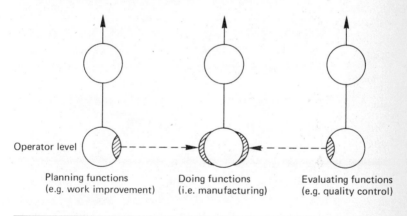

Operator level

| Planning functions | Doing functions | Evaluating functions |
| (e.g. work improvement) | (i.e. manufacturing) | (e.g. quality control) |

---

and evaluating activities, presently completed by support functions,
should be reassigned to those currently responsible for the doing tasks.
In this way, not only does such an action lend support to the arguments
put forward in the last section but it also provides a tangible common-
sense illustration of the effect this can have. These actions facilitate the
materialisation of productivity bearing improvements and at the same
time create greater job interest for all concerned.

It releases specialists from 'non-specialist' work and gives operators work which involves the three important dimensions which make up meaningful tasks by broadening their responsibilities and allowing them to both plan and evaluate the work they carry out.[9] Although these changes bring small returns in themselves, the cumulative effect can be enormous and the contribution made to providing manufacturing's strategic contribution, significant.

Cascading overheads

Linked to both the structure of work and role of specialists within an organisation, companies should seek to push work as far down the organisation as possible. Coupled (as is the concept of work structuring dealt with in the last section) to an investment by the firm in the training of the individuals involved, as with all these and similar ideas, the systematic cascading of overheads will help to redress the imbalance beween salaried and other staff which exists in many companies today, whilst also providing those involved with a more meaningful task.

This principle involves changing the levels at which decisions are made and allowing people to decide on how best to complete tasks once they have been given the relevant parameters and information involved.

Quality circles or productivity improvement groups

As part of the organisational changes advocated here, the introduction of quality circles or productivity improvement groups needs careful consideration. The necessary care in evaluating their role and contribution, however, has not always been exercised by those Western companies which have adopted them. In many instances they have been perceived as panaceas and as such have been evaluated and implemented at an operational level and not as part of a strategic organisational change to draw out the continuous improvement potential of the shop-floor.

The concept of quality circles (their name derives from the fact that quality was Japan's initial, major, manufacturing problem after the Second World War, hence the change in name by some organisations to productivity improvement groups) emanates from Japanese business practice. It illustrates the impact of participation on the productivity increases which can be achieved in all aspects of performance by systematically involving workers in the improvement of quality, productivity and similar operations activities. This form of worker involvement in Japan has been growing rapidly. A review of the period from 1965 to 1983 shows a steady increase in the number of circles and their membership during these years – see Table 6.1 below.[10]

TABLE 6.1
The growth in Japan of quality circle members and membership between 1965–83

Year	Number of	
	circles	members
1965	4 930	70 920
1974	65 477	664 458
1983	173 953	1 490 629

By the late 1970s, many other countries in the world were adopting this approach. It was recognised as a way of providing the systematic involvement of the workforce and the returns on the investment of training given and time spent were impressive and numerous. Many reviews of the adoption of quality circles are available.[11] However, the distinction had not been drawn in many firms between a major organisational change adopted as an operational response, to one adopted as part of a strategy-led response to improving the effectiveness of manufacturing. This has led some reviewers to conclude that their observations suggest that 'in many US organisations ... quality circles are already in the adoption–disappointment–discontinuation cycle that has been characteristic of many other managerial fads'.[12]

The failure of UK manufacturing companies to recognise the value of the shop-floor's contribution is widespread. The use of quality circles or productivity improvement groups, however, is an aid to redressing this imbalance and 'tapping what is probably our most underdeveloped asset – the gold in the mind of our workers'.[13] For this to be effective, however, the company needs to be genuinely committed to the principle of continuous improvement and to seriously accept that this can only be achieved by participative management. The structures then need to be developed to make the *principle* work in *practice* and then to support its development throughout whilst not interfering with the nature of that development. In this way, companies are able to start tapping into their collective wisdom. The change, however, is a strategic one. It accepts that there are significant benefits to be derived from detailed, operational improvements, that implementing improvements quickly and effectively must be on a participative basis and that people, as a group, have the ability to evaluate each others' ideas and develop them.

Participative management, however, is not a soft style. It is both demanding and results-orientated. The difference is embodied in the changed views of work and relative contribution of those involved. Functions and groups of people who are high potential contributors need to be clearly identified. Similarly, other functions and groups need to be placed in their relative positions on the continuum depicting these features in terms of the business needs. Fulfilling potential or eliminating low contributors will bring noticeable improvements.

6.8 Some Key Areas of Operational Control

Infrastructure development is a wide-ranging area and the aspects addressed in this chapter are not meant to provide either a comprehensive or even a representative coverage. They have, however, been chosen because they constitute some of the important aspects of manufacturing infrastructure. Also, their treatment is intended to offer guidelines on how to develop other areas within the manufacturing strategy of the company concerned. In this section, therefore, only three facets of operational control are covered. The first, quality, has been selected because of its important role as either a qualifying or order-winning criterion. The second, inventory control, was chosen because often it is the biggest single asset in a manufacturing company's balance sheet. The final aspect, control of manufacturing, has been addressed because of its role in delivery performance, another important qualifying or order-winning criterion. In addition, the conclusion of the chapter discusses a payment systems development chosen because of its inherent role in the motivation of people to achieve the relevant performance criteria to be provided by manufacturing and as an example of how all facets within infrastructure need to develop within a strategic overview.

6.9 Control of Quality

Although in many instances, quality is a qualifying criterion in manufacturing strategy terms, its impact on market share is more dramatic than probably any other single factor. The fortunes of Jaguar Cars is a clear example. For many years, Jaguar had been producing cars whose product reliability was considered poor. A concerted effort by the company and its suppliers improved the level of quality significantly. Over a relatively short period of time, Jaguar was able to meet the qualifying criterion requirements of quality and stopped losing orders to competitors due to this factor. The rise in sales was substantial. In 1984, it achieved record export sales and its best home market sales for many years.

Operational decisions in the past to separate the total responsibility for quality from the person responsible for completing the task were not recognised at the time in terms of the strategic consequences that might arise. In project and jobbing, however, this division has rarely, if ever, been introduced. In continuous process, quality checks have been built into the process thus retaining the link between the doing and evaluating task within the process itself. However, in batch and line, the union between the responsibility for completing the task and achieving the required levels of quality whilst argued to be intact, in reality are quite separate (see Table 6.2).

Obviously, the most appropriate time to check conformance to the specification is when the item is made. However, under the systems currently used in batch and line processes, work is checked in a time period following its production. Depending upon the length of time between production taking place and quality being checked or at what stages quality checks are taken will have a direct bearing on a company's ability to minimise the repercussions of below quality work.

This, therefore, raises two important issues concerning quality which need to be agreed by manufacturing at the corporate level and then form part of manufacturing's response to the business need.

1. *A reactive or proactive approach to quality.* The first issue is to determine whether to adopt a reactive or proactive approach to

TABLE 6.2
Responsibility for quality control and the type of process

Type of process	The task	Responsibility for quality
Project and jobbing	The task and quality are normally integrated in the skills of the person	Usually vested largely in the performance of the task or provision of the service. Primarily the person responsible for this part of the process plus supervisory support
Batch and line	Work has been deskilled to reduce amongst other things, labour costs. Inspection and later quality control introduced	Theoretically the responsibility is still vested in the person providing the task with supervisory, quality control and inspection support. In reality, quality control and inspection are seen as being responsible for quality.
Continuous process	Quality is determined by the process and, therefore, reintegrates quality into the task	Usually built into the process as an integral part of the design. The facilities to monitor the quality are usually controlled by the same person who is responsible for other aspects of the task

Source: Terry Hill, *Production/Operations Management*, p. 267.

quality. In the former, the emphasis is towards detection with the objective to prevent faulty work being passed on to subsequent processes. In this way, the costs involved in rectification, scrap, returned products and non-repeat business will be minimised.

A proactive approach, on the other hand, emphasises prevention rather than detection. It requires allocating resources to make products right first time, more of the time. This is achieved by reviewing the quality of both design and conformance in order to identify the factors affecting these two features. Quality control is then designed around this analysis.

2. *The responsibility for quality.* The responsibility for quality concerns two separate issues. The first concerns defining the departmental responsibilities throughout the process. The second, the responsibility for measurement.

In recent years the distinction between quality assurance and quality control has become more marked. Quality assurance is the function charged with the task of developing the quality structure and the responsibilities and activities within that structure, together with establishing procedures to ensure the organisation meets the agreed quality levels for its products. Quality control is that aspect of quality assurance which concerns the practical means of securing product quality as set out in the specification.[14] The separation of roles between the people completing the work and those given specific responsibility for checking the quality achieved, albeit as a back-up activity, has been in force for a number of decades. This separation in many organisations has been further emphasised by the reporting systems which have developed (see Figures 6.3 and 6.4).

In order to facilitate manufacturing's task an infrastructure change has to be implemented. Quality control needs to revert to the set of activities for which manufacturing is responsible whilst the quality checks need to form part of the operators' role.

The gains are considerable both in terms of costs, customer relations and job interest. However, it will not happen overnight. Traditions die hard and the investment in training needs to be clearly recognised. However, with the responsibility for good quality work now back where it belongs, companies can also move from the reactive approach which they invariably adopt and one which is almost dictated by the existing departmental and on-line responsibilities for quality, to the proactive approach necessary to ensure that manufacturing will be able to provide the quality requirements which current and future markets demand.[15]

6.10   Control of Inventory

In most manufacturing companies, inventory is very substantial. However, the methods used to control it are often casual. They lack the
level of sophistication or insight appropriate to an item which stands at
some 30–40 per cent of most companies' total assets. Whilst decisions
to use funds for plant and equipment, for instance, are normally carefully monitored, the relative effort and attention given to the control of
inventory is, by and large, too little and too late. Increases in inventory
happen and concern to exercise due control over this sizeable asset
comes after the event. This is owing to the fact that inventory control is
based on a number of operational activities without the strategic overview of control warranted by an investment of this size.

There are two general characteristics about inventory which illustrate,
above all, the level of business disinterest in its control and the underlying perspectives on which existing controls are built. First, many
companies take complete physical counts of stock on as few occasions
as possible, often as little as twice a year to coincide with the financial
accounting periods. Furthermore, when the date for stock-taking
approaches it is common practice to create an unrepresentative picture
of inventory inside the business by holding-off purchases at the front
end and moving existing inventory inside the business itself. The
rationale for this is to reduce the inventory holding *per se* and so reduce
the size of the clerical task involved. Manufacturing companies therefore look on these tasks as a chore and not an opportunity to collect
valuable data essential to the control of what is often the biggest single
asset category on their balance sheets.

Secondly, inventory breakdowns are normally expressed in terms of
the stage the material has reached in the process: namely, raw materials/
components, work-in-progress and finished goods. This choice, however,
is made solely to facilitate the evaluation of inventory as an input into
the profit and loss account and balance sheet. Thus, the outcome of
this data-collection exercise is viewed primarily as a provision of information to the accounts function and not as an important opportunity
to create the basis for controlling this large asset.

The purpose of having inventory in a business is to provide a set of
advantages which reflect its needs. Depending on what constitutes the
needs in the market-place and the agreed manufacturing requirements
within the business, the size and spread of inventory will differ. Effec-

tive control, therefore, is based upon an understanding of why inventory is held where it is and what functions it provides. Currently, however, many companies attempt to control inventory by global, across-the-board mandates over short time periods. With this approach, neither the control nor time dimensions reflect the reality of manufacturing.

Function of inventory as a basis for control

There are two broad categories of inventory: corporate and mainstream. Corporate inventory (accounting often for some 20 to 25 per cent of the total holding) is the name attributed to those categories of inventory which do not provide a manufacturing function.[16]

The types of corporate inventory are numerous and will reflect the nature of the manufacturing company involved. Typical, however, of their types are:

- sales inventory to meet customer agreements
- sales inventory owing to actual sales being lower than forecast
- marketing inventory to meet a product launch
- purchasing inventory incurred to achieve quantity discounts
- corporate safety stocks caused by uncertainty of supply (e.g. possible national or international strikes)
- slow-moving category under various related subheadings.[17]

In order to control corporate inventory, information on the stock-holding by category is required. Thus, the recognition, categorisation and separation of this category into its appropriate type have to be completed. Once known, targets can be set in line with the business needs (and this obviously may not always be a reduction), responsibility for its control can be charged to the appropriate function and inventory can be monitored. A company is then able to understand the return it receives for its investment, decide on the value for money associated with that holding and also use this information as part of its overall review of functions, customers, policies and the like.

The function of mainstream inventory is to facilitate the manufacturing process at all its stages. However, in order to exercise meaningful and effective control, the types of inventory within this category need to be understood and the relevant holding recorded against the various types involved.

To do this three important aspects need to be recognised:

1. *The dependent/independent demand principle.* Where the rate of issue for an item does not directly relate to the use of any other item, then it should be treated as an item with an independent pattern of demand. Examples include finished goods and factored items. Conversely, items where the demand is linked to the use of other items are said to have a dependent demand pattern. For example, components and sub-assemblies. This distinction is drawn to ensure that companies recognise that whereas the demand for independent items will have to be arrived at through forecasting or similar techniques, the demand for dependent items can be calculated.

2. *The functions provided by mainstream inventory.* Holding mainstream inventory provides a number of distinct functions within manufacturing. These need to be distinguished and inventory data collected accordingly. The functions are:

   - *Pipeline inventory.* Inventory exists because of the need to transport inventories around the system. Pipeline inventory is that which is in the system to link geographically separate parts of the manufacturing process, including subcontracted work

   - *Cycle inventory.* Cycle inventories occur because of managements' attempts to produce in lot sizes. In order to gain the manufacturing advantage of reduced set-ups, order quantities are schedules. Part of that quantity is to meet actual requirement and part may exceed current demand. All quantities above one constitute cycle inventory but they need to separate further between actual requirement and excess requirement.

   - *Buffer inventory.* Because demand or supply times vary, there is a need to protect the business against such variations. The higher the service level or the lower the incident of stock-outs preferred, then the greater are the quantities of buffer inventories which have to be provided.

   - *Capacity-related inventory.* Inventory is a way of transferring work forward to be sold in a future time period. The most obvious use concerns a company with known seasonal patterns of sales. Where a company decides to keep manufacturing capacity relatively steady, it is able to cope with the varying levels of forecast demand by planning to hold capacity-related inventory.

   - *Decoupling inventory.* In jobbing, the skilled person responsible for completing the task links the various operations involved as part of the process. Similarly, in both line and continuous process, the design of the process links each operation to the one before and the one after. However, in batch, the design is to provide a number of functionally laid out sets of processes which are not dependent one to another. The reason is to allow one set of processes to work independently and, therefore, more efficiently. The way this is achieved is by investing in inventory which decouples each set from each other set of processes.

Control can now be exercised by establishing the amount of inventory held by function and within geographical areas (i.e. related to machines or machine groups) and systematically reducing the holdings involved.

3. *The 80/20 rule.* A review of inventory based upon a Pareto analysis* will almost certainly reveal that some 20 per cent of the items will account for about 80 per cent of the value. Using this as the basis for an ABC classification allows a company to exercise tight control over the relatively few items which are high in value. However, on the low value items, excess buffer inventory holdings allow the controls to be simple and the records to be minimal.

Based on these three perspectives of inventory, the control exercised can now reflect the important, the large and the relevant. Once a business knows why and how much inventory is being held it can divert attention, effort and the level of control accordingly. Two examples to illustrate this approach will help to amplify the issues involved.

1. A company involved in manufacturing low-volume, standard products had 24 per cent of its total assets tied up in work-in-progress despite a sophisticated scheduling system being in operation. The products involved comprised hundreds of standard labour hours over many processes, including assembly, and were subject to schedule changes by customers. An analysis of its work-in-progress revealed levels of decoupling inventory which were a distinct over-provision of this function. The 80/20 rule typically prevailed. As responding to customer schedule changes was determined to be part of the manufacturing's task, the company took several decisions concerning its high inventory levels. An ABC analysis on work-in-progress by product enabled it to cut back on cycle inventory and to deliberately

---

*A Pareto analysis orders the data from highest down to lowest. The list provided then helps show the 80/20 relationship which exists between the data being reviewed.

shorten the process lead time for high value components and sub-assemblies. In future, high-value parts were made strictly in line with a customer's orders and were accelerated through the various processes by giving them priority. Low-value components and sub-assemblies were made in excess of requirements and scheduled into the process well in advance of delivery needs. In this way, the advantages of cycle inventory were achieved for many items at least-inventory investment. Similarly, they were now schedule to 'meander' through the processes in a controlled way but offering efficiency opportunities without incurring correspondingly high inventory investment.

2. A plant which was part of a large group of companies received an across-the-board corporate directive to reduce inventory by 15 to 20 per cent in a given time period. The plant involved manufactured optional features for vehicles. However, in order to make a sale, the customer required short delivery response owing to minimising the off-the-road time for any vehicle. In order to provide this distinct order-winning criterion, the products had been designed to have a high proportion of standard parts and sub-assemblies to gain some economies of scale and to maximise coverage of the wide range of products involved, whilst minimising inventory holdings. Manufacturing, to meet this short lead time, needed to hold all parts in stock so as to reduce the overall process lead time and allow itself the time to respond to the market. Only when inventory's role within the manufacturing strategy was explained was the corporate directive rescinded.

Finally, when reviewing inventory holdings it is important to look at Table 3.1 (pp. 70–1). This table illustrates how the implications for inventory holdings in terms of raw materials/components, work-in progress and finished goods would differ with each choice of process. Therefore, as a starting point the trade-offs involved between inventory investment, plant utilisation, efficiency and other operational factors need also to be taken into account when reviewing the fundamental decisions addressed in Chapter 3. However, this in no way precludes a company from changing the mix in trade-offs which surround inventory investment. The description of just-in-time production systems given later provides an alternative approach to managing processes. However, in so doing it picks up a fresh set of trade-offs for manufacturing and the business which, on the plus side, include a sharp reduction in inventory levels. It is essential, therefore, that the manufacturing strategy debate concerning process choice and the role of inventory in this configuration (see Table 2.2) explains and amplifies the implications for the business and the critical nature of the trade-offs involved.

6.11   Control of Manufacturing

There are a wide range of issues and concerns which could be addressed in this section – many of them to do with the complex detail of planning and control systems. Those who feel the need for this detail are referred to the reading list at the end of the chapter.[18] In this section 'control' is treated from a strategic viewpoint aiming to assist the manufacturing executive with those key strategic insights which will enable him to direct the development of systems appropriate to both the market opportunities/needs and the manufacturing process requirements.

The strategic issues concerning the design and development of manufacturing control systems are dealt with under the following headings:

1. Market related criteria.
2. Process requirement criteria.
3. Levels of control within an organisation.
4. Choice between push or pull systems.

The first two concern factors which influence the type of control systems required to support the corporate strategy, while the second two deal with strategic design principles.

Market related criteria

The contention that process and infrastructure need to be developed to support the key features of manufacturing's strategic role has been the underlying theme throughout the book. The control of manufacturing is no exception.

Many companies, however, design or develop controls without a strategic overview. They are normally designed before the level of manufacturing complexity has been reviewed and established, without an eye on the order-winning criteria in the market-place and on the basis of a firm's own internal processes, and unrelated to either its suppliers or customers.

Although control systems affect a number of trade-offs within manufacturing (for example, levels of inventory and process costs) the most important strategic dimension concerns their role in achieving the required levels of delivery speed and reliability. However, both these aspects of performance have a customer perspective (e.g. speed of delivery response) and a supplier perspective (e.g. ability to respond to demand changes). Hence, it is important that executives should ensure that control system design relates not only to the firm's own manufacturing processes but also to its suppliers and customers. In addition, where delivery speed, for example, is an order-winning criterion then the control systems must be designed to allow delivery performance to be monitored throughout the process not only in terms of control but also in terms of highlighting areas of potential improvement and perceived weakness.

Similarly, having established the delivery performance of its major competitors, the control of manufacturing has to be designed to facilitate the measurement of its own achievement and to provide timely warning of potential delays in delivery sensitive markets.

Process requirement criteria

Process choice not only has the implications for manufacturing outlined in Table 3.1 (pp. 70–1), but has many important implications for control as well. It is important, therefore, for companies to understand these implications and particularly to recognise that one overall control system, classically advocated by specialists, will not be an appropriate way forward.

For example, in project, these one-off tasks require a control which is able to plan resources to the site, their use on site, and in the case of equipment and plant, their release after use. In addition, it will incorporate the control of all the activities involved in completing the task and must be able not only to monitor progress but also to assess the impact of unforeseen delays and changes on the project as a whole in terms of its agreed completion date. This distinct set of needs has been reflected in the development of sophisticated network analysis techniques which provide the sensitive monitoring demanded and purpose-made control to meet the characteristics of this one-off provision.

As with project, jobbing and batch require order-status information (i.e. the progress to date on an order compared with the schedule) as a key feature of an appropriate control system. Normally jobbing, as it is largely under the control of one person, can obtain this feedback quickly with an assessment of any overruns involved. However, batch is far more complex. In functionally laid out processes, handling a wide range of products, with many operations, is compounded by the fact that many businesses using a batch process have invested in decoupling inventory to allow individual machine utilisation to be maximised by enacting the principle that *materials wait for machines*. This best ensures the highest possible utilisation of both machines and labour. *One significant trade-off is the increased level of control complexity*.

With both line and continuous process, the nature of the control task changes. The essential requirement concerns the flow of components and materials to the start point of the process. In itself, an easy control problem, but often one which is very difficult to enact owing to a dependence on suppliers and, typically, internal batch processes to meet agreed component and sub-assembly schedules.

In many companies, several processes exist within manufacturing to meet the differing volume requirements of markets. As already mentioned, the approach to designing a manufacturing control system in the past has been typified by two important features. These two aspects, moreover, are so critical to the level of control which can be and is achieved that they are essential prerequisites in effective control design.

1. The level of process complexity must first be agreed. The question of process positioning addressed in Chapter 5 is one strategic dimension which in itself determines the size of the control task. The data base provision which underpins manufacturing control is itself directly related to a company's internal span of process.
2. The facets of control within processes require different individual responses. In many firms, a single control system has been installed on the basis that it reduces the investment involved. This leads to a position where instead of the complexity of reality being addressed by the control system, the reverse happens. In order to simplify the control problem application and hence reduce costs and speed up installation, the complexity of reality is left to the users of the system to cope with. The result is a system which typically is under used, bypassed with alternative, clerically-based control activities and one which falls into disrepute.

TABLE 6.3
The major levels of control, the tasks involved and the different levels

Level of control	Features	
	Some strategic and operational issues	Level of organisational responsibility
Long-term planning	Long-term (five years on) capacity planning. Involves important strategic issues such as following or leading demand in the provision of manufacturing capacity and the supply of skill requirements to support anticipated technical developments.	Strategic
Aggregate planning	Designed within the long-term plan. Consists of establishing feasible medium-term (up to two years) plans to meet agreed output levels in a situation where capacity is considered to be relatively fixed. Often requires critical adjustments to the relevant demand and capacity variables (e.g. into or out of market segments, workforce levels, shift patterns, inventory and order backlog).	Strategic
Short-term control	Detailed capacity, planning and purchasing activities, working several time-periods ahead.	Production control function

| Day-to-day control and delivery | Meeting delivery schedules once the control parameters and information have been provided. Includes procurement against purchasing agreements, inventory analysis, and short-term delivery and capacity changes. | Shop-floor |

Levels of control within an organisation

The control of manufacturing differs in terms of the time horizons involved and detail required. It is essential, therefore, for companies to use these natural divisions as a way to delineate between levels of control and so ensure that the structure and emphasis in design and the responsibility levels in the firm are selected to reflect these distinctions. To more fully appreciate some of the important strategic and operational issues in designing control systems, Table 6.3 illustrates some of the major characteristics of the planning and control task in terms of the activities involved and the appropriate level in the organisation where responsibility should ideally be placed.

Table 6.3 depicts four levels of control. *Within each level the objectives and activities are fundamentally different* and require this difference to be reflected in the control system appropriate to each level. To further accentuate some of the more important features embodied in Table 6.3, a few of these are highlighted.

- It is most important that aggregate planning alternatives are agreed at the executive level as the trade-offs embrace strategic differences. For instance, demand changes need to be assessed in terms of their fit within the agreed marketing strategy, whilst the implications of manufacturing alternatives need to be clearly identified in terms of people, cost and complexity.
- The move to a shop-floor responsibility for the day-to-day control of manufacturing is in line with the arguments and ideas raised earlier in this chapter. Only here can an up to date, on-line assessment be made of capacity and, given responsibility for both delivery achievement and manufacturing performance, then the most sensible trade-

offs in any circumstances can best be made at this level of the organisation. Once the necessary information is to hand, those responsible
for manufacturing will arrive at the most sensible decision.

Choosing between push or pull systems

The major design and development issues within manufacturing controls concern the basic distinction between what are known as push or
pull systems. The basic distinction between these two types of system
is that a push system loads jobs into the factory in line with appropriate
finish dates, whereas a pull system creates schedules of work in line
with priorities.

The choice of system depends on several factors, including whether
a company manufactures to a make-to-stock policy or against order
backlogs, the complexity of the manufacturing process and the availability of computers to provide data handling capacity. Where a company makes a relatively simple product on a make-to-stock basis then
it would be able to use a push system on a manual basis. Based on sales
forecasts for a period and the end-of-period finished goods stock
envisaged it would be able to calculate its component requirements and
assembly programme, and load the system accordingly.

However, for companies with more complex products and working
on an order backlog principle then, before the advent of relatively
cheap computer power, many companies in this situation used (and
many still do) a planning and control system which worked on the
basis of a *pull* system. The principle on which this type of system is
based is that customers place orders with a company. These are then
broken down into their make-in and bought-out details and the availability of parts is checked. From this check a shortage list is created
and this forms the basis for manufacturing priorities.

In the West, the main developments, especially to cope with the
latter type of manufacturing situation have centred around a well
planned, computer-based *push* system of manufacturing planning and
control. The push system is based on the preparation of a multi-period
schedule of future demands for the company's products (known as a
master production schedule). The computer then breaks down these
schedules into detailed manufacturing and purchasing schedules. The
phrase 'push system' refers to the fact that these detailed schedules
push work into manufacturing in line with appropriate finish dates and

process loadings. In this way it requires manufacturing to produce the required parts and to push them on to the next process until they reach the final assembly stage. The name given to this push system is materials requirement planning (MRP).

A push system based upon orderly schedules offered considerable advantages over the disruptive, customer-waiting features of the earlier pull system. Scheduled production seemed like good management when compared to a system of priority lists, frequent changes and an army of expediters.

Although an MRP system relies on forecasts being largely correct and restricted customer schedule changes, the inventory levels normally associated with this type of system tend to be lower overall than the previous pull systems and less likely to include slow-moving items.

These advantages seemed to heavily favour the widespread use of computer-based push-systems, especially with the falling cost of computers. However, the pull-systems developed in several Japanese manufacturing companies combine the features of control and low inventory. The Toyota production system is the most widely known of the just-in-time (JIT) systems. The principle behind JIT is simple – produce and deliver finished goods just-in-time to be sold, sub-assemblies and components just-in-time to be made into finished goods, and purchased components and materials just-in-time to be made into components and sub-assemblies. The JIT ideal is not to have materials in the system which are inactive, thereby carrying unwarranted costs. To achieve this idea, Toyota's JIT production is supported by an information system based on 'Kanban' and a series of production method improvements which allow the concept of production and delivery quantities to move nearer towards the ultimate goal of one single unit.

Kanban (meaning card) is the Toyota name for its inventory replenishing procedure which forms part of this pull-system. In essence, the assembly line calls off the parts it needs by releasing a card (a Kanban) once parts have been withdrawn to meet current production needs. This card then becomes the authority to produce a replacement quantity by the section concerned. To do this, it in turn withdraws the material/components necessary to make the replacement batch. In so doing, it too releases a card(s) into the previous parts of the process, and so on. Hence, parts are pulled through the system only as required. An authority to produce (a Kanban), therefore, is required before a section can commence work on a replacement quantity. This essential discipline and control is achieved because the companies using these systems have reset the trade-offs involved in terms of inventory, utilisation of plant and labour efficiency. In the case of the latter, Japanese companies, by making non-doing tasks an integral part of each operator's job, are able to provide alternative tasks which constitute a legitimate part of the person's work. Thus, labour efficiency does not have the same narrow definition which is currently held in most UK and US manufacturing companies.

In addition to Kanban, the Japanese companies using JIT also devote great attention to production method improvements as well as establishing stability of call-offs and close liaison with suppliers. High on the list of method improvements is decreased set-up times with phase one aimed at achieving the SMED (single minute exchange die) system before aspiring to an OTED (one touch exchange die) system which would lead to the exchange of a die being achieved within 60 second.[19]

Some important issues when considering MRP and JIT

The development of either MRP or JIT systems have their own drawbacks. Not only are MRP systems costly but they take a long time to install. The creation of data bases and the installation and tailoring of MRP systems to the particular manufacturing company is time consuming with the result that they do not normally bring any significant results in the first two years of their development.

For a JIT system to reach the stage of development to provide the level of advantages described in Japanese applications, however, would also be time consuming. As Shigeo Shingo explains it took Toyota twenty years to implement improvements within its own plants and only then did it dispatch people to train and execute improvements within their suppliers' production systems. This phase took ten years before the system was formally adopted 'as a total system for Toyota Motors and the parts' suppliers'.[20] This does not imply that these time series would prevail for any company starting from scratch, but Figure 6.6 does show the Kanban installation schedule at a company, which implies both sequence and timescales depending upon the size and complexity of the plant.[21]

Two important aspects are highlighted in this schedule. The first is that it took some twelve months to achieve the implementation on the basis that adequate support staff were provided. The second is that JIT and Kanban appear right at the end of the schedule. They are, in fact,

FIGURE 6.6
Kanban implementation schedule at LM Ericeson

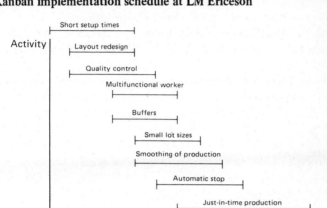
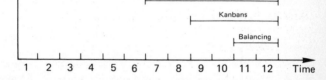
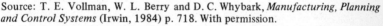

Source: T. E. Vollman, W. L. Berry and D. C. Whybark, *Manufacturing, Planning and Control Systems* (Irwin, 1984) p. 718. With permission.

a by-product of the previous activities which underpin essential development phases.*

Thus, it is most important to realise that there are no short-cuts. One general manager, attracted by the tangible advantages of JIT announced to one of its component suppliers (itself a part of the same division within the group of companies) that his company wanted daily deliveries. However, when questioned about his own company's notorious schedule changes and the need to fix these (a prerequisite for JIT to work is very stable schedules) the reply was that they would only be fixed for two days ahead. The lack of understanding on which this approach is based focused attention on the fact that the substantial advantages inherent in JIT do not come free. Furthermore, it is important to recognise that the Kanban inventory control system is also only

*Note: a corresponding schedule with similar tasks and timescales was advocated by Shigeo Shingo in his book on the Toyota Production System.

suited to very stable production schedules usually associated with repetitive manufacturing. In Toyota, the production plan has a one-year horizon and the master production schedule is frozen for one month, with the following two months specified by car models.

A final comment on MRP and JIT concerns the important issue of investment and return. As mentioned earlier, MRP systems are expensive to install and the returns are a long time coming. Based upon a computer application, MRP also tends to be applied to existing manufacturing facilities and processes (with their inherent level of complexity) without undertaking an extensive review of what is currently required. Whether current products should be made in the future or existing processes should be changed or reduced are not normally an integral part of the approach. The result is that expensive data bases can be created which may not be needed, and complex systems overlaying unnecessarily complex processes. With JIT, on the other hand, the process is systematically simplified. It is based on a manual system, low computer-based systems support, with the steps involved aimed at simplifying the process (i.e. reducing complexity), and thereby bringing rewards at each stage.

There is a tendency for executives to assume that they must live with the current level of complexity within a business. They perceive the solution to its control through the introduction of specialist know-how and complicated systems. No one tells them otherwise. Once the level of complexity is assumed as given, then it follows that specialists must be correct in advocating computers to handle the complexity and to advocate seeking the gains which come from integrating the computer data bases and thus availing themselves of the added advantages of computer systems over manual controls. The 'no-one-has-ever-got-fired-for-choosing-IBM' syndrome. However, these are serious trade-offs, based upon the premise that existing complexity cannot be altered. However, whatever control solution is adopted, it is essential that the current position is first reviewed in order to lower the level of complexity where possible before designing the control systems to be used.

6.12   Conclusion

As an example of strategic infrastructure development, the JIT production system within Toyota has all the classic hallmarks. It works well because Toyota has demonstrated that it understands the need to reconcile the three major phases in its business – the before phase (its suppliers), the owned phase (its own processes) and the forward phase (the sale of cars through its networks). It works because Toyota has managed its forward phase in such a way that it freezes schedules and hence demands or requires little change in its own or its suppliers' processes. In this way it has cushioned its manufacturing core from the instability of the market-place, thus preventing it from being exposed. The stability so created means that Toyota is able to demand exact deliveries, so much a feature of the JIT production system. Toyota in this way has earned this favoured position in the before-phase by establishing the necessary prerequisite for these gains in its own processes and the forward phase of the total system. It can, and does, therefore, demand these benefits from suppliers because it freezes the owned and forward phases and forces the inventory forward and out of the system rather than the other way round.

Many UK and US car companies do not appreciate these essential links. They show due sensitivity in the forward phase because they require to generate goodwill and motivate their distributors to sell more cars. In the before-phase, however, the converse happens. They believe here that to threaten suppliers is the posture which will bring best results. And this is a very telling difference.

Providing a clear manufacturing strategy for the business enables those responsible for infrastructure development to work from a common base in a common direction to meet a common requirement. Historical or personal, in some instances almost esoteric views, therefore, fall by the wayside to be replaced by a strategic underpinning of infrastructure. The consequence will not only be to provide relevance by meeting the needs of the business but also to provide continuity by ensuring that the long-term requirements are an integral part of current thinking and decisions. What militates against this is that without a strategy-based approach, these wide multi-functional areas are more open to personal judgements, more prone to fixed ideas and swayed by the argument of what is more readily available from the point of view of specialist provision than what needs to be provided to meet the dimensions of manufacturing. Thus, the interactive nature of the dynamics within manufacturing not being the responsibility of any one specialist or support function is not at the forefront of the argument or the application. The responsibility for this is clearly and wholly manufacturing's. Thus, by underpinning these with a clear and well argued manufacturing strategy, the direction and mechanism for common evaluation will be provided.

On an entirely practical basis, the development and introduction of a payment system illustrates how any facet of infrastructure can and needs to be designed to support a company's competitive strategy and not in keeping with the efficiency orientated perception of manufacturing's strategic role.

A medium-sized manufacturing company wished to replace its existing payment scheme for hourly-paid employees which had fallen into disrepute. The initial proposals centred on a classic productivity-based scheme involving individual bonus-related earnings. When it recognised the need to develop this in the context of a manufacturing strategy, the company postponed work on the scheme until the necessary, earlier work was completed. Two order-winning criteria were highlighted – delivery speed/reliability and price. With these now forming the basis of the manufacturing task, the scheme which was eventually developed reflected these criteria. Delivery performance now accounted for half the potential performance earnings, while the other half was for improvements in productivity. Furthermore, in order to encourage a broader view of work, the payments were made twice a year and on a factory-wide achievement related to attendance time.

The shape and emphasis, therefore, now more accurately reflected the needs of the business and in this way encouraged an important part of manufacturing's contribution by the way it was designed.

Notes and References

1. T. J. Peters and R. H. Waterman Jr, *In Search of Excellence: Lessons from America's Best-run Companies* (Harper and Row, 1982).
2. R. H. Hayes and S. C. Wheelwright, *Restoring Our Competitive Edge: Competing through Manufacturing* (Wiley, 1984) p. 32.
3. Ibid., p. 33.
4. T. J. Hill *et al.*, 'The Production Manager's Task and Contribution', CRIBA Research Paper No. 94, July 1981, University of Warwick, included a survey of the *Sunday Times* from 1970–79 that revealed of all the advertisements where salaries were given for production, sales, accounting/finance and personnel, the median salary offered to production managers was lowest on four occasions in 1970, 1972, 1973 and 1978 and joint lowest (with personnel managers) in 1971. Only in 1977 was it the highest within this group. In fact, in 1975, the average salary for personnel managers was £1000 more

than that offered to production managers. At the director level the picture was worse. Compared with sales/marketing and accounting/ finance, the median salaries offered to production/manufacturing directors were lowest on six occasions and never once the highest. Accounting and finance on the other hand, were second in 1970 and then top in each of the following nine years. One obvious consequence is that young managers on reviewing this position will be attracted away from the line functions by higher rewards and quicker promotion. To turn this round will take many years.

5. 'A New Target: Reducing Staff and Levels', *Business Week*, 21 Dec. 1981 pp. 38–41.
6. Peters and Waterman, *In Search of Excellence*, p.306.
7. 'A New Target', *Business Week*, 21 Dec. 1981, p. 38.
8. This and some of the other concepts discussed here are taken from a set of well developed work structuring principles which have been presented in various unpublished papers, 1979–81 by P. C. Schumacher, Schumacher Projects, Godstone, Surrey, UK.
9. A key feature of quality circles (dealt with later in this chapter) is that those involved not only implement their ideas but also evaluate the gains they yield. In fact, this is one of the few key elements of a quality circle listed by Professor Asbjørn Aune, Norwegian Institute of Technology in Trondheim and quoted in J. R. Arbose, 'Quality Control Circles: the West Adopts a Japanese Concept', *International Management*, Dec. 1980, pp. 31–9.
10. These figures are provided in a year by year review of the adoption of quality circles within Japanese business – *Forman Quality Control*, No. 256 (1984) p. 59.
11. Other references to the adoption and outcomes of quality circles include 'Why Does Britain Want Quality Circles?' *Production Engineer*, Feb. 1980, pp. 45–6; three articles published in S. M. Lee and G. Schwendiman (eds) *Management by Japanese Systems* (Praeger Publishers, 1982), Part II. Quality Circles, pp. 65–118; Terry Hill, *Production/Operations Management* (Prentice-Hall, 1983) pp. 271–2; R. J. Schonberger, *Japanese Manufacturing Techniques: Nine Hidden Lessons in Simplicity*, ch. 8, 'Quality Circles, Work Improvement and Specialisation', pp. 181–98; and R. E. Cole, 'Will QC Circles Work in the US?' *Quality Progress*, July 1980, pp. 30–33.

In addition, J. R. Arbose in his editorial 'Quality Control Circles: the West Adopts a Japanese Concept' (see note 9), provides a wide-ranging list of savings achieved from applications in various countries, a checklist for starting-up, and Professor Kaoru Ishikawa's list of the eight tools of problem analysis in which group leaders need to be trained.
12. R. Wood, F. Hull and K. Azumi, 'Evaluating Quality Circles: the American Application', *California Management Review*, vol. XXVI, no. 1, Fall 1983, pp. 37–53.
13. Arbose, 'Quality Control Circles', p. 31.

14. British Standard Glossary of Terms used in BS. 4778, 'Quality Assurance' (1979), 19.1.
15. There are many references to the advantages to be gained and examples of the results of such decisions. These include Toyohiro Kona, *Strategy and Structure of Japanese Enterprises* (Macmillan Press, 1984), ch. 7, 'Competition Strategy', pp. 194–6; JETRO 'Productivity and Quality Control: The Japanese Experience', no. 30 1981; Schonberger, *Japanese Manufacturing Techniques; Nine Hidden Lessons*; D. A. Garvin, 'Quality on the Line', *Harvard Business Review*, Sept.–Oct. 1983, pp. 65–75; C. Lorenz, 'A Shocking Indictment of American Mediocrity', *Financial Times*, 17 Oct. 1983; J. M. Juran, 'Product Quality – a Prescription for the West', *Management Review* June 1981, pp. 9–20.
16. See Hill, *Production/Operations Management*, pp. 175–9 for a more detailed discussion on the types of corporate inventory and their control.
17. Ibid, pp. 178–9.
18. G. W. Plossl, *Manufacturing Control – the Last Frontier for Profits* (Reston Publishing Company, 1973); T. E. Vollman, W. L. Berry and D. C. Whybark, *Manufacturing Planning and Control Systems* (Irwin, 1984); O. W. Wight, *Production and Inventory Management in the Computer Age* (CBI Publishing, 1974).
19. Shigeo Shingo, *Study of Toyota's Production System from an Industrial Engineering Viewpoint* (Japan Management Association, 1981) p. 77.
20. Ibid., p. 295.
21. A plan to introduce JIT and Kanban is also provided by Shigeo Shingo, ibid, p. 332, showing similar time-scales.

Further Reading

Aoki, M., (ed.), *The Economic Analysis of the Japanese Firm* (North-Holland, 1984).

Cole, R. E., 'Permanent Employment in Japan: Facts and Fantasies', *Industrial and Labor Relations Review*, 1973, pp. 615–30.

De Jong, J. R., 'The Method in Work Design. Some recommendations based on experience obtained in job redesign', *International Journal of Production Research*, 16, 1, 1978, pp. 39–49.

Johnson, R. T. and Ouchi, W. G., 'Made in America (under Japanese Management),' *Harvard Business Review*, Sept.–Oct. 1974, pp. 61–9.

Schumacher, E. F., *Small is Beautiful* (Blond Briggs, 1973).

Thurley, K. and Wood, S., *Business Strategy and Industrial Relations Strategy*, in their book 'Industrial Relations and Management Strategy', Cambridge University Press (1983) pp. 197–224.

Accounting and Financial Perspectives and Manufacturing Strategy

7

Two common denominators are used in manufacturing businesses as the basis for control and performance measurement. The first is the time base on which manufacturing principally works. Product mix and volumes, capacity calculations, performance measures in terms of efficiency, utilisation and productivity all normally use the basic measurement of time. The second common denominator is that of money. At the corporate level forecast activity levels, performance measures, levels of investment and similar activities use the money base. The importance, therefore, of getting the correct links between the time-based and money-based measures is self-evident. Correct not only in terms of being accurate but also in terms of reflecting the key perspectives associated with the business itself.

The money-based denominator issues which this chapter addresses are controlled by what, in many companies, is frequently one of the least-developed functions, that of accounting and finance. Often living on the approaches established when business activities were very different, this area has not really faced up to resolving many of the important changes in business with appropriate developments. This chapter highlights a number of areas which need to be addressed from the point of view of both manufacturing and overall strategy. It will link the areas of manufacturing and corporate strategy with accounting and finance and illustrate some of the key issues which need to be developed and the essential direction which these improvements need to take. In addition, it will show the ways in which manufacturing strategy will influence, and in some cases, facilitate, some of these changes whilst also drawing attention to the essential nature of manufacturing's needs and the accounting and financial information provision.

The purpose of this chapter is to make a number of critical observations about the impact on manufacturing of finance and accounting practices. The observations are made from a manufacturing executive's perspective and it is, therefore, acknowledged that they may well be provocative when examined by the professional accountant. But, if this causes debate between manufacturing and finance executives the purpose is achieved, because the solutions to the issues addressed must be worked out in the context of a particular company's corporate and manufacturing strategies. Having said that the financial systems in a business can, and do, have a major impact on manufacturing's ability to develop and maintain effective competitive strategies, then one essential objective of the finance function must be to give manufacturing the capability to measure and accurately assess its performance relative to major competitors and the competitive value of investment proposals. The chapter deals therefore with these two broad areas of interaction between finance and manufacturing. First, the effect on manufacturing strategy of investment appraisal methods and secondly, how management accounting systems critically affect the control and performance measurement of manufacturing operations.

7.1 Investment Decisions

The approach to developing a manufacturing strategy was explained in some detail in the earlier chapters. One important consideration which was highlighted in those explanations was the level of alternative investments associated with different decisions (see Figure 7.1). Many organisations, bounded by cash limitations, need to commit their scarce resources wisely. However, the criteria for assessing the level or nature of this critical corporate decision have rarely been arrived at with the care and in-depth analysis which is warranted. In many companies, investment decisions though initially chosen or stimulated by corporate competitive requirements are finally evaluated solely by accounting measures and methods of appraisal. The interaction of these financial measures on strategy and the consequent investment decisions are illustrated by reference to the framework introduced in Chapter 2.

FIGURE 7.1
When developing a manufacturing strategy for a business, the restrictions imposed at both ends of the procedure by the necessary financial considerations are rarely understood or their interaction acknowledged

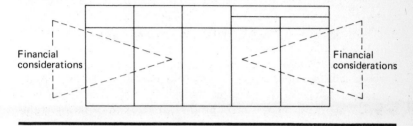

Accounting methods of investment appraisal are generally based upon one important premise – the relative return on capital associated with each investment proposal under review. With capital investment in limited supply and capital rationing a widespread consequence, the argument to invest predominantly on the basis of return is not only built into the appraisal system itself but invariably is reinforced by the discussion and argument which will take place. In this way the figures will themselves unwittingly support investment return as the predominant or even exclusive measure on which to assess these key corporate strategy decisions.

The consequences of this undue weighting have been felt by many companies and the ramifications within manufacturing industry have been widespread. The necessity to question this view of investment decisions has stimulated a series of well argued articles and papers which illustrate the simplistic nature of the accounting perspective and challenge its unevaluated application. As early as 1974, Dean declared that 'because of our obsessive concentration in short-term gains and profits, US technology is stalemated'.[1] Hayes and Abernathy's 1980 article said it all in the title 'Managing our way to economic decline'[2] and again with Garvin, Hayes captured the essence of the issues in the article 'Managing as if tomorrow mattered'[3] in which they make, amongst other things, a concerted challenge on current accounting approaches to investment appraisal. They provide a detailed argument to support their view that companies have increasingly turned to sophisticated, analytical techniques to evaluate investment proposals.

The long-term result has been that many of the managers involved have 'unintentionally jeopardised their companies' future, and they summarise the consequences with the conclusion that 'investment decisions that discount the future may result in high present values but bleak tomorrows'.

7.2   The Need for a Strategic View of Investments

The key shift in emphasis which companies need to adopt when evaluating investments is to move increasingly towards a strategy-based review. What constitutes a sound investment needs to be measured by its contribution to the agreed corporate strategy and not by how well it meets the criteria laid down by a set of accounting rules and evaluations. Simmonds in one of several critiques of current management accounting observes that

> the emphasis ... which accounting and finance have placed on return on investment over the years has subtly transmuted into a widely- and deeply-held belief that return comes from the investments themselves. ... The truth is much different. Sustained profit comes from the competitive market position. New production investment to expand sales must imply a change in competitive position and it is this change that should be the focus of the investment review. Without it, the calculations must be a nonsense.[4]

This sleight of hand has been detected by all too few companies. The consequence has been that increasingly the key factor by which investment proposals have been assessed has swung away from strategy considerations towards levels of investment return *per se*. Return must be defined in terms of improved long-term competitiveness rather than just short-term measures.

Changing the basis of investment appraisal is both complex and fraught with difficulties. It is one of those issues in which manufacturing executives have traditionally felt relatively weak and where those who control the cash are professionally very strong. The debate has, therefore, been one-sided with manufacturing the casualty by default. The argument that investments must provide a quick pay-back are financially (and emotionally) attractive! They tend, however, to totally over-simplify the investment issues at stake and fail to drive executives towards determining and analysing those fundamental criteria which constitute the components of competitive strategy.

A short section on investment can only begin to open up the debate from the manufacturing perspective by providing some guidelines which manufacturing can use to raise key questions. Hopefully finance executives will also use them to develop their own appreciation of the strategic issues involved in manufacturing investment decisions. Six key contentions are made each of which is expanded to give substance but none can be claimed to be comprehensively examined. They are:

1. Investment decisions must be based on order-winning criteria.
2. Excessive use of ROI distorts strategy-building.
3. Government grants are not necessarily golden handshakes.
4. Linking investment to product life cycles reduces risks.
5. Manufacturing must test the validity of forecasts.
6. Investment decisions must quantify infrastructure requirements.

Investment decisions must be based on order-winning criteria

The impact of investment policy and appraisal methods on manufacturing's strategy contribution to the competitiveness of a business is clearly significant. If high hurdle rates are imposed then it will invariably lead to a decreasing capital investment. In times of capital rationing the argument put forward to support high return on investment thresholds is that they facilitate the process of creaming off the more attractive investment proposals and hence enable a company to equate the best opportunities with available funds. But this line of argument fails to assess the relevance of investment proposals in the context of an agreed corporate strategy. The result, at best, is a hit and miss play between agreeing essential investments as part of manufacturing's strategic contribution and, at worst, the failure to trigger off essential investments if manufacturing is to provide its important contribution to market-share objectives.

For instance, delays in appropriate investment will lead to a position where costs do not decline as expected. The result would be a falling off of achieved experience curve gains (see Chapter 4) and, if the delay itself and extent of the investment requirement are large, then loss of market share will eventually follow.[5]

Manufacturing strategy arguments for process investment to meet order-winning criteria other than price and the associated low-cost manufacturing task, come up against the difficulties of accounting and finance-based rationale. Proposals, for instance, to invest in processes which increase production flexibility when customer response and delivery speed are the key order-winning criteria will be difficult to prepare in an appraisal system where return on investment is paramount. Similar forces will also work against facilities focus, irrespective of the importance in its role within manufacturing's support of the business needs. Other accounting and financial perspectives will also militate against the pursuit of focus in manufacturing. The desire and strength of argument by the accounting and finance function to manage earnings and cash flows by smoothing cyclical business swings carries substantial weight. However, focused manufacturing requires a greater degree of interaction between manufacturing and sales/marketing which will, as a consequence, lead to a higher level of shared dependence between these two prime parts of a business. One result is that it will increase the argument against smoothing with the dynamics of sustaining and improving market share becoming of greater significance and carrying more weight of argument than the smoothing preferences of accounting and finance.[6]

Investments such as computer-aided design (CAD) provide an example of the limitations in the accounting approach to investment appraisal. CAD is usually evaluated on the cost savings attributed to its introduction. However, a significant gain associated with this investment is the speed of response to customer changes, particularly in a make-to-order business. Often this increased competitiveness is not recognised by a company as part of its corporate strategy. So, the contribution that CAD can make in corporate strategy support will neither be evaluated as part of the investment appraisal nor will it usually be systematically developed and exploited at all stages in the business.

Excessive use of ROI distorts strategy building

Companies in the UK and USA, highly sensitive to the view of the stock market and shareholders of short-term declines in profits, have become all the more prone to adopting a short pay-back posture. Furthermore, in times of low profit performance, the pressure invariably increases to affect short-term recovery programmes as a way of demonstrating improvement and management action. In turn, the argument to set high thresholds can win the day where inadequate strategic direction and agreement has been reached. With its back to the wall, clutching at straws seems highly attractive at the time, made even more so by the £ or $ signs associated with promised higher returns on investment. But, investments in manufacturing processes and infrastructure taken out of their critical strategic context can commit a company for years ahead in an inappropriate direction. Rarely in practice are investments assessed after they have been installed to determine the extent to which reality measured up to the proposals and to identify why any significant disparities arose. Whilst not proposing that hindsight is a substitute for foresight, such an assessment would provide a most important review of the effectiveness of these critical decisions. These analyses would not only assess the actual level of return but also enable a company to measure the extent to which past investments have supported the corporate strategic requirement.

The approach to investment appraisal in Japan and West Germany has a different basis. When they invest they are often prepared to sacrifice the short-term for longer-term profits which accrue from market share and increased volumes. In this way they demonstrate two important differences in approach. The first is that they avoid the delusion that in an imprecise environment, numbers are precise and thereby reliable, and thus by using numbers, assume that the risk is reduced. The second is that to run a successful business, risks need to be taken.

Ohmae summarises the clear difference in approach between Western and Japanese businessmen by illustrating, with examples, the investments made by two Japanese companies and concluding that 'in neither case, however, is any attention given to return on investment (ROI) or payback period, let alone to discounted cash flow. In both, the dominant investment criterion is whether the new business is good for the corporation as a whole'.[7] He then continues to illustrate these differences by posing such questions as

How many contemporary US corporations relying on ROI yardsticks would have embarked on the development of a business that required a twenty year incubation period, as did Nippon Electric Company with its computer and semiconductor businesses? . . . Would Honda have so obstinately persisted in using its motorbike profits to bring its clean-engine vehicle to market if it were a corporation that measured the ROI of each product line and made its decisions accordingly? In fact, would any manufacturers be entering

the four-wheel vehicle market in today's environment if ROI were the investment criterion?[8]

A by-product in many companies of the emphasis on ROI in the corporate evaluation of investments has been an increasing tendency to view these proposals as a series of one-off, unrelated events, and not, as invariably they are, characterised by strategic sequence. Only when companies review investment decisions in the light of their corporate strategies, and, in turn their marketing and manufacturing strategies, will the essential cohesion be established. Until this happens, companies will be in danger of investing in ways which will not give them the necessary synergistic gains of strategic coherence. An example of what happens is provided by a company involved in the manufacture of office equipment and supplies which, over the years, had added on capacity in a piecemeal way. The result was a company with seven manufacturing units in the same road, only two of which were interconnected. Buying up premises as they were required made, on paper, a better return on investment than resiting the business. However, the costs of handling and transport between units added complexity and overhead duplication. The position was only assessed when a new chief executive called a halt to the proposal to add another part to the 'rabbit warren'.

Government grants are not necessarily golden handshakes

With disproportionately high unemployment rates in certain parts of the UK and the impact of declining primary as well as secondary sectors of the economy, successive governments have, most understandably pursued a policy of trying to attract manufacturing as well as other activities to these areas in order to redress the national imbalance. In a similar way, they have persuaded organisations to take on ailing companies or parts of companies to avert significant instances of primary and secondary redundancy. In addition at plant level, governments have attempted to stimulate or support investment in manufacturing companies as a way of helping to increase their competitiveness in world markets. In each instance, the carrot has been a generous system of grants and other awards. Many companies, attracted by the size of the hand-outs and the cash and return on investment gains they represent, have decided to take up the offer and relocate or establish all or parts of their business in one of a number of distressed areas, take on a relatively large piece of manufacturing capacity at one go, or invest in numerical control equipment to improve their manufacturing process capability. Where clear strategic parameters have not been established by these companies and the evaluation of proposals has rested largely on the attractiveness of its return or cash injection, then companies have all too often rued the day when the decision was made. Bound by a minimum period of residence, by the relative size of the investments involved or by the desire to save face, at least in the short-term or while the custodians of the decision still have responsibility for the business concerned, companies find themselves hidebound. Examples are numerous.

One carpet company vertically-integrated into yarn production instead of continuing its then current policy of buying from a number of yarn suppliers. The mill selected was in a remote area and at some hundred miles distance from the carpet plants of the parent company. Besides all the difficulties associated with recruitment at all levels in the mill and the distances involved in what was a 'linked' process, it also incurred one additional and fundamental problem. The decision to split the processes into yarn and carpet manufacturing was made on the basis that it was a natural break in the processes involved. However, the manufacturing company had established its niche in the quality end of the markets. By separating the business at the natural break provided between the sets of processes involved the manufacturer had facilitated the investment-orientated arguments. But, at the same time, the essential quality control link had been broken between yarn spinning and carpet manufacture, both of which were now a common, corporate responsibility. Thus, a manufacturing split based upon processes had ignored the essential qualifying criterion of producing high quality carpets. The quick feedback and opportunity for close liaison were not easy to exploit. In the early months, justifying the investment from both parts of the total business became top management's preoccupation. Reality, however, proved more difficult to handle than the orderlines implied in the integration proposals.

A medium-sized company having decided to establish a subcontract machining facility was attracted to change its location decision from the industrial site of its first choosing to one some twenty-five miles away. The carrot offered was that the latter had a development classification attracting a high level of grant and expenditure exemptions. This alternative proved significantly more attractive to the executives, bank and other financial institutions who all developed a fixation towards the impact it made on ROI, profit and cash flows. However, only when the order-winning criterion of delivery speed was clearly imposed into the debate did these accrued financial advantages pale into insignificance. Without the sales, the calculations had no foundation.

Finally, a large UK manufacturing company having itself great difficulty in achieving adequate profit margins was persuaded to absorb part of another group of companies. The cash injection offered as part of the government proposal to avert job losses, swung the balance. The difficulties of absorbing such a large addition to manufacturing capacity, matching systems, controls and other parts of the infrastructure besides the production processes involved, added to the company's already difficult task. The rationalisation which ensued cast serious questions on the fit between the decision and the strategic needs and direction of the existing business.

Linking investment to product life cycles reduces risk

Many companies entering markets for existing replacement or new products make decisions on process investment which need to reflect the forecast demands for those items at the various stages in its life cycle. As explained earlier in chapter 3 (pp. 80-1) most products do not move from jobbing, to batch, to line levels of volume over the life cycle. In fact for this to happen is rare. Companies assess the market or base their forecast volume requirements with customers and have to plan their investments in accordance with the relevant volume parameters established by these procedures. It does not make sense for them to invest at one level of volume and then re-invest in line with their own or increased share in the light of subsequent market growth. However, the difficulty inherent in these decisions is the judgemental nature of predicting the future. Where a high level of certainty exists there is less difficulty in matching the process investment to eventual product volumes. However, in areas of uncertainty and given the characteristic ways of appraising investments and evaluating the various alternatives, companies invariably place themselves in a yes/no decision situation. With long delivery times for equipment, this position is further aggravated. Commitments have to be made months, sometimes years, in advance of the scheduled launch. However, an alternative to this can be

FIGURE 7.2
Alternative approaches to investment decisions

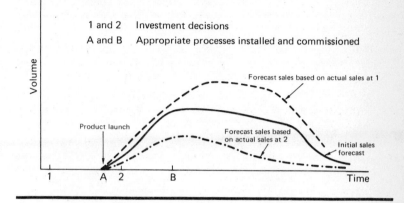

considered in many situations. Figure 7.2 shows a projected life cycle for a product.

At 1, process investment decisions would have to be made and purchase orders raised in order for the plant to be installed and commissioned to meet the intended product launch at A. The alternative approach is to delay the process investment decision until 2, hence allowing sales forecasts to be amended in line with the actual sales to date and the revised projections. The trade-off embodied by adopting this second approach is that the process choice would be more in line with the requirement. In this example, the new forecasts could be higher, lower or somewhat near the same as the original forecast. Hence, the eventual investments would be more in keeping with the actual sales levels. To do this and yet minimise investment would require that existing processes could cope with the manufacturing task to point B. The company would thereby not be able to meet the level of manufacturing costs necessary to yield adequate margins and, in this way, the trade-offs between loss of profits in the period between A and B and the risk of inappropriate investments being made, would have to be assessed.

Manufacturing must test the process implications of product life cycle forecasts

A particular point to be made with regard to investments is that in many instances, investment proposals rarely cover each main phase of a product's life cycle. Yet, manufacturing's task is to produce the product over each phase of this cycle and respond to the consequent variations in volumes. Returning to Chapter 4 on focus, the importance of distinguishing between product and process focus (see Figure 4.2) brings with it the need to provide alternative sets of processes. However, not only does the production engineering function classically ignore the change in the manufacturing task towards the end of a product's life cycle, but also the potential process investment requirements which are associated with this change are ignored. Hence, many companies find that they are required to retain high-volume plant to meet low-volume requirements. Manufacturing, faced with this mismatch does the best it can. Unfortunately, the need for the business to look at the alternative approaches is not recognised. What happens is that manufacturing uni-laterally chooses the solution which makes sense in the light of the production difficulties, constraints and performance measures, only to be changed in circumstances where the trade-offs involved in that choice have come under corporate scrutiny (for example, the inventory holding associated with making order quantities in excess of sales call-offs or requirements). Given that the order-winning criteria associated with the volumes involved at these stages in a product's life cycle are invariably different (see Figure 7.3) then the process choice appropriate

---

FIGURE 7.3
Product life cycles, order-winning criteria and process investment interact

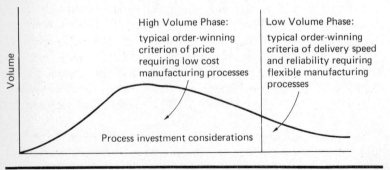

High Volume Phase:

typical order-winning criterion of price requiring low cost manufacturing processes

Low Volume Phase:

typical order-winning criteria of delivery speed and reliability requiring flexible manufacturing processes

Volume

Process investment considerations

to these stages should be realigned, if manufacturing is to be able to provide the essential criteria at each stage of a product's life cycle. Thus, the investment proposal needs to include the processes necessary to effectively manufacture (in line with the varying needs of the market) throughout each stage.

The viability of a proposed product introduction should be over the whole of its life cycle and so include the investments necessary to cope with the same time period. This does not happen. It is assumed that the process installed for the high volume phase is the only requirement. Where existing processes can cope effectively with the change in volumes, the costs involved with this transfer (often quite high) also need to be recognised in the initial stages and included as part of the corporate assessment.

Investment decisions must quantify working capital and infrastructure requirements

Many investment decisions are distorted in two ways. On the one hand, they ignore intangible, difficult-to-evaluate reductions or benefits which accrue from the investments. Whilst on the other, they underestimate the working capital needs associated with each proposal and often ignore altogether the infrastructure costs which will be involved. The tangible nature of the investments associated with the equipment, plant and support services involved in a process have led to a clear identification of the costs involved. However, many areas of investment directly associated with the capital expenditure being proposed have been overlooked or ignored in the past and, in many instances, are understated or assumed to be unnecessary at present. Only in the last five to ten years have companies required a statement of the additional inventory necessitated by the process proposals under consideration. The drive by most companies to reduce inventory in the late 1970s has been one important stimulus for this change. Even so, many proposals understate inventory. This is due to the fact that those involved in the preparation of a capital expenditure proposal are invariably not responsible for inventory levels within manufacturing. This leads to a significant underestimation of the levels which will actually be needed to sustain manufacturing.

The effect on the infrastructure requirements which will emanate from particular manufacturing process investments is often either underestimated or not evaluated when expenditure proposals are prepared. The failure is often that those responsible for either the control of manufacturing or the achievement of required levels of performance are not the same as those who prepare the proposals. Thus, an oversimplified review of infrastructure requirements is made. The consequence of this is that any increase in complexity goes unrecognised and the assumption is made that existing systems, controls and structures are not only appropriate but are also adequate. The incremental nature of such assumptions leads to a deterioration in a company's ability to control and assess its manufacturing function and the eventual overhaul of one or more parts of its infrastructure. The costs associated with such developments can involve high expenditure. For example, one company estimated that to install a revised manufacturing control system in a typical plant cost upwards of £200 000.

Where a company is starting with a green-field site on which to make a single product, then its investment decisions will usually take full account of the need for services, systems and controls with regard to all the major aspects of infrastructure. However, most companies are more complex and are generally investing in existing plants or introducing products to be made in already up-and-running processes. Usually, investment considerations when introducing a product are more akin to the following examples:

1. The decision to enter a market will require an investment in all the processes necessary to manufacture the product in question. Whilst similar to the green-field site example referred to above, the product in this instance will be assumed to use existing site services, support systems and overheads. However, this assumption belies reality. It ignores the increase in complexity and corresponding demand placed upon the non-process aspects of manufacturing which go hand-in-hand with the decision and the resulting deterioration of the effectiveness of existing systems and structures.
2. Most product introductions also generally use parts of the existing manufacturing processes. In these instances, therefore, the problem is compounded by the fact that there will be an increase in both inventory and in the complexity brought on by the shared use of existing processes and infrastructure and the interplay between them.

7.3   Operating Controls and Information

In order to assess its current performance a company needs control information which reflects the key areas of its manufacturing task. However, although there is a lot of information collected and recorded, many companies fail to clearly separate the difference between records and control.[9] Furthermore, 'the development of the marketing orientation [in many companies] has led to an increase in the amount of market-based information available to management. In contrast the paucity and limited availability of relevant internal information is striking'.[10] One key problem area is that of management accounting. Although money is used as the common denominator to assess both current and future corporate performance this function is often lacking in relevance and sensitivity towards changing circumstances.

7.4   The Simplistic Nature of Accounting Information

The accounting information provided in most companies can be characterised in a number of ways. In the first instance it is historically-based. Although this is an inherent part of cost information, it seems to induce an attitude within accountants and an acceptance by the business that it is not of paramount importance to produce information which is relevant and as close to reality as can be achieved. The second characteristic is that invariably the information provided is primarily focused on management accounting relating to the business as a whole rather than the management control of manufacturing. This leads to the inadequate provision of information which is not only of a critical nature in itself but also is perceived by management as the basis for assessing performances and on which to make future decisions.

In broad terms, accountants primarily work on the basis of norms. They choose averages to simplify the measurement task. The procedure then is to compare each part of the business to a norm. However, the global nature of these comparisons hides the key to control. By failing to go back to the information from which the average has been drawn, the checks made obscure the level of performance achieved. As averages are a compilation of many parts, it is important to be able to assess the level of performance within each part. The argument put forward in defence of the approach adopted is that to collect and update data in this way would be very time-consuming and expensive. Therefore, it is necessary to simplify the procedures and tasks involved in order to make some sense of reality and to be able to report within an acceptable time-scale.

Reality, however, is complex. The controls need to reflect and measure reality. The accountants' approach is to simplify reality by simplifying the controls used. In this way they are able to account for all the parts, yet cope administratively with the task and also meet the audit obligation of 'accounting for everything in a systematic way'. However, the basis for control in companies needs to reflect the complex business issues and not the tasks required by company law. Hence, the controls need to reflect the size and importance of the area concerned – detailed controls for the significant areas and simple, broad-brush controls for the insignificant areas.

Several, general examples will serve to illustrate these points.

- Most companies use total sales turnover as an indicator of successful performance. Invariably this leads to a situation where the contribution of individual products is not rigorously examined. In profit and loss account terms, the top line becomes the measure of sales performance, whereas the bottom line, the measure of manufacturing performance. What fails to be clearly distinguished is that the two performances are inextricably linked. The consequence of the lack of distinction between the two reinforces the argument by marketing of the need to retain all products. The simple measure of the marketing performance fails to distinguish the relative contribution of each product. Hence, the conclusion that all sales are equally good business.
- It is usual for manufacturing's task to be based on a proposed or forecast level of volumes. Invariably the volumes experienced differ from period to period, and over time. However, rarely are costings provided for the different volume levels involved. It is essential to establish costings for the varying levels of throughput. In this way, the costings appropriate to the volume levels experienced will be used. This will then allow a company to assess a period's performance in a more exact way and to establish the reasons for the level of achievement recorded.
- Accounting systems should reflect the type of processes being used. As shown in Table 7.1, the treatment of costs, pricing and the development of accounting procedures and controls will vary. The

TABLE 7.1

Some of the different accounting approaches depending upon the type of process

Aspect	Type of process	
	General-purpose	Dedicated
Overhead		
Recovery	Process or product orientated	Blanket rate per standard hour
Control	Complex control: needs to assess the impact of product mix and volume changes, alternative routings and other similar factors	Simple variance control derived from comparing actual to standard unit volumes
Costs		
Set-ups	Direct to product	Overhead rate based upon machine utilisation
Process scrap	Specific to the process or product	Blanket allowance
Quality	Direct to product	Overhead rate established
Tooling	Direct to product	Overhead rate established
Maintenance	Direct to process	Overhead rate established
Basis for pricing	Product cost basis	Contribution basis
Development of accounting procedures and controls	Bottom-up	Top-down

Source: based on ideas developed by Clive Turner Associates, 5 Meriden Road, Hampton-in-Arden, West Midlands

costing structure and performance reporting system needs to take account of these differences in order to distinguish between the provision of sensitive cost information and the measurement of performance.

● Plant decisions constitute a high business risk due to the size of the investment, the forecast sales basis for that decision, and the flexibility/process cost trade-offs involved and their relationship to the market. However, the accounting policy on depreciation reinforces this risk where it is classified in relation to the type of plant rather than the life of the product for which the plant is to be purchased. Typically, plant is depreciated by rules of thumb accounting classifications. For instance, one large manufacturing company used the rules in Table 7.2 which had been arrived at by historical usage and precedents.

TABLE 7.2

Item of plant	Typical number of years over which plant was depreciated in all parts of the company
Tool room equipment	25
Presses	20
Automatic lathes	15
Numerically controlled machines	10
Machining centres	5
Test	
dedicated	5
general-purpose	10

The gains which accrued from having common accounting procedures belied the simplistic nature of this policy. As a consequence, this sizeable asset becomes detached from its essential business orientation in order to accommodate the administrative requirements of the accounting function and policies involved.

7.5   The Need for Accounting System Development

Attempting to improve the competitive nature of their performance, many UK companies are paying greater attention to improvements in quality, processes, inventory holdings and work-force policies as essential measures to effect this change. However, there is one major area which normally receives little attention. 'Most companies still use the same cost accounting and management control systems that were developed decades ago for a competitive environment drastically different from that of today[11] When trying to assess the level of contribution provided by each product as a prerequisite for judging what steps to take, many companies find that the accounting information provided fails to differentiate between them. Whilst everyone knows that higher volumes decrease costs and product proliferation increases them, rarely are these essential trade-offs differentiated within accounting procedures. Classically, the core areas generate the substantial parts of a business. However, in order to assess the trade-offs associated with product breadth and focus, companies need appropriate information to help them arrive at sensible decisions. Non-core products are characteristically marginal in their contribution to a firm.

Far worse than this, they may create added cost which will be hidden by an average allocation to all products and customers. As a consequence, the essential core business may be deemphasized or overpriced, while the marginal extensions of the product line and customers served may be underpriced or over-emphasized in their importance. This may be true even though a real competitive advantage exists in the core business while there is no comparable advantage in the extension coverage.[12]

The impact on business competitiveness can be significant.

Allocate, not absorb overheads

The accounting practice which leads to this situation is the application of the allocation and absorption approaches to overheads. In most manufacturing companies overheads are between 30 and 50 per cent of total costs and are usually increasing both in themselves and in terms of their relative size. Yet, all too often the bulk of these are absorbed. A review of one manufacturing company revealed that some 80 per cent of total overheads were absorbed. As these costs accounted for over 40 per cent of the total, the implications were alarming. The reason why overhead costs are predominantly absorbed is that it involves less administrative work and system maintenance than alternatives. Many accountants abuse this principle still further, by using one overhead absorption rate for several parts of the business involved, and often absorbing on a single rather than the number of bases necessary to reflect the business and improve the relevance of the information provided. One company within a group of manufacturing companies comprised seven sites ranging from raw material holding and distribution through spares/low volume manufacturing, high volume manufacturing and distribution of finished goods to a customer. Overheads for all seven companies were pooled and were then absorbed at one common rate for each site based upon the single factor of direct labour hours. Faced with declining profits, the group executive turned to the basic performance evaluation of each site. The answers told them very little.[13]

A business needs more sensitive information at all times. The only meaningful way to account for this sizeable set of costs is to reflect reality. It needs not only each site accounted for separately but also the distinction drawn between products within a site. It is essential, therefore, for accounting functions to adopt the policy of allocating overheads wherever possible.* As a general rule, a minimum target of allocating 80 per cent of total overheads should be the initial aim. The consequences would be that then only a relatively small portion of total costs would need to be spread on an absorption basis.

Adopting the manufacturing strategy principle of plant-within-plant and focused factory would, therefore, work in both ways. It would enable the company to more easily identify the overheads associated with each part of manufacturing and similarly would enable the company to assess the contribution to the whole business provided by each part. Furthermore, this change brings with it a shift from the principle of accounting for overheads on a functional basis to a dedicated overhead allocation. Thus, instead of the costs involved in providing a support function being summarised as a total for that function, it changes to a policy of accounting those overheads which are dedicated to or are directly associated with a part of manufacturing. Not only

*Overhead allocation involves the 'allocation', 'apportionment' or 'allotment' of overhead costs to the appropriate cost centre or cost unit. Overhead absorption is achieved by dividing the costs involved on a suitable basis (e.g. standard labour hours, direct clocked hours, direct labour costs, material costs or floor space) and then spreading them on a pro rata basis in line with the common factor which has been chosen.

does this now enable a company to assess more clearly the contribution of its different parts, but in times of change it will enable a company to take out or increase the vertical slice of overheads associated with that part of the process under review. Thus, it allows change to take place in a more orderly and sensible way. Accounting decisions are now more in line with manufacturing strategy needs. It avoids accentuating the already wide gap between the support needs of manufacturing activities and the perceived role of support functions. Thus, as overhead costs are now clearly identified with a particular sector of manufacturing, the level and nature of support can be agreed to meet the current needs of that sector and reflect any changes identified in the future.

A further refinement to these changes involves making any functional overhead into a business unit. This then enables a business to move away from the position where an accountant or accounting procedure spreads the unallocated overhead on some arbitrary basis in order to make the books balance to a position where each part of the business declares a budget for the amount it intends to purchase from each overhead function. The gains are obvious.

Beware, however of the counter-argument put forward by accountants that these changes are difficult to accomplish and lack a high degree of accuracy. These changes will, in fact, enhance the value of and contribution made by this information in the light of the business needs both in terms of relevance and accuracy.

Create business related financial information

Another area where changes in the accounting system would lead to sizeable advantages to a company concerns the need to provide business-related information. As a necessary input into developing both a marketing and manufacturing strategy, accounting information is rarely designed to provide analyses which would form an integral part of each strategy formulation. Some examples of key marketing information include:

- *Customer sales and profitability.* An assessment of both the sales and all costs associated with selling to and supporting major customers would enable a company to establish the true worth of these relationships.

- *Market share and profitability*. Identifying the value of sales in each market, its relative size and the level of profitability for each market segment would be an essential input into formulating a market plan.

For the manufacturing side of the business, information rarely provided by existing accounting systems would, in turn, offer invaluable insights in the strategy formulation. For example:

- cost estimates of manufacturing at varying levels of throughput
- capacity analyses identifying the contribution of each product in terms of any bottleneck or limiting factor in manufacturing's existing capacity – known as analysis of contribution by limiting factor. This would enable companies to assess proposals to increase capacity and to decide how best to allocate existing capacity in the meantime
- cost estimates for supplying items outside the normal product range

Budgeting is a further area where strategic perspectives can be phased into the management accounting procedure. Although many businesses use budgets as one of the building blocks of its corporate assessment, traditionally the system adopted does not indicate those areas which are the core of the corporate strategy. Similarly, the effect of its decisions to engage in any corporate strategic thrust or defence is not indicated or highlighted in this basic performance summary.

Finally, the need to separate out those costs incurred by manufacturing but not induced by manufacturing decisions are seldom reflected in the control statements provided by the accounting system. Excess manufacturing costs incurred as a result of a change in schedule to meet a sales or customer request, for instance, are not shown under their own separate headings, e.g. 'manufacturing excess cost due to customer schedule change'.

Provide performance related financial information

The third area of development concerns the provision of accurate performance-related information. Budgets, by definition, are out of date by the time they are completed. It is necessary, therefore, to revise the budget figure by using the latest information. In this way, the basis for establishing and assessing levels of performance is changed from a budget to a latest-estimate basis. One clear example of this is the use of flexible budgeting which changes the cost base in line with actual volumes and alters the basis for related cost information (e.g. overhead absorption).

The last illustration concerns the distortions which businesses experience as a result of the way in which inventory values are calculated. In many situations, inventory de-sensitises cost information by becoming a cost buffer. Most accounting systems assume that costs are held in the value of work-in-progress as calculated in the system. What often happens is that accumulated cost excesses are discovered when the inventory is physically counted at the end of period stock-taking and then recorded as an inventory or stock-taking loss. As inventory is physically counted in many firms but twice a year, control or responsibility is not easy to establish.

7.6 Conclusion

In many companies the link between process investment decisions and the need to provide supporting infrastructure in the form of control systems is not appreciated. This distinction arises from the fact that decisions about processes are not only tangible but they are also taken at a different phase in the decision sequence (see Table 7.3). On the other hand, the sizeable investments associated with manufacturing process decisions of working capital and infrastructure are often obscured for exactly the opposite reasons – they are less tangible and occur in the operating phase of the installation.

Furthermore, when a process investment is installed on the shop-floor a distinct accounting change takes place. At the pre-operation stage highlighted in Table 7.2 a process is singularly evaluated in great detail as part of the investment appraisal system and is cash-flow orientated. However, once installed this same process will no longer be treated as an individual item in accounting control terms. Instead, it will be controlled by a number of broad brush accounting systems based on profit. It will become just part of a functionally based set of assets and costs comprising a range of investments, different in terms of usage, degree of dedication to the manufacture of specific products, age and support system requirements. The change in accounting treatment highlights the contrasts involved and the necessary high level of control in the pre-operation phase compared with the lack of sensitivity in the global controls once the asset is being used.

TABLE 7.3
The three phases in an investment programme showing the sequence involved, the nature of the investment and the tangible nature of each phase

Phase	Time-scale	Features of the investment	Tangible nature	Features of evaluation and control
1	Pre-operation	Fixed assets in the form of plant, equipment and associated installation costs	High	Constitutes taking one investment in isolation. Traditional investment appraisal techniques used which are *cash-flow* orientated
2	Operating	Supporting working capital in the form of inventory		The investment now becomes an integral part of the business summary. It reverts to revenue accounts which measure *profit* to investment as the
3		The service and support overheads necessary to provide an appropriate level of infrastructure	Low	basis of control or assessment. Control of individual investments now relatively loose – rarely have post audits

Source: based on ideas developed by Clive Turner Associates.

What then are the ways forward? These comprise changes at two levels in the organisation. At the top, many executives have perceived their role in accounting and finance in a different form. Often they become involved or even spearhead activities designed to generate earnings by financial transactions. This has the major drawback of diverting management effort and interest away from the business core. They become more distant from the prime profit-generating activities of a manufacturing business. They start to control from a distance. Without the understanding of each firm's strategy, they feel unable to contribute to the essential developments which must be made in the tough competitive climate of manufacturing. They feel exposed and become less able to evaluate the necessary long-term alternatives. As a consequence, they increasingly exert pressure by short-term measures and assessments. Lower down the organisation, plant executives being measured by the success of the business in the short-term often respond by adopting similar opportunistic patterns of behaviour such as reducing expenditure or withholding investments in order to increase profits and improve cash flow in the short-term. Similarly, groups of companies often monitor investments centrally and against a common set of criteria. However, they leave the post-assessment to be taken at plant level. Seen as part of their role, the group executives' action reinforces the predominant role of financial measures when assessing investments and weakens the key responsibility link between the investment decision and its future evaluation. The need to decentralise these responsibilities could not be more strongly argued.

The way forward is through the emergence of strategy-based decisions and controls. Accounting and manufacturing need to determine together the investment criteria and day-to-day accounting control provision which should be adopted. Not only will this reinforce the orientation of manufacturing towards its key tasks but also provide information which is both relevant and current. This growing awareness of the need for strategic management accounting[14] needs to be accelerated if companies are to be able to make sound manufacturing and other strategy decisions based in part, on these essential details. It is most necessary, therefore, that firms stem the apparent drift away from their manufacturing focus.

Perhaps a final lesson which UK and US companies may consider is that 'in Japan, perpetuation of the enterprise, not profit, is the driving force. As Toshiba's Okano puts it: The company is forever'.[15] Although in no way implying that this should be adopted as the UK or US corporate value system, it highlights one essential difference. Strategy is the driving force; survival and success will only be achieved through a strategic orientation and this must become the pattern by which companies both give direction and assess current and future performance.

Notes and References

1. R. C. Dean Jr, 'The Temporal Mismatch – Innovation's pace vs Management's Time Horizon', *Research Management*, May 1974, pp. 12–15.
2. R. H. Hayes and J. Abernathy, 'Managing Our Way to Economic Decline' *Harvard Business Review* July/Aug. 1980, pp. 67–77.
3. R. H. Hayes and D. A. Garvin, 'Managing as if Tomorrow Mattered', *Harvard Business Review*, May–June 1982, pp. 71–9.

4. K. Simmonds, 'The Fundamentals of Strategic Management Accounting' (unpublished) p. 13 based upon a paper entitled 'Strategic Management Accounting' presented to the Institute of Cost and Management Accountants' Technical Symposium, Pembroke College, Oxford, 6–8 Jan. 1981.
5. Several authors highlight these type of consequences including Boston Consulting Group:s Perspective, 'The Experience Curve – Reviewed: II History', S. Rose, 'The Secrets of Japan's Export Prowess', *Fortune*, 30 Jan, 1978, pp. 56–62 and Simmonds, 'The Fundamentals of Strategic Management'.
6. This argument also forms part of S. C. Wheelwright's Research Paper No. 517, 'Facilities Focus: a Study of Concepts and Practices Related to its Definition, Evaluation, Significance and Application in Manufacturing Firms', Graduate School of Business, Stanford University, 12 Dec. 1979 p. 55.
7. K. Ohmae, 'Japan: from Stereotypes to Specifics', *The McKinsey Quarterly*, Spring 1982 pp. 2–33.
8. Ibid., p. 3.
9. T. J. Hill and D. J. Woodcock, 'Dimensions of Control', *Production Management and Control*, Mar./Apr. 1982, vol. 10, no. 2, pp. 16–20.
10. K. J. Blois, 'The Manufacturing/Marketing Orientation and its Information Needs', *European Journal of Marketing*, vol. 14, 15/6, pp. 354–64.
11. R. S. Kaplan, 'Yesterday's Accounting Undermines Production', *Harvard Business Review*, Jul./Aug. 1984, pp. 95–101.
12. Boston Consulting Group Perspective No. 219, 'Specialization or the Full Produce Line' (1979).
13. Kaplan, 'Yesterday's Accounting Undermines Production', p. 96 provides another example of what, all too often, is a common situation
14. K. Simmonds, 'The Fundamentals of Strategic Management Accounting'.
15. Ohmae, 'Japan: from Stereotypes to Specifics', p. 7.

Index

ABC analysis – inventory   185
Accounting   201, 218–25

Backlog of orders   *see* Order
    backlog
Batch (process)   62–4, 66–71,
    76–81, 83, 87–8, 94, 179–
    80, 189, 210
Batch quantity   *see* Order
    quantity
Buffer stock/inventory   71,
    75, 78
Bureaucratic style   71, 73, 77,
    93, 102
Business implications of process
    choice   *see* Trade-offs

Capability   71
Capacity   71, 72, 75, 77, 122,
    210
Capital investment   *see* Plant
    investment
Capital rationing   205
Cascading overheads   176
Centralised   71, 77, 93
Choice of process   *see* Process
    choice
Complexity   99–105, 107,
    149, 189, 214, 216

Component inventory   *see*
    Inventory
Computer-aided design (CAD)
    206
Continuous process   64–7,
    69–71, 78–81, 179–80
Contracts   *see* Long-term con-
    tracts
Control of inventory   *see*
    Inventory, control
Corporate objectives/strategy
    38–40, 42, 53–6
Corporate marketing decisions
    see Marketing strategy
Cost direct   71, 74–5, 78–9
    labour   *see* Cost, direct
    low manufacturing   75,
        77–8, 90, 109–11, 120–3,
        125, 127, 130–1
    material   *see* Cost, direct
    overhead   71, 74–5, 79, 120
        130
    reduction   *see* Cost, low
        manufacturing
Customer order size   *see* Order
    quantity
Customer/supplier relations   *see*
    Customer/vendor relations
Customer/vendor relations   152

227

Decentralised 71, 74, 93
Delivery
  reliability 41, 48, 70, 73, 109
  speed 41, 47–9, 54, 70, 73, 109, 210
Dependent/independent demand principle 184
Direct numerical control (DNC) 83–4
Discounted cash flow 207
Dog-leg profile 91–5, 159

Effectiveness 27, 36, 57
Efficiency 27, 36, 57, 120, 186
  see also Labour efficiency
Eighty-twenty (80/20) rule 165, 170, 185
Entrepreneurial style 71, 73–4, 93
Experience curves 112–38
  see also Learning curves
Export–import ratios 4, 14

Fads – management *see* Panaceas
Finished goods inventory *see* Inventory
Flexibility *see* Flexible process
Flexible budgeting 222–3
Flexible manufacturing systems (FMS) 76, 82–6, 89–90
Flexible process 64, 71–2, 74, 82–4, 86–7, 89–90, 104, 111, 152, 206
Focus
  process 109–12
  product 109–12
  progression 112, 138
  regression 108, 112
  see also Focused manufacturing, Process focus, Product focus
Focused manufacturing 99–112, 127–38, 206
Functional layout *see* layout
Functional teamwork concept 174–6

General-purpose equipment/ plant 73, 82, 86, 88, 109–10, 217
Government grants 208–10
Group technology 82, 85–8

Hurdle rates 205
Hybrid processes 81–90

Imports (of manufactured items) 5
Independent demand principle *see* Dependent/independent demand principle
Infrastructure 23, 28, 31, 40–4, 52, 68, 71, 73–9 91, 94, 101–3, 105, 122, 147, 155, 158–98, 210, 213–4
Internal span of process *see* Span of process
Inventory
  buffer 184
  capacity-related 184
  component/raw material 71–2, 77, 182, 186
  control 182–7
  corporate 183
  cycle 184–5
  decoupling 184, 189
  finished goods 71–2, 77–8, 182, 186
  mainstream 183
  pipeline 184
  turnover 131–2
  work-in-progress 71–2, 77–8, 83, 87, 105, 182, 185–6
Investment appraisal 202, 204, 207

Jobbing 62–3, 66–71, 73–4, 76, 78–81, 94, 179–80, 189, 210
Joint ventures 151
Just-in-time (JIT) production 155, 186, 193–7

Kanban 193–6

Key manufacturing task   71-2, 74, 93, 109-10, 162

Labour
    efficiency   123
    standards   121
    utilisation   71, 74
Layout
    functional/process   83, 86-7, 189
    product/line   83, 86-7
Lead time, total   74
Learning curves   113, 121
    see also Experience curves
Line   64-70, 73-6, 80-1, 83, 86, 94, 179-80, 210
Line layout   *see* Layout
Long-term contracts   151

Machining centre   76, 82-3, 89-90
Make-to-order   74, 77
Make-to-stock   77
Management fads   *see* Panaceas
Manufacturing
    exports   3
    output   2
    proactive role/response/stance   25, 27-8
    reactive role/response/stance   25, 27-8, 32-3
    strategy   23-7, 35-6, 38-57, 91, 96, 100, 100-11, 123, 137, 141, 159-60, 163, 165, 187, 201-2, 205, 208
    volume   *see* Volume
Marketing strategy   38-43, 55, 94-5, 101, 134, 208
Materials requirement planning (MRP)   193-6
Mix mode assembly   82, 88-90

Numerical control (NC) machines   76, 82-4, 86, 88-90

One-off process   *see* Jobbing
One-off products   79

One touch exchange die (OTED)   194
Order backlog   74, 192
Order quantity   63, 70, 75-7, 92
Order size   *see* Order quantity
Order-winning criteria   23-4, 40-1, 43-56, 66, 71-3, 91-2, 101, 106, 108-10, 112, 166, 178, 187, 205-6, 210, 212
Organisational profile   163
Overheads – absorption *v.* allocation   219-21

Panaceas   103, 177
Pareto analysis   *see* Eighty-twenty rule
Payback   204, 207
Payment scheme/system   121, 178, 198
Plant
    investment   *see* Process investment
    mission   137 (*see also* Manufacturing task)
    utilisation   65, 71, 76-7, 105
Plant-within-a plant (PWP)   107, 137
Price/price sensitive   41, 46, 54, 70, 72-3, 75, 78, 92
Process analysis/choice   23, 28, 31, 40-4, 52, 59-96, 160, 188, 217
    flexibility   *see* Flexible process
    focus   *see* Focus process
    investment   71-2, 74-8, 83, 87, 89-90, 122, 136, 172, 202, 212-14, 223
    layout   *see* Layout
    positioning   141-56, 164, 189
Product
    focus   *see* Focus, product
    layout   *see* Layout
    life-cycles   32, 46, 108, 144-5, 210, 212-13
    profile   90 (*see also* Profile analysis)
    range   64-6, 71-3, 78, 90-2
    volume   *see* Volume

Production
  control: pull systems 192;
    push systems 192
  planning: aggregate 190–1;
    day-to-day 191; long-
    term 190; short-term
    190
  volume *see* Volume
Productivity
  labour 7, 9, 121
  multi-factor 7
  national comparisons 6–9
  plant-level comparisons 9–14
  single factor 7
  total factor *see* multifactor
    above
Productivity improvement groups
  see Quality circles
Profile
  analysis 89–95
  mismatch *see* Dog-leg pro-
    file
Project (process) 61–2, 66–73,
  79–81, 179–80, 188–9

Qualifying criteria 49–51,
  71–3, 178–9, 209
Quality (product) 41, 47, 109
Quality
  circles 176–7
  control 179–81, 209
  proactive approach 179–81
  reactive approach 179–81
  responsibility for 179–81

Raw material inventory *see*
  Inventory
Return on capital *see* Return on
  investment

Return on investment (ROI)
  91, 203, 205–8, 210

Set-ups/Setting-up 63
Single minute exchange die
  (SMED) 194
Span of process 141–56, 164
Standardisation 105, 120
Substitution (component/
  material) 120

Trade-offs (and business implications of process choice)
  53, 61–7, 71, 85, 88, 90,
  102–3, 107, 110, 147,
  149, 152, 159, 165, 186,
  188–9, 191, 196, 211
Transfer lines 82, 85, 88–90

Umbrella pricing 119
Unit *see* Jobbing
Utilisation
  labour *see* Labour utilis-
    ation
  plant *see* Plant utilisation

Vertical slicing 147–8
Volume 67, 71–2, 75–7, 80–3,
  86–88, 93, 103–4, 106,
  109, 112–25, 144, 210,
  212–13, 216
  definition 64–6

Work structuring 122
Working capital 213
Work-in-progress inventory
  see Inventory